After his court appearance, a defiant PW Botha held a press conference in the court, clearly basking in the national and international attention after years in obscurity. He wagged the familiar finger again, and warned: 'Don't awaken the tiger in the Afrikaner, the consequences will be grave.'

I was standing a few metres away, and said to him: 'Mr Botha, has nobody ever told you that there aren't any tigers in Africa?' Those of us who thought the old coot had become senile and slow were in for a surprise. He took three steps towards me, punched me in the chest with his famous finger, and said: 'Yes, but if there were, you wouldn't have been one of them.'

It was a good retort, and everybody laughed. And then he went off about 'this man' – still punching me with his finger – who had 'spent his life making trouble for everyone' and 'stirred up feelings where he shouldn't have'. I sometimes miss the old guy.

Pale Native

Pale Native

MEMORIES OF A RENEGADE REPORTER

MAX DU PREEZ

ZEBRA

Published by Zebra Press
an imprint of Struik Publishers
(a division of New Holland Publishing (South Africa) (Pty) Ltd)
PO Box 1144, Cape Town, 8000
New Holland Publishing is a member of Johnnic Communications Ltd

First published 2003

1 3 5 7 9 10 8 6 4 2

Publication © Zebra Press 2003
Text © Max du Preez 2003

Cover artwork © Hardy Botha

PUBLISHING MANAGER: Marlene Fryer
MANAGING EDITOR: Robert Plummer
EDITOR: Ronel Richter-Herbert
COVER AND TEXT DESIGNER: Natascha Adendorff
TYPESETTER: Monique van den Berg
INDEXER: Robert Plummer
PHOTO RESEARCHER: Carmen Swanepoel

Set in 10.5 pt on 13.5 pt Minion

Reproduction by Hirt & Carter (Cape) (Pty) Ltd
Printed and bound by Paarl Print, Oosterland Street, Paarl, South Africa

ISBN 1-86872-372-0

www.zebrapress.co.za

Log on to our photographic website www.imagesofafrica.co.za for an African experience

Contents

Photographs between pages 152 and 153

History is against you, my brother

IT WAS LATE in 2002. My professional options had become fewer and fewer, and my bank manager more and more agitated. Perhaps it was time for me to get a job after years of being an independent operator. An exciting job right up my alley was advertised, but I hesitated: I had never, since starting to work as a journalist in 1973, applied for a job. I was always offered jobs, started my own projects or worked as a freelancer. But friends and colleagues encouraged me, and in the end I sent in my CV.

The interview with the panel was interesting. I quickly realised I probably knew a lot more about my (and their) craft than they did. I had done this kind of job several times before with considerable success.

But it quickly became clear to me that the interview was a charade. What I'd feared was going to happen, was happening. I was not black. I could not even try to be black. My parents and their parents and grandparents were white-skinned. I could change my personality, my qualifications, my appearance – I could even have a sex change. But I could not change the colour of my skin, ever.

I sat through the rest of the interview, mechanically answering their questions, but my mind was elsewhere: the New South Africa about which I'd dreamt so much, worked so hard to help achieve and was enjoying living in, was finally turning its back on me. Of course it wasn't the first indication I'd had that this was happening to me, but the situation had never been as simple and clear-cut as this.

It wasn't a comfortable feeling.

Early the next day, one of my interviewers, an old acquaintance who, ironically, had once unsuccessfully asked me for a job, phoned. 'You and I know you're ideal for this job, Max,' he began uncomfortably. I let him sweat a bit. 'But I'm sure you'll understand it is politically and strategically impossible to appoint a white person. We have to go black now.'

And then my friend said the magic words that led me to writing this book: '*History is against you, my brother.*'

History. My personal history: what has happened to me, who I have been, what I have said and done. My family's history through more than three centuries of living in Africa. My tribe's history: colonialism, struggle, apartheid, *baasskap*. My country's history: oppression, division, conflict, liberation. My continent's history, the history of my species on this planet. My-story.

History is against me, my old comrade had said. That is quite a serious thing to say to someone. You're done, my brother, and there's nothing you can do about it – utterly inexorable, like some sort of super-universal karma.

I remembered something that had puzzled me greatly when I was a child: the biblical declaration that the sins of the fathers would be visited on their sons for generations. As a youngster I wondered what kind of god would punish a boy for what his father and grandfather had done. Perhaps it was that god who had now turned history against me, who was making me pay for the sins of the fathers of my tribe over many generations.

It was during this time that I heard, for the first time in years, from an old colleague and partner in crime, who e-mailed me from Oxford. Why on earth did he leave paradise, I asked him. His e-mail replied, 'The Big Wheel of History had turned. That's all. I'm not crying. It was right that the wheel turned. You can't blame the wheel for the fact that it crushed me. *As ek kyk na al die arme undignified poepholle wat probeer vasklou het, is ek bly ek het fokof gekies*' [When I look at all the poor undignified arseholes who tried to cling on, I am glad I chose to fuck off].

He reminded me of the slogan I'd used when the newspaper I had founded and edited was eventually crushed and had to close: *Ons fade nie, ons fokof* [We don't fade away, we fuck off]. That was my credo; it was nice and simple, and I lived by it.

And now that history has turned against me, am I going to fade or am I going to fuck off? Where would I go? Or am I going to be a poor undignified *poephol* trying to hang on? And what does that mean?

The more important question lurking beneath all this was: Was there no role left for me, in the prime of my life, to play in my country because a black majority was in charge and I had a white skin? Is History, this thing that has now become almost personalised in my head, saying I don't belong in Africa? Or perhaps that I can stay, as long as I shut up and am a good, loyal subject? Am I, in the words of my country's president, 'a colonialist of a special kind'?

Have I become a *bywoner*, a tenant farmer, in the land I am so passionate about?

My friend in Oxford and many other friends and former colleagues had chosen to leave the country. Only once before had this option been put before me: an offer of an academic post at a Dutch university. I fantasised for about five seconds about teaching nubile young *Hollandse meide,* and then said no. It wasn't even patriotism or a sense of duty or responsibility that prevented me from ever considering leaving South Africa. It was just unthinkable. If you transplant a fifty-year-old kameeldoring tree, it will wither and die. Its root system goes too deep to dig out. Just as I cannot change the colour of my skin, I cannot become an American, European or Australian. I would be an alien forever, like a polar bear in the Pretoria Zoo. My soul is African. My skin colour is the only European thing about me.

Yes, this 'history-is-against-you' thing really bugged me. Suddenly, I suffered a midlife crisis, an identity crisis and a nobody-loves-me-any-more crisis all at the same time.

The next day I walked to the top of the mountain on my piece of land in the Eastern Free State and had a bottle of wine all on my own with my dog by my side. I peered over the Mautse Valley all the way to the misty blue Maluti Mountains in the distance. King Moshoeshoe's country. As a child my father had told me many fascinating stories about Mosesh, as he was known, the founder of the Basotho nation, who never lost a war. In my small world in the rural Free State, King Moshesh had undoubtedly been my biggest hero, perhaps like Superman had been for my son.

In the cliffs around me was the spectacular art of the world's oldest people, the San, or Bushmen, who lived here for thousands of years. Only a handful of these remarkable naturalists survive today.

The valley below me was once, almost two centuries ago, strewn with the corpses of tens of thousands of people, the victims of a massive social and military upheaval involving the Zulu and Sotho peoples. Eight decades later, this was the theatre of war between the Boer and the Brit. The British, as part of their scorched earth policy, burned down most of the farms and homesteads around me. My paternal grandfather fought in that war in these parts as an officer of the Republic of the Orange Free State, and ended up a prisoner of war in Ceylon. He came back such a sick man that he died a few months before my father was born.

I, too, had almost died prematurely, at the foot of this very mountain. In 1989 a senior officer of the South African Defence Force lay waiting for me, his Russian assassination rifle trained on my front door, where I was expected to arrive at any moment. I was a traitor to my people: I had sided with the enemy, the black communists of the African National Congress (ANC). But something came up, and I only arrived two days later. He didn't wait. I only know about this because he confessed to me years later.

My mother died when I was an infant and I never knew much about her family. I do know that her great-uncle, Paul Kruger, spent some time in this region as a child of the Great Trek. Some forty years before Kruger became the president of the

Zuid-Afrikaansche Republiek north of the Vaal River, around the 1840s, he was asked to negotiate a peace treaty with King Moshesh on behalf of the Orange Free State. He must have travelled right past this way, probably down the valley just below me, on his way from Pretoria to Thaba Bosiu, Moshesh's mountain stronghold in the foothills of the Malutis.

I own a yellowed, first-edition copy of his memoirs, called *The Memoirs of Paul Kruger, Four times President of the South African Republic – Told by Himself*, published by T Fisher Unwin in 1902. According to Kruger, he met the king on top of the mountain, where Moshesh rebuked him for believing his military successes were due to his own bravery. Rather, the king said, 'it was the dispensation of God'.

Kruger wrote: 'Now, as Moshesh was at that very moment speaking of the dispensation of God and using pious words, I said to him: "But, if you are so devout, how do you come to have more than one wife?" Moshesh replied: "Yes, I have just about two hundred; but this is not half so many as Solomon had."

'To which I made answer: "Yes, but you surely know that, since Christ's time, and according to the New Testament, a man may have only one wife."

'Moshesh reflected for a moment and then said: "Well, what shall I tell you … it is just nature."

'In the evening, I sent for Moshesh again to come to me. Moshesh came, but this time dressed like an ordinary Kaffir, that is, not in European clothes. When he came in, I called him: "Why is Moshesh so long in coming? Can't he come when I send for him?"

'Moshesh answered: "I am Moshesh".'

Three words, but a full explanation. Yet I'm not sure my great-great-uncle understood it. Many decades later, other men like Moshoeshoe looked their white adversaries in the eye and said: 'I am Sobukwe.' 'I am Biko.' 'I am Mandela.' The Verwoerds, Vorsters and Bothas could not grasp that they were saying, 'I am an African. The soil under your feet has belonged to my people long before there was a Europe or an Asia or an America. I represent a civilisation as old as humanity.'

On 27 July 1987, I was sitting in a small hall in Dakar, Senegal. A man, banned and in exile, walked to the microphone to introduce himself to a group of fifty or so nervous white people on a visit from South Africa. He gave a new version of 'I am Moshesh.' He said, 'I am Mbeki. I am an Afrikaner.' (Twelve years later, Thabo Mbeki was elected president of South Africa.)

African/Afrikaner. The first human being on record who described his own identity as someone from the African continent was a young white man in March 1707. Hendrik Biebouw and three of his friends had had too much to drink and were caught racing wildly on their horses through the streets of the tiny village of Stellenbosch. *Landdrost* [magistrate] Johannes Starrenberg hit the teenager with a cane and ordered him to leave. Biebouw shouted: 'I shall not leave, I am an Afrikaander, even if the magistrate beats me to death or puts me in jail.' Five years later, a Dutch colonial document referred to locally born burghers [citizens] as 'Afrikanen'.

Yet, as black South Africans became a more coherent group demanding political rights, the same people who first called themselves by the name of the African continent started identifying themselves as 'Europeans'. It said so on the segregated park benches and public toilets: 'Europeans Only'.

African/Afrikaner. I am both. I call myself after my continent twice. I wish I could otherwise. It is the reason I am in the predicament I am now. During the apartheid years, my fellow Afrikaners deeply resented me because I associated so strongly with the African part of me. Now, after our liberation, fellow Africans only want to see the Afrikaner side of me.

I am a native of this land, but unlike most other natives, I am pale.

The tongue of my heart and my soul is a tongue born in Africa and called after Africa, but after many decades of abuse it is now resented by many as the tongue of alien invaders.

Ja-nee, I thought, sitting on top of the mountain. Africa is not a place for sissies. I was born into a rough neighbourhood. It has no time for sulkers, little mercy for people who act as victims. Have I become one of those despicable, snivelling, so-called liberals who expressed their disdain at the crudities of apartheid but had no stomach for a robust, raw and energetic free South Africa?

The energy that I feel gushing from the soil, my African soil, through my foot soles and into my spirit tells me who I am. The ancient mountains and valleys around me whisper to me that I am where I belong. Forces much greater than loud-mouthed politicians and my own fears and insecurities have placed me exactly here at this time. I am who I should be and where I should be.

My soul is not the soul of a *bywoner*.

So it came that I snapped out of my malaise and decided to let my mind wander over my history, my country and my experiences as a journalist over thirty years. I had the great privilege of having been an eyewitness to one of the greatest human stories in modern history.

That's all this book tries to be: the wanderings of a mind with a very short concentration span, in a small and personal way trying to make sense of big questions around history, fate and identity.

PART I

Sins of the fathers

I

A very strange tribe

I WAS ABOUT fourteen or fifteen years old, which means it was around 1965. I was sitting on the stoep of my family home in the Free State town of Kroonstad, where I was born and went to school. I don't remember much about my childhood, but this one incident is so clear in my memory I can describe the peeling paint on the patio furniture and the dahlias in the garden, the smells of a Highveld afternoon.

With me were my father and one of his friends. I have no idea why I was allowed to listen in on the conversation, because in those days children were supposed to be seen, not heard. 'Are you counting teeth?' was the odd saying when children eavesdropped on the conversations of adults. For some reason, I was allowed to count teeth on this day. Or perhaps they didn't even notice me.

My father's friend was, as I understood it, an emissary from the Afrikaner elders in the town, sent to talk to my father about his behaviour. My father was a pious, God-fearing family man, but he had one habit that disturbed his peers. My father was an elder of our congregation in the Dutch Reformed Church, responsible for keeping the books of the congregation's missionary work. Once a month, Reverend Ernest Buti, the black minister, parked his ancient pick-up truck in the street in front of our house and walked the long garden path to the front door. He was bringing the books and the slips of his mission's expenses and revenue to be checked and filed by my father.

My father would meet Buti at the front door, shake his hand and ask him to sit down on the stoep, or invite him to the *sitkamer* [living room]. If any one of us children were around, we would also greet him by hand: 'Good day, *moruti*' [reverend]. While they were discussing the *moruti*'s work, my mother (my father married again when I was about six) would serve rusks and coffee. After business had been concluded, my father would walk the reverend through the garden to his bakkie, shake his hand, and then he'd be off.

This upset the Afrikaners in our town I learnt from the conversation on the stoep. It was not regarded as proper behaviour for an Afrikaner in the rural Free State in the 1960s to shake the hand of a black man, meet him at the front door and serve him coffee and rusks in the same cups and plates whites used. He personally did not mind it much, my father's friend said, but why did my father have to do it in such a public way? It was only upsetting the good folk of the town. Why could the reverend not stop at the back of the house and go in the back door?

My father, a man with a short temper, was livid. I remember him saying, 'The *moruti* is a servant of God. If I did not treat him with respect, it would be showing disrespect to God. Is that what you people want me to do?'

I remember being intensely proud of my father. I don't remember if my juvenile mind registered that his statement was just and moral, or if I simply liked the fact that my father had made a stand.

The conversation then calmed down and turned to the ordinary things male Afrikaners talked about: rugby and the weather. We were looking across the big lawn that ran all the way to the street, with no wall or fence. We watched a truck with a dozen or so black workers on the back driving up the street. It turned the corner too fast, and the workers had to scramble to keep their balance. As the three of us watched this, my father remarked, 'A pity he didn't go faster. We would have been rid of a few more *kaffirs*.'

I couldn't believe what I had just heard. I looked at my father, laughing at his joke with his friend. How could a man who had just defied his own society, in fact risked being ostracised by his own people on the question of treating black people humanely, turn around a few minutes later and utter such unspeakable racism? How could he himself use the derogatory word for black people that had always been the most taboo word in our family?

This bizarre schizophrenia prevalent in my tribe has gone on to puzzle me all my life.

I have often looked on in amazement at how Afrikaners who held extreme racist views and supported apartheid in its most rigid form, related to their black employees or neighbours or people in public office in the most humane and courteous manner.

I have seen close, almost brotherly relationships between conservative white farmers and their black workers. I have met right-wing Afrikaners who would go out of their way to help black people in need. I have also seen racist behaviour and violence in its most extreme form.

I have also seen Afrikaners switch from the right-wing Conservative Party – and in one case even the Afrikaner Weerstandsbeweging – to being enthusiastic card-carrying members of the African National Congress, who call their friends in the party 'comrade'. I consider all these things and then admit to myself: I really don't understand the Afrikaner psyche.

My parents had instilled in all their children's minds how important it was to respect other human beings. No kind of racist remark or talk was ever allowed in our home. I had seven siblings, and not one of them went on to be a standard Afrikaner nationalist with all the racist undertones it implied at the time. My two elder brothers became *dominees* [ministers] and progressive missionaries, and my elder sister married a left-wing theologian.

My father spoke Sesotho fluently and knew quite a lot about Sotho history – his tales of the proud King Moshoeshoe inspired me decades later to research this remarkable man and make a documentary about him.

There was a strong anti-Jewish sentiment among Afrikaners during my youth. The Jews were the Hoggenheimers, the *Groot Geldmag* [big money power] who helped keep Afrikaners down, and many of them were communists siding with the black majority against the whites. My father, who had been active in the fiercely anti-Semitic Ossewa Brandwag militia in his younger days, clearly did not share these views.

In 1967, when I was still in high school, we were listening to the one o'clock news on the radio during the family lunch, when news came of Israel's Six Day War. I knew very little then of what was going on in the Middle East, but I think I was trying to prove to my father that I was clever, and made some kind of remark about the poor Palestinians suffering under the vicious Israelis.

My father became very angry. He stood up from the table and shouted down at me, 'Nobody insults Israel in my house. Don't you ever say anything against Jews in this house.' (I found out years later that when he as a young man from a very poor home could not find any kind of job during the Depression of the 1930s, he was taken in by old Mr Goldblatt of Goldblatt Wholesalers in Kroonstad, and developed a deep affection for the Goldblatt family.)

So my father appeared to be less prejudiced than the rest of his generation of Afrikaners. He was a fair and generous man. And yet, when I came into open conflict with the National Party government in my late twenties and early thirties, my father closed himself off from me and we did not exchange more than a few words in many years. He was, I thought, traumatised by his community's view that his son was some kind of traitor to the *volk* [nation], a fellow traveller of the country's communist enemies. He was deeply disappointed that I did not go the way of my *dominee* brothers who were serving God, or my other brothers who earned good money in the business sector.

I was a disappointment and an embarrassment to my father. Some time during the late eighties, the local newspaper did a story on my father. I got to see a copy of the interview much later. He told the reporter about his children: his eldest daughter was a teacher married to a Pretoria academic, his two eldest sons were *dominees*, his middle son was … and then I realised he had skipped me. I was the editor of a newspaper at the time, but he preferred to deny my existence.

It wasn't a pleasant feeling, and I never really believed my brothers' explanation later that it was the newspaper's oversight, not my father's. Of course, I never discussed it with him.

I lived with this kind of resentment until I was in my late forties. Then one day I had a call informing me that my father was going to undergo a small operation at a Pretoria hospital, coinciding with his eightieth birthday. I went to see him, and for the first time since I was a child, had a pleasant conversation with him about more than rugby and the weather.

On his way to the hospital, he had seen the newspaper posters on the lamp poles with the story that I had been kicked out of a fairly high-profile job at the SABC the previous day. I told him that my fight with the SABC was about the principle of journalistic freedom and independence.

He touched my shoulder and said he was proud of me. He said that I should know he was always proud of me and always knew I was serving the truth, even when the government he had voted for all his life was trying to paint me as some kind of crazed enemy of the people.

His operation went well, but a few days later he developed unexpected complications. When I saw him again, he was on his deathbed.

I travelled back to Kroonstad for his funeral. I was surprised to see several black people sitting in the church. I was even more surprised that a black minister paid a warm and moving tribute to my father. I also spoke. I am very used to public speaking and spent years as a television anchor. But on this day I had great difficulty speaking.

I looked at the assembled congregation in front of me. I felt the bile of resentment, even naked hatred, push up in my throat. I recognised some of the people from my childhood, now much older. In their faces I saw the faces of PW Botha and his ministers and apparatchiks and his police generals and his foot soldiers. I started shaking and could not speak.

These are the narrow-minded, bigoted, ignorant, arrogant people who dragged my country into the depths of human humiliation and oppression. This is my enemy. These are the people who painted me as some kind of deviant psycho.

I tried to control myself so as not to embarrass my family again. You are the people, I said to the congregation, who made my father suffer because of what I was doing. But why did I become different from you? Why was I fighting against what you stood for? Blame this man, and I pointed to the coffin. Blame my father for what I came to stand for, because he taught me that all people deserved dignity, deserved to be treated with respect. You are here because you loved and respected him; you should also respect that side of him, I said.

Schizophrenia. Utter contradictions.

The last Afrikaner government called me an enemy of the people, and only a few years later, so did the ANC government.

A hundred years ago, my ethnic group was one of the most loved and admired people in the world. Paul Kruger, my maternal ancestor, was eulogised all over

Europe, America and Russia. The nations of the world could not get enough of this quaint tribe of simple, proud people who stood up to the mighty British Empire.

A mere fifty years later, these same people became the single most hated and resented ethnic group in the world. The international community declared the ideology to which they clung a crime against humanity. Sanctions and boycotts were instituted against them. It became a shameful experience for most white South Africans to go through customs at London, New York or Paris and to have to show their South African passport.

Darlings to pariahs in two generations: how did that happen?

And then these very same evil people did something extremely rare, if not unique, in history: they negotiated themselves out of power and handed over the reins of government to the party they had fought violently until five years before. The leaders whom they had jailed for decades and vilified as evil tools of communism soon became their heroes, too: Nelson Mandela, Walter Sisulu, Desmond Tutu.

Many learned (and some not so learned) people have tried to explain how it came about that the once oppressed Afrikaners turned into relentless oppressors themselves and embraced a vicious ideology of complete racial separation. I understand the explanations, but I still don't understand my tribe. They are almost defined by their inconsistencies, ambivalences and contrarieties.

I love them and I hate them at the same time. But I am one of them.

2

About ancestors

I NEVER HAD the urge to research my family history. It never mattered to me who exactly my ancestors were – I vaguely knew that they were a rough bunch of white people with beards and strange clothes and little education, and that was enough for me.

From the time I was very young I had a gut instinct that the leaders of my ethnic group were lying to me. I did not know the truth and I could not articulate my instincts, but I knew I should not believe *them*. I did not believe my history teachers, because my experiences of the glorious people they described to me indicated otherwise. The Church in which I grew up lied to me. I knew the things the *dominee* and members of his church council were up to, and I often sat in church shaking my head inwardly when I looked at their pious faces.

I remember seeing huge barbed-wire fences going up around the fuel tanks in our town after 1960, with police and soldiers on guard everywhere. I was told that the 'location', as the black township was known, had become a dangerous place for whites. I asked what was going on. I was told that black people planned to rise up and kill white people. I looked at the black people I came into daily contact with, and I knew I was being lied to.

The only stories I did like from the Afrikaner history that I was taught were the stories of Christiaan de Wet and Koos de la Rey, two brave and cunning generals during the Anglo-Boer War. And I was fascinated by the story of how the Zulu king Dingane killed Voortrekker leader Piet Retief and his party. I wondered how it felt to be a handful of white people facing a horde of half-naked Zulus with murder in their hearts. But I also wondered if there was a part of the story that I wasn't being told. Cold-blooded murder such as that, and for no reason at all, seemed odd to me.

As a child I always had the feeling that I was born in the wrong place at the wrong time. I deeply resented the severe restrictions and discipline forced on me, and I could not wait for the day I would leave school to start my 'real' life. I felt uncomfortable in my strict Calvinist family home, and I felt very out of place in the schools I attended. I never had one good friend until I went to university. Since leaving school, I've never had contact with anyone with whom I went to school.

I did sometimes try to fit in and be accepted, especially to get girls, but mostly I accepted my plight as an outsider. At one stage, I think I was about fifteen, I firmly believed that this was God's punishment for all my sins.

So my ties to my community and my ethnic group were rather tenuous. There has not been a single day in my life that I did not know and feel that I was an Afrikaner, and I never resented the fact, but when I looked at them as a group, I often thought they were intolerant, narrow-minded, xenophobic and obsessed with hero worship. These emotions, of course, made it much easier for me as a young journalist to learn the truth about my society, and to then live my life in opposition to apartheid and exclusive ethnic nationalism.

So I never had an urge to know more about my ancestors, my family or 'my people' until late in my life.

Two events changed my mind. The first was stumbling across a mystical figure from central South Africa in the mid-eighteenth century, Mohlomi. I had never heard of him before, but I came across this little-known character while researching the life of King Moshoeshoe. Mohlomi opened my eyes; he made me look at and appreciate the concept of ancestors.

Mohlomi was born around 1720 (four years before German philosopher Immanuel Kant, eight years after French philosopher Jean Jacques Rousseau). Mohlomi was the grandson of Monaheng (also known as Kali), the Koena chief who led his people into the Caledon Valley, which now forms the border between South Africa and Lesotho. Before that, only the Bushman (San) lived in that area.

During his initiation, probably around 1736, Mohlomi had an extraordinary vision. One night the roof of the initiation hut opened up and Mohlomi was transported to the heavens on the back of a giant eagle, where he was met by a great assembly of the *Balimo*, the souls of the departed ancestors. The *Balimo* told him his land was in trouble and that he had been chosen to do something about it. He was taught how to live as a man and a chief and sent back with the words, 'Go, teach your people love, respect and peace.'

Mohlomi spent the rest of his life doing that. Armed with only a walking stick, he walked to all centres of civilisation in southern Africa at the time (horses were unknown to these parts until about 1820). We know that he walked to Delagoa Bay, today's Maputo; to Great Zimbabwe; to the Tswana settlement near Kuruman; to the Ulundi area in KwaZulu-Natal; to what later became known as the Transkei. He lived off the veld and, according to legend, had many close encounters with lion, cheetah, buffalo, rhino and elephant.

Mohlomi's philosophy was later described as *botho*, translatable as compassionate humanism. He taught people to greet each other by raising an open right hand to show they had no weapon, and to call out '*Khotso!*' [peace] – a custom that has survived to this day. He lectured chiefs to protect women and children and to abstain from smoking marijuana and drinking sorghum beer. And he preached democracy: 'A chief is a chief only by the grace of his people,' was one of his famous sayings.

But he was most concerned about southern Africa's main problem at the time: hostility and armed conflict between chiefdoms. Some of his famous sayings that endured were 'Peace is my Sister' (women occupied a tenuous social position at the time and had to be cherished), and 'It is better to thrash the sorghum than to sharpen the spear.'

Mohlomi, who never in his life met a white man, was also responsible for establishing the concept of diplomatic immunity in southern Africa – something that hardly existed in most parts of Europe at the time. He declared – and it became the custom – that messengers between chiefs should never be attacked. Even if it is a messenger from your worst enemy, you are not allowed to kill him; instead, you have an obligation to give him food and shelter and help him on his way. In the years of great conflict that were to follow, this custom was mostly respected, even by great warriors such as Shaka and Mzilikazi.

Evidence indicates that the chiefs took Mohlomi seriously, rather than seeing him as a weirdo, mainly because he was a famous medicine man who actually helped the sick get better, as well as a wonderful storyteller. He was a chief in his own right, but apparently not a very hands-on one. He preferred to wander the subcontinent and let the elders of his clan rule. His kraal was at Ngoliloe, in the district of what is today the Eastern Free State town of Marquard.

Mohlomi was a remarkable man. There were very few, if any, leaders or philosophers in the world at the time who preached love, tolerance, women's rights, peace, democracy and abstinence. He was a black Confucius, but his civilisation chose, because of their way of life and the fact that they were cattle farmers who moved around a lot, to relate their stories and philosophies orally, rather than writing them down. That is why very few people today are conscious of this deeply spiritual man who lived in Africa. He would have been a famous New Age guru if he lived today.

The story fast-forwards to 1786, to a village roughly about 100 kilometres north-east of Ngoliloe, called Menkhoaneng, where a boy was born to Mokhachane, chief of the tiny Mokoteli clan, and his wife Kholu. His name was Lepoqo. Through his mother and his paternal grandmother he was also related to the great chief of the Koena, Monaheng/Kali, Mohlomi's grandfather.

Lepoqo was destined to become one of Africa's greatest sons ever. In fact, we could call him the first Nelson Mandela. But he achieved greatness under another name.

Lopoqo was a troubled and aggressive boy. It was almost as if he always knew he was destined to be a great leader of people and was frustrated at being a mere herd boy in Menkhoaneng.

Shortly after his initiation around 1804, Lepoqo decided to prove himself to his age-mates and led them on a successful raid against the neighbouring village of Chief RaMonaheng, a man who had given the Mokoteli people lots of trouble over the years.

When Lepoqo returned with dozens of fat cattle, a praise singer chanted that by taking his cattle, Lepoqo had shaved RaMonaheng's beard, the symbol of his manhood. 'Shwe, shwe,' the praise singer imitated the sound of the razor on the beard – and so gave Lepoqo the name by which he became famous: Mo-shwe-shwe, or Moshoeshoe as it is spelled in Sesotho. Moshoeshoe composed a new verse in his own honour.

Ke 'ena Moshoeshoe Moshoashoaila oa ka Kali
Lebeola le beotseng RaMonaheng litelu
[I am Moshoeshoe, the Shaver, descendant of Kali
The barber's blade that shaved off RaMonaheng's beard]

But the young Moshoeshoe's burning ambition to be chief and his frequently violent temper bothered his grandfather, Peete. If Moshoeshoe were to become a good chief of the Mokoteli people, something drastic had to be done. Strong medicine, said Peete, was the only answer. And the most famous medicine man in the whole region was Mohlomi.

It is said that Mohlomi immediately sensed that Moshoeshoe, later abbreviated to Moshesh, was destined for great things. Despite the long queue of people waiting for his advice and medicine, Mohlomi spent several days educating Moshesh. You need the wisdom of the *Balimo*, not medicine, he told Moshesh.

According to the research of a historian who later became the prime minister of Lesotho, Ntsu Mokhehle, Mohlomi told Moshesh that he was destined to be a great chief and leader of many clans. He told Moshesh, 'Learn to understand men and know their ways. Learn to bear with their human weaknesses and shortcomings. In their disputes, adjudicate with justice and sympathy. Your closest friends should be the children. The poor and the troubled need you more than those with wealth and status. The land you shall rule should be a home to travellers and fugitives. Always be slow to take up arms – lean heavily on the rod of peace.'

Mohlomi warned Moshesh to be sceptical of sorcerers. He often played a trick on his own people: he would hide an item somewhere and then summon those who called themselves seers to find out who stole it. They would throw their bones and then pick a culprit, whereupon Mohlomi would bring out the item with the warning that these people should not be trusted. In later life, Moshesh often played the same trick on some of his senior advisers.

Mohlomi was equally strict in his advice that no one should ever be killed because he or she was accused of being a witch. This was a universal problem at the time, even in so-called Enlightened Europe: the last record of a person accused of witchcraft and executed by the state was in Portugal in 1811. Mohlomi's advice was something Moshesh always adhered to, and he campaigned against witch-hunts.

Eventually Mohlomi declared that Moshesh's tuition was over. He presented Moshesh with a spear and a shield as symbols of authority, and in an unusual gesture for such a famous and powerful man, took off one of his earrings and gave it to Moshesh. Then he put his hands on Moshesh's shoulders, rubbed his forehead against the young man's, and said: 'All the knowledge and wisdom with which *Molimo* [God] and the spirits of our ancestors have blessed me, are now yours also.'

Peete and Moshesh's father, Mokhachane, both soon noticed a marked change in the young man's behaviour. It was as if he had found the path that he had longed for, as if he was starting to channel his considerable energy differently now.

Proof that he was a changed man came a few months later. A man in a village near Menkhoaneng killed his own son, mistaking him for an intruder. The chief asked Moshesh's father to bring some of his men to help kill the killer.

The young Moshesh intervened. Would the man who kills the killer then not also have to be killed, and the man who kills that man also, he asked to the astonishment of all who knew him. The man's life was spared.

Back to Mohlomi. On his deathbed, in 1818 or 1819, Mohlomi had another vision, one that truly disturbed him. He told his wife, Maliepollo, and the elders gathered around. 'After my death, a cloud of red dust will come out of the east and consume our peoples. The father will eat his children.'

About a year later, his prediction came true: a period of ten years of brutal conflict between chiefdoms and groups, starting among the Nguni-speakers in the east, with a domino effect right into the Caledon Valley and as far north as present-day Mozambique, Zimbabwe, Tanzania and Malawi. Hundreds of thousands of people died, and more were uprooted. It was called, in Sotho, the *Lifacane*, or in Zulu, the *Mfecane* – the great upheaval – and it inscribed the names of a few leaders forever onto the pages of southern African history: Shaka, Mzilikazi, Matiwane, Manthathisi, Sekonyela, Mapangazita. And Moshesh.

It is my considered opinion that if there had not been one strong stabilising force in South Africa at the time, one great leader who gathered and united people rather than take part in the killing himself, South Africa would have looked a lot different today. Many more people would have died, and the conflict would probably have engulfed the southern parts of the country as well. The resistance the black inhabitants of southern Africa mustered when white trekboers started moving onto their land from about 1838 would probably have been a lot weaker.

Moshesh was that leader. Applying Mohlomi's philosophy and advice, he ensconced himself and his small chiefdom on top of a virtually impenetrable flat mountain top, Thaba Bosiu, and collected and gathered individuals and groups fleeing from the *Lifacane* – even groups of cannibals, including the group that captured and ate his beloved grandfather, Peete. He quickly became famous all over southern Africa for his masterful, sometimes genius diplomacy. He ruled wisely and peacefully, and within a few years had established a prosperous nation, the Basotho. His territory later became the British Protectorate of Basutoland, now the independent kingdom of Lesotho. His subjects and their descendants were the only people inside the geographical borders of South Africa who were never subjected to apartheid.

Moshesh deserves the title of 'the Nelson Mandela of the nineteenth century'. (A remarkable spiritualist and sangoma who lives in the caves in the Mautse Valley, Thikhilalana, says on the day of Mandela's inauguration as president in 1994, she saw him right there in front of her, shaking hands with King Moshesh.)

White South Africans are so utterly ignorant of this side of their nation and their history. This is what one of the great white intellectuals of the twentieth century, Dr Hendrik Verwoerd, said on 10 March 1960: 'The fundamental reality being disregarded is that without white civilisation, non-whites may never have known the meaning of idealism or ambition, liberty or opportunity.' Mohlomi and Moshoeshoe and many other African philosophers and kings knew as much or more about all these things than Verwoerd's Dutch ancestors who lived during their time.

Mohlomi and Moshesh made me aware of the importance of ancestors, of the value of understanding those who came before you. I started to realise that I could not make sense of my society if I did not understand what events and which people shaped and influenced our attitudes and memories.

In recent years I found myself going back to this theme again and again. On 26 January 2001, I wrote about it in my column for the Independent Newspapers Group:

> If white South Africans really knew and understood the true history of the people of this country, they would have acted very differently the last few decades – and they would have been far more tolerant and less selfish and self-obsessed now that we have a democracy.
>
> Equally, if the present leadership of the ANC and the new black elite appreciated and respected the true history of the people of this country, they would not have been so power-hungry, greedy and arrogant.
>
> I have spent the last two days on Robben Island directing two television documentaries on the history of the struggle for democracy. I'm writing this from a house formerly occupied by an apartheid-era prison warder. Today I listened to eight former political prisoners, who spent their best years on this island, telling the stories of their lives and their time in prison.
>
> These men did not only obliterate the creeping sense of pessimism that has recently threatened to overwhelm me about the affairs of my nation.

They actually inspired me anew to believe in the magic of what we as a nation have achieved here on the southern tip of Africa, and to recommit myself to working for the preservation and development of that magic.

Moving around on this island also brought me another insight: white people shy away from the history of this country and deny as much of it as often as they can, because they feel threatened by it; they think of it as an attack on them. They don't want to know about the ugly parts of the early colonial history when the Khoi and San were brutally subjugated and Africans dispossessed. That means they cannot accept the proud and beautiful stories of the Khoi leader Autsomato or of Adam Kok, Shaka, Dingane or Moshoeshoe as their own. They think only the history of Jan van Riebeeck or Piet Retief or Paul Kruger is their history, and then they have to glorify these figures, despite the evidence, to be proud of them. Because how can you be confident and proud of who you are if you despise the history of your ancestors?

If Thabo Mbeki can express his admiration for the early Khoi leaders and of the Afrikaner women of the Anglo-Boer War, as he has done, and Jakes Gerwel can speak proudly of the Zulu, Xhosa and Basotho heroes of the previous century, as he has done, then certainly white South Africans can decide to also own these heroes, to accept those parts of our history as their own. The fact that I am an ethnic Afrikaner surely doesn't disqualify me from claiming the resistance of fellow South Africans against colonialism, injustice and apartheid as my history, because I'm a South African and an African before I'm a white or an Afrikaner.

There needs to be a very fundamental mind shift: whites should, and should be helped to, break the mould of them as a separate group inside this nation. Embracing the amazing history of our liberation over many generations would be a good first step, and would replace the paralysing feelings of guilt, however hidden and denied, with pride and a commitment to make this country work better. Nobody in the world deserves to be forever condemned to being the evil offspring of despised colonialists and racists.

I dream of the day our young people of different groups and races can believe in a shared history. The day a young Afrikaner can talk of his proud ancestor King Moshoeshoe who built a nation and was never defeated, or a young black person of his ancestor Christiaan de Wet, the cunning guerrilla fighter who gave the mighty British a run for their money a century ago. In a small way, we have that already: most whites are intensely proud of Nelson Mandela, even though their own kin threw him in jail, and many blacks accept people like Joe Slovo and Beyers Naude as their own heroes. It is true of most nations: you don't have to be in the same ethnic bloodline of the great men and women of the past to own them as heroes. Thabo Mbeki has expressed his deep association with the early Khoi leaders and of Afrikaner women of the Anglo-Boer War very eloquently in his 'I am an African' speech. The fact that I am an ethnic Afrikaner doesn't disqualify me from claiming the resistance of fellow South Africans against colonialism, injustice and apartheid as my own history, as I do.

The history of the early Khoi and San who clashed with the first European seafarers and colonialists is my history. The history of Shaka and Ngqika and Hintsa and Sekonyela and Adam Kok is my history, as is the history of Slagtersnek and the Great Trek and Blood River. All these people are my ancestors, the fathers (and mothers) of my nation who came before. I don't have to like them or agree with what they did for them to be my ancestors, they just are.

We should not over-romanticise our history, and we should never allow anyone to manipulate it to serve any kind of political or other purpose. But we should also resist the attempts of academics, politicians and others to try to separate our past into little ethnic boxes, to make separate histories with 'good guys' and 'bad guys', 'good tribes' and 'evil tribes'. History writing should not be about demonising and glorifying, but about facts, perspectives, contexts, attitudes and interactions.

We should claim our common history as South Africans, otherwise we will remain the victims of the past.

3

European gentlemen

DISCOVERING THE FASCINATING history of slavery at the Cape Colony in the seventeenth and eighteenth centuries was the other thing that stimulated my desire to delve into the past, and particularly my own and my ancestors'. I started researching slavery at the Cape after a moving visit to the old slave island of Gorée off the Senagalese coast in 1987.

The easiest way for a slave woman to get her freedom was to marry a white settler. There were thousands of marriages across the colour line in the first century of colonialism at the Cape, I read to my astonishment. Could my Du Preez, Kruger or Saayman (my paternal grandmother's maiden name) ancestors have been among them? I tried to find out. (I do not know my maternal grandmother's maiden name.)

Not a lot has been written on slavery in South Africa. It is probably the one part of our history least known to citizens. And yet, by 1834, when slavery was abolished, there were 36 169 slaves in the colony. That represented a large chunk of the total population living in the Cape Colony in that period. Between the importation of the first slaves shortly after 1652 and the abolition of the overseas slave trade in 1807, about 60 000 slaves were brought to the Cape. Historians and social commentators of all groups seem reluctant to fully explore and explain this part of our history. Why, I wonder. Does it make them uncomfortable?

Understanding the history of slavery in South Africa and the white attitudes towards slaves is, I firmly believe, absolutely crucial if one wants to understand the unfolding white attitudes in the nineteenth and twentieth centuries that resulted in de jure apartheid after 1948. Most historians teach us that the interaction between the Xhosa and the settlers on the eastern frontier of the colony was the primary formative influence on racial attitudes. My understanding is that the pattern of racial relations had by then already largely been established.

A South African historian who has researched and published on slavery, Hermann Giliomee, appears to agree with this view. He writes in his monumental work *The Afrikaners, Biography of a People*: 'Negative views of blacks ... were part of the identity map of burghers well before they met blacks on the frontier. So was racial apprehension. Burghers were not so much afraid of a general slave uprising as of their own slaves murdering them or setting fire to their houses. The insecurity springing from life on isolated farms produced the phobias that were to mark white society in the centuries to come.'

What made slavery more evil than any other form of oppression or discrimination is the fact that it reduced a human life to an object, to property.

One of the most profound pictures painted of slavery was, ironically, by US president George W Bush on the same Gorée Island during his African tour in July 2003.

He said: 'At this place, liberty and life were stolen and sold. Human beings were delivered and sorted, and weighed, and branded with the marks of commercial enterprises, and loaded as cargo on a voyage without return. One of the largest migrations of history was also one of the greatest crimes of history.'

Those who survived the voyage, Bush continued, were 'displayed, examined and sold at auctions across nations in the western hemisphere. They entered societies indifferent to their anguish and made prosperous by their unpaid labour. There was a time in my country's history when one in every seven human beings was the property of another. In law, they were regarded only as articles of commerce, having no right to travel, or to marry, or to own possessions.'

The spirit of the African slaves did not break, Bush said. And then he said something that is equally true of slavery at the Cape Colony: 'Yet the spirit of their captors was corrupted. Small men took on the powers and airs of tyrants and masters. Years of unpunished brutality and bullying and rape produced a dullness and hardness of conscience. Christian men and women became blind to the clearest commands of their faith and added hypocrisy to injustice.'

When the settlers arrived from Holland, Germany and France, they brought with them the attitudes of Europe. They believed in personal freedom, and the sanctity of property rights was central to that freedom. Slave owners included their slaves on inventories of property with their cattle and sheep. Good Christians and liberal-minded colonials believed that slaves had to be treated well, but never questioned the right of one human being to wholly own the life of another. And remember: slaves were always black people.

Most white men in the colony owned slaves: two-thirds of the burghers in Cape Town and three-quarters of the farmers in the districts of Stellenbosch and Drakenstein owned slaves by 1795.

A peculiar feature of the relationship between slave and master at the Cape at that time was the custom to have slave women wet-nurse the white babies. Giliomee reports speculation that this intimate relationship between white boys and slave women 'could, in later life, find expression in [white men] being more at ease with black women and even preferring sex with them than with white women'.

Now here's a thought: those men who got their milk as babies from a black woman, who grew up with her intimate body smell and warmth, went on to use her as a piece of property when they became adults. This must do serious damage to one's soul. There is not one instance on record where one of these men had freed his surrogate mother when he took over the household.

Unlike in America and Europe, an active abolitionist or anti-slavery movement never developed in South Africa. This contributed to the fact that a human rights culture and a proper liberal movement also never really developed in South Africa, not until the late twentieth century. That is one reason why a system such as apartheid could be implemented.

Until very recently, most white South Africans believed – because historians told them to – that the trekboers on the eastern frontier decided to migrate into the interior of South Africa in 1835 (the Great Trek) because of their fierce sense of independence – they merely wanted to throw off the yoke of British colonialism.

It is true that they loathed the colonial authorities. It is also true that they felt threatened by the lack of physical security and vulnerable to Xhosa incursions. But on closer analysis it becomes clear that the abolition of slavery on 31 August 1833 played a major role in the trekkers' decision. Trek leaders such as Gert Maritz had many slaves, but it was about more than simply losing out financially.

The abolition of slavery was experienced as an assault on the trekboers' way of life and a violation of their basic right to property. It fuelled their resentment of the British, and they saw the ending of slavery as the hated 'philanthropists' getting the upper hand in determining British policy in the colony.

Great Trek leader Piet Retief himself declared in 1836 that the trekboers 'were deprived in most cases of the services of their servants, and which in the present distressing times cannot fail to have a most prejudicial effect upon their agricultural pursuits in general'.

But I believe the most important factor at play was that the abolition of slavery threatened their sense of being untouchable masters and overlords; their long-held views on race and class. Their superior racial identity was integral to the view that they had on life, society and themselves. This undermining of their communal psyche started in 1828 with Ordinance 50, which determined that no free inhabitant of the colony could be forced to work or have his freedom of movement curtailed on the grounds of his race or skin colour. It became known as the Magna Carta for the Khoikhoi.

Of course, some would say that the handing over of government to the black majority in 1994 was a similar shock to Afrikaners' racial sensibilities – and led to the Second Trek, this time to Australia, Canada and elsewhere. But that would perhaps be an oversimplification.

But back to the slave question.

From my earliest youth, I remember that when you really wanted to insult someone, you would say: Only two Krugers (for example) came to South Africa. The one never had children; the other one married a black woman.

The premise of this widely used insult was that Afrikaners were a pure white race and that having black blood – 'a touch of the tar brush' – made you inferior.

In his 1947 book, *Regverdige Rasse-apartheid*, the influential academic G Cronjé wrote that the mixing of races was 'highly undesirable' because it would lead to an 'inferior' group of people. They would have congenital weaknesses to, among other things, alcoholism. (Perhaps he had a point: the super-Afrikaners of the Afrikaner Weerstandsbeweging seem to have a serious weakness for brandy and Coke.)

Much later, a minister in the ruling National Party cabinet and later founder of the Conservative Party, Dr Andries Treurnicht, wrote in his book *Credo van 'n Afrikaner*: 'Never since the founding of the nation [*volksplanting*] in 1652 were people of colour accepted in the ranks of the Afrikaner volk nor were they accepted as part of the white community.'

The National Party's Programme of Principles, published in 1914, declared: 'In our attitude towards the Natives the fundamental principle is the supremacy of the European population in a spirit of Christian trusteeship, utterly rejecting every attempt to mix the races.'

Lily-white Afrikaners. One only need consult the exhaustive research of JA Heese (*Die Herkoms van die Afrikaner*, published in 1971) and HF Heese (*Groep sonder Grense*, published in 1984) to establish that as a concept, pure-white Afrikaners never existed.

The first documented marriage between a white settler at the Cape and a slave was that between Jan Woutersz and Catharina of Bengal in 1656. (Slaves did not have surnames; they were identified by the places where they came from.) Jan became a caretaker on Robben Island, where their child was born in 1657. Jan, Catharina and their children lived in the white settler community with no discrimination.

Most slaves at the Cape were from India, the East Indies or Madagascar, but there were also slaves from Angola, Guinea and Mozambique.

In 1658, Jan Sacharias, a freeburgher, married Maria of Bengal. Maria belonged to medical officer Pieter van der Stael, but Sacharias bought her freedom in order to marry her. In the document that was submitted to the Political Council, it was pointed out that Maria could speak and understand Dutch and that she already had a rudimentary knowledge of the Christian Reformed religion. Their daughter, Maria, was baptised in the Fort in 1660.

The first documented marriage between a white man and a Khoikhoi woman took place in 1664. Pieter van Meerhoff was a Danish soldier and medic employed by the Dutch East India Company (VOC) who arrived in the Cape in 1659. He married Eva, a Khoi woman who spoke Dutch and Portuguese and was part of Jan van

Riebeeck's household. Because she did such good work for the VOC as an interpreter and intermediary with Khoikhoi chiefs without getting paid, the company decided to throw her a wedding party and contribute to her dowry. After Van Meerhoff's death, Eva found herself lost between the two cultures. She became a prostitute and an alcoholic, and was detained several times on Robben Island, where she died in 1674.

In 1669 Arnoldus Willemsz Basson married Angela of Bengal. She became the matriarch of all Bassons in South Africa and many other Afrikaans families.

There are also marriages between freed slaves and white women on record. One example was Christoffel Snyman, son of the freed slave Antony of Bengal and Catharina of Palicatte, who married the daughter of a prominent Huguenot, Marguerite de Savoy. Most of today's South African Snymans are their descendants.

It was more difficult to establish how many white settlers had relationships with slaves without getting married. In some cases these could be traced through the registers of christened children. Jan Herfst (many descendants were later called Herbst) baptised his son Johannes in 1685. The mother was an African slave, Cecilia of Angola. He later had another child with Lijsbeth, daughter of Louis of Bengal, whose mother was an African slave from Guinea. All these descendants became part of white society.

Other extramarital relationships between slaves and settlers are traceable from court documents. Jan van Riebeeck suspected his slave Maria of Bengal of having a relationship with constable Willem Cornelis. On Sunday night, 23 August 1660, Van Riebeeck and two witnesses caught the lovers in bed. Cornelis was hauled before court, where he was fined and fired. (Three hundred years later, this act of spying on people in bed was repeated hundreds of times during raids on 'mixed' couples under the Immorality Act.)

My favourite story of such relationships is the story of the Cape beer brewer Willem Mensing, who was in love with a black slave from Madagascar, Tryntje. Tryntje's owner, a Cape society woman, tried her best to keep the two apart, even forcing Tryntje to sleep with her in bed or chaining her for the night in the attic. But love knows no restrictions, and in 1712 Tryntje had Willem's baby. We'll get back to Willem a little later.

Armosyn Claasz of the Cape (slaves born in the Cape were referred to as 'van de Kaap') was born in 1661 in the VOC's slave lodge. Her mother was an African slave, probably from Angola. In 1688 she had a son, Claas Jonasz, baptised. Most of his descendants became part of the white society – the Afrikaner families Brits, Van Deventer, Slabbert, Fischer and Carstens count among them.

Armosyn's daughter Manda Gratia's father was an African slave and she was very dark-skinned. But she was also very talented, and became the matron of the slave lodge at the age of thirty-five. By 1714, Manda Gratia had had four children with white men: Johannes, Frans, Pieter Cornelis and Magdalena Geertruy.

Armosyn's youngest daughter, Magdalena Ley, was also born out of a relationship with a white man, and she was baptised in 1697 as a slave child belonging to the VOC. Magdalena married Hermanus Combrink in 1720 and became the matriarch of all Combrinks in South Africa. Other Afrikaner families with close blood ties to Magdalena are Ackerman, Nel, Alberts and Grobbelaar/Grobler.

Remember the story of Hendrik Biebouw, the first man on record to call himself an Afrikaner? His father, Dietlof Biebouw, had a daughter with his slave lover called Diana in 1687; thus she was Hendrik's half-sister. She later married an Odendaal, and all Odendaals in South Africa today can trace their roots back to them.

Then there is the story of the son of Abdulbasi, the Rajah of Tambora. His name was Ibrahim Adehan. He wasn't a slave and it isn't known why he came to the Cape, but according to church registers he was baptised as a Christian on 2 November 1721 – under the Dutch-sounding name of Abraham de Haan. On 20 September 1722 he married Helena Valentyn, daughter of Hercules Valentyn from the west coast of India, and Cecilia of Bengal. Their daughters, Sara, Louise and Maria, and son Abraham, all married white people.

Church records also registered the conversion and baptism of one Juko, a Chinese man, on 19 February 1702. He changed his name to Abraham de Vyf, and married Maria of Batavia in April 1702. His daughter, Leonora, married Andries Bacsktroo in 1712, and after his death married Nicolaas Jan Mulder. What are the chances that they are the ancestors of the late National Party cabinet minister Connie Mulder and his two sons, who now lead the Freedom Front in parliament?

One reason for the unexpectedly high number of marriages between white settlers and slaves was that there was a serious shortage of white women at the Cape in those early years. The VOC's first priority was to import soldiers, sailors and officials, and of course women didn't qualify.

It was mostly soldiers and lower class company officials who married slaves, and after 1657 the burghers who were released from the VOC's employ and allowed to farm for their own account [vryburgers]. Apart perhaps from the French Huguenots, who arrived from 1688, the whites at the Cape came from poor, struggling families in Holland and Germany and were not highly educated. These were the people who stayed, because most of the senior officials in the VOC went back home or were posted to another colony.

According to Prof HF Heese, the colour of a person's skin or their race didn't mean automatic exclusion from material and social progress in the early years at the Cape, as long as he or she was not born as a slave. Membership of the Christian church made assimilation into the European society much easier. Muslims and Hindus found themselves outside this main stream, and even where they were light-skinned because of intermarrying, they were shunned.

All children born before 1795 (the date of the British occupation of the colony) from marriages between white men and slaves grew up in white society and were accepted as 'white'.

By the beginning of the eighteenth century, there were several 'Euro-Asian' and 'Euro-African' families who were accepted as white. At the Cape, the Bassons and Vermeulens were influential families, and among the trekboers there were the descendants of Johannes Antonissen of Bali, of David Hoon, who was the son of Sambouw of Madagascar, and Johannes Claasen, son of Claas of Malabar.

Marrying a white man was the easiest way for a slave woman to obtain her freedom and improve her social and material position. But she had to become a Christian first, because most of the slaves were either Muslim or Hindu. A slave woman's child with a white man would be born a slave, unless the white man accepted the child as his own and bought his or her freedom.

Not only were there more white men than women in the colony, there were almost twice as many male slaves as females. On the farms outside Cape Town, the best chance male slaves had to find a wife was among the Khoikhoi. A child between a slave and a Khoi would be born free, but could be forced to work on the farm for a period. These offspring were called Baster Hottentotte, and they occupied a very low position on the social ladder. Descendants of white and Khoi relationships were called Basters, and they enjoyed much more freedom than the Baster Hottentotte. The Basters formed the nucleus of the later Rehoboth Basters who still live south of Windhoek in Namibia, and the Griqua.

Between the two main cultural-economic groups, the Christian European group and the Muslim or 'Cape Malay' group, another group existed at the Cape: some were slaves, some former slaves, some were 'Baster Hottentotte', some were the offspring of white and black liaisons but were not claimed by their white fathers. This in-between group was later called the 'Cape Coloureds'.

By the end of the eighteenth century, the pattern was firmly established in the Cape Colony: white meant dominant and prosperous, dark meant inferior and poor. This pattern was strengthened even more under British rule, and remained valid in the whole of South Africa for two centuries.

In fact, many of those early patterns continued until very recently. Sexual intercourse outside marriage was outlawed in the Cape, but very rarely did white men get punished for it, and when they did, it was a mild punishment. Black men did not have it that easy. In 1695 a freed slave, Jan of Batavia, was found guilty of having had sex with a young white woman. He was sentenced to corporal punishment and then banished to twenty years of hard labour in Mauritius.

In 1713 a black slave, Anthony of Mozambique, was found guilty of raping a young white woman. The court found that it was a crime of 'despicable enormity' because he was a heathen and she was a Christian. His sentence? He was tied to a cross, his skin was pinched off his body with red-hot iron instruments, his back and bones were then broken while he was still alive, and then he was decapitated. His body was fed to the vultures and his head was put on a stake for everybody to see. Talk about sending a clear message.

Hypocrisy on racial issues among whites is the other pattern that struck me while reading all these amazing tales. Remember the story I told earlier of Willem Mensing who had the love affair with Tryntje of Mozambique? Remember the marriage between Marguerite, daughter of a prominent Huguenot, and Christoffel Snyman, son of two East Indian slaves?

Just after 1700, a group of Stellenbosch farmers complained to the authorities that they felt threatened by the non-white groups in the colony. The Khoikhoi would attack 'the Christians' at the slightest opportunity, they stated in their petition, as would the 'Caffers, Moulattos, Mesticos, Casticos and all the black riff-raff [*swart gebroeidsel*]'. They expressed their disgust at the number of racially mixed marriages and concluded that 'Ham's blood' [*Chams bloed*] was 'not to be trusted'.

One of the petitioners was the very same Willem Mensing who could not keep his hands off the black Tryntje, and even had a baby with her. Another petitioner was the father of Marguerite, the prominent Huguenot Jacob de Savoye, who at that stage was already the grandfather of several 'mestico' children. These men cursed their own blood.

It made me think of a story Van Zyl Slabbert told of his time as Leader of the Opposition in the South African parliament. Referring to Dr Andries Treurnicht, whom I quoted earlier on the topic of racial purity, Slabbert writes in his book *Afrikaner/Afrikaan*: 'A frontbencher in his party once said in parliament, to the great entertainment of his fellow party members, that only two Slabberts came to South Africa: the one died without children, and the other one married a black woman. Not long after that there was a woman in my parliamentary office. She wanted me to help her get an American visa. She worked in the South African Navy and I suggested to her that it would be easier getting it through government channels than through the opposition. She said it was too risky, because she had a relationship with a black American diplomat and that they were in love. In that case, I suggested to her, it would be easier to do it through him. No, she was afraid it would be exploited for sensation. I asked her what made her so special. She replied, "I am Andries Treurnicht's daughter."' (My translation.)

Prof. Heese found that there were more than 1 200 marriages between white and black or people of mixed blood between 1652 and 1800. He calculates that Afrikaners have at least 7.2 per cent 'non-white' blood in their veins. His breakdown of Afrikaner genes by 1837 looks like this: Dutch 35. 5 per cent; German 34.4; French 13.9; Asian/African/Khoi 7.2; British 2.6; other (Scandinavian, etc.) 2.6; and unknown, 3.5 per cent.

But what about my direct family? The Du Preez patriarch, Hercule, arrived from France via Holland in 1688 and became a wine farmer on De Zoete Inval, now the prosperous town of Paarl. He spelled his name Du Pré (I've even seen the spelling Des Pres), but as happened with several other Huguenot surnames, half-literate Dutch clerks corrupted the name on official forms. Along with the more famous Adam Tas, Hercule was involved in a revolt against Governor Willem Adriaan van der Stel in 1706 – the governor described him as 'a most malicious and dangerous character'.

Hercule's grandson, Philippe, married a woman of mixed blood (her mother was a freed slave), Isabella Potgieter, in 1727. The couple had several children.

On the Saayman side, my father's mother's family, I had more luck – I can even claim Khoikhoi ancestry. Daniel Zaaiman, as the surname was then spelled, married Pieternella Meerhoff, daughter of the Khoi woman Eva and the Dane Pieter van Meerhoff. They had two sons, Johannes and Christiaan. And in 1712 a Pieter Zaaiman married the daughter of a slave and a white man, Anna Marie Koopman.

On the Kruger side I found that Jacob Kruger married Jannetje Kemp, who was not white, in 1718. But there had to be a lot more of that in the Kruger family – does Paul Kruger look even remotely Aryan in any of the photographs you have seen of him? I don't think so.

In the church and colonial records checked by the two professors Heese, the following typical Afrikaans families appear on the list of white men who married black, Asian or mixed-blood women: Ackerman, Alberts, Badenhorst, Basson, Beets, Bester, Beyers, Bezuidenhout, Blom, Bodenstein, Boonzaaier, Boshoff, Botha, Brand, Brink, Brits, Buys, Claassen, Coetzee, Combrink, De Bruin, De Jager, De Klerk, De Vries, De Wit, Du Plooy, Du Preez, Ehlers, Eksteen, Erasmus, Esterhuyzen, Fouche, Gerber, Geyer, Geyser, Goosen, Gous (Gouws), Harms, Hertzog, Heyns, Hoon, Hugo, Human, Jacobs (Jakobs), Jansen, Kemp, Kleynhans, Klopper, Kock, Kok, Kotzé, Kroukamp, Kruger, Landman, Lombaard, Lotter, Lourens, Maartens, Matthee, Meyer, Minnie, Mostert, Mulder, Muller, Oberholzer, Odendaal, Oosthuyzen (Oosthuisen), Pieterse, Pretorius, Reynders, Roelofse, Scheepers, Scholtz, Serfontein, Slabbert, Smit, Smuts, Stapelberg, Steenkamp, Swart, Van Deventer, Van der Schyff, Van der Merwe, Van der Westhuizen, Van Dyk, Van Graan, Van Tonder, Van Wyk, Van Zyl, Veldsman, Vermaak, Vermeulen, Visagie, Visser, Volschenk, Vos, Vosloo, Wassenaar, Welgemoed, Wentzel, Wepener, Wessels and Zaaiman (Saayman).

During the harshest years of apartheid, the late fifties to the late seventies, the National Party government instituted bizarre tests to be used by officials responsible for classifying citizens according to race. They measured noses, cheekbones and lips and applied the 'pencil test': pushing a pencil into a person's hair – if it stays, the hair is too curly to qualify as that of a white person. Still, stories abound of families split in half, some classified as coloured, others as white.

It must have happened in my family too, because Du Preez is not an uncommon surname among people once classified as coloured, especially in the southern Cape. (In the United States, most people with my surname seem to be black, like the popular musician Champion Jack Dupree).

It is so easy to demonstrate how supremely ridiculous race is as a way of separating people. Culture and language make sense, yes, but race is a nonsense. And yet white South Africans always had this persistent obsession with race. But we should also remember that their ancestors arrived in the Cape 350 years or so ago with the views on race and class prevalent in Europe at that time. The Afrikaners did not invent racism; they just perfected it, to paraphrase an advertising slogan of South African Airways.

4

Five dead men

THE FRENCH AND GERMAN parts of my family lost their mother tongue within two generations, and soon they were speaking a simplified, creole version of Dutch that had developed among the slaves and the servants, later called Afrikaans. What a supreme irony that the main symbol Afrikaners employed to define their ethnic nationalism was the creation of black people.

My Du Preez, Saayman and Kruger forefathers were among those who became freeburghers, and most of them moved towards the eastern Cape as agricultural land in the districts around Cape Town became scarcer. They resented the Dutch colonial authorities; after 1795 they hated the British colonial authorities even more.

The land was beautiful and the land was good. Returning to Europe never even crossed their minds. It was everything Europe wasn't: it was wild and free and big and it was theirs. They had no sense that they were invading other nations' land, and it never occurred to them that perhaps they had no right to be there. This was the way of the world in the eighteenth century. They saw themselves as frontiersmen, as pioneers taming a new corner of the world. They occupied the land at will – the Khoikhoi could muster very little resistance, and the Bushmen who did, simply got shot. The settlers lived by the Bible and the gun.

And then they met a whole different group of local people. They were proud cattle farmers, but they were also fierce warriors. They had a complex culture, an intricate system of hierarchy involving kings, chiefs and elders, and they had a clear legal system.

That's not exactly what the trekboers saw. They saw a horde of strange, primitive heathen people who did not wear clothes made of cotton or wool, who did not use horses or horse carts or ox wagons, who were very black and used a language they had never heard before. The Xhosa people saw an equally strange, pale people who showed no respect but had firearms and who came to steal the land they had used for centuries. They did not understand each other, so they feared each other.

In the words of Alan Paton, the Xhosa 'became part of the Afrikaner mind, just as the advancing whites became part of the black mind'. Most trekboers could not imagine any other relationship than a hostile one, one of white master and black servant. That's all they knew. The next few decades saw incessant conflicts between the two groups, then known as the Kaffir Wars, today called the Frontier Wars. The scene was now set for the conflict between white and black that has still not been resolved completely.

But everything wasn't always as simple, as black and white. Allow me to tell you a story from these times that will illustrate how things were often not as they seemed.

The first story played itself out between 1813 and 1816: the Slagtersnek rebellion (Slagtersnek translates as 'Butcher's neck'). It ended with the hanging of five trekboers by the British colonial authorities. It became an important day in the Afrikaner-nationalism calendar: an example of British cruelty towards peace-loving, defenceless Afrikaners.

In the weeks before the outbreak of the Anglo-Boer War in 1899, General Jan Smuts wrote that Slagtersnek was 'the first beacon of blood' between Boer and Brit. In 1906, a monument was unveiled to commemorate the rebellion. The man who was to be the first National Party prime minister of South Africa in 1948, Dr Daniel Francois Malan, said at the unveiling that the Afrikaner's 'century of injustice' had started with Slagtersnek. 'Through Slagtersnek a patriotism started growing in the hearts of Afrikaners from which we still reap the fruits,' Malan declared.

In April 1813, a Khoi worker named Booy complained to the deputy magistrate of Cradock, Andries Stockenström, that his employer, farmer Freek Bezuidenhout, refused to pay him his full wage and kept him on the farm against his will. Bezuidenhout explained in a letter that Booy had caused him a lot of damage, and he wanted to recoup it. Stockenström persuaded Booy to return to the farm and asked the local *veldkornet* [equal to a lieutenant], Philippus Opperman, to draw up a new contract between the two.

But soon Booy arrived back at Stockenström's office, complaining that Bezuidenhout had assaulted him for laying a charge against him. Stockenström issued a summons for Bezuidenhout to appear in Cradock. Bezuidenhout wrote back that he couldn't make the trip, but Booy was free to go – all he wanted was one heifer for the damage Booy had caused him. Booy denied he owed Bezuidenhout anything. *Veldkornet* Opperman sent Booy with a letter to Bezuidenhout, but Bezuidenhout simply beat him up.

Stockenström again summoned Bezuidenhout to appear in court, and sent several messengers to deliver the summons. Bezuidenhout told them all to go to hell. Stockenström, only twenty-three years old at the time, saw this as a rejection of his authority. He discussed it with Governor Lord Charles Somerset, who agreed that stern action was required. Bezuidenhout was told to appear before the Circuit Court in Graaff-Reinet on 5 October 1814. But, in the meantime, a fellow farm worker murdered Booy, whom he caught having sex with his wife. Bezuidenhout feared that he would be held responsible for Booy's disappearance, and didn't pitch up in court. He was sentenced to one month in jail for contempt of court.

Four white military officers and twelve *pandoers*, Khoikhoi soldiers, were sent to arrest Bezuidenhout. They arrived on his farm early on 10 October 1815. Bezuidenhout, his son Hans and a visiting young man, Jacob Erasmus, took their rifles and hid in a cave. Bezuidenhout started shooting at the *pandoers*. One of the officers, Lieutenant Frans Rossouw, tried to persuade him to give himself up, but he swore at them and started shooting again; one of the *pandoers* then shot and killed Bezuidenhout. The soldiers retrieved the body, arrested Hans and Jacob and left for Graaff-Reinet in a hurry.

Bezuidenhout's son Hans was sentenced to a caning and six months in jail. Erasmus was freed, because he did not fire a shot.

Back on the Bezuidenhout farm, the funeral was held. Thirty people attended, among them Freek's brother Hans, his brother-in-law Cornelis Faber and the Prinsloo neighbours Piet Kafferland and Groot Willem. According to the writer Thomas Pringle, the mourners had a 'drunken orgy' afterwards, although the Afrikaner historians who wrote on the incident did not mention this. It is not known whether this happened before or during the 'drunken orgy', but Freek's brother Hans got up and swore that he would take revenge on what he called the murderers of his brother: Stockenström, *Veldkornet* Opperman and Lieutenant Rossouw.

About two weeks after Freek's death, a fiery man called Hendrik 'Kasteel' Prinsloo arrived on the Bezuidenhout farm. He was given his nickname as a youngster, when his father was imprisoned in the Cape Town Castle for organising a small uprising against the British authorities. Because of this, Kasteel had a deep-seated hatred of the British. He accused the men of the area of being cowards – only good enough to be hit by their women.

Kasteel made a broader case than avenging the death of Freek. He said the trekboers should also rise up because the British favoured the Khoikhoi over the whites; that the Black Circuit, a court that heard complaints from black workers against their employers, was a conspiracy against the trekboers; and that the British were depriving the farmers of new land.

The rebellion was beginning to take shape. But perhaps this is a good time to take a closer look at some of the characters involved.

Freek Bezuidenhout himself had three children, but was never married. His son Hans's mother was not a white woman, so the community called Hans a Baster. The woman who lived with him at the time of his death was also a black woman. Freek, so the gossip in the area went, also had a preference for Xhosa women, and often spent long periods of time among the Xhosa. His brother Coenraad was also living with a Baster woman.

Cornelis Faber, Hans Bezuidenhout's wife's brother, spent years among the Xhosa because the police wanted him. He only came back when an amnesty was declared. He also lived with Xhosa and Baster women. Stephanus Bothma was banished from the colony for five years for fraud.

The truth is that most of the Slagtersnek rebels were a rough bunch without the narrow racial hang-ups of the rest of their frontier community. Several of them had better friends among the Xhosa than among the whites in the region. One source states that the Xhosa men in some kraals were 'on first-name terms' with Faber and the Bezuidenhouts; according to some stories, Freek and Coenraad Bezuidenhout and Cornelis Faber loved to occasionally visit the kraal of Chief Gaika, where they had drinking buddies and girlfriends. Unlikely heroes for Afrikaner nationalism, aren't they?

Kasteel Prinsloo, Cornelis Faber and Hans Bezuidenhout started recruiting men to join their uprising. But they had another card up their sleeve: they planned to get their Xhosa friends to rise up with them against the British. They first negotiated with a petty chief with whom they had spent many hours drinking, a man called Jalousa, but then Faber led a deputation to Chief Gaika, whom they knew well. But the chief wasn't going to get involved in the white man's squabble: he stalled for time and said he had to consult with other chiefs before he could make a decision.

The same factor that two centuries later would sink the seditious plans of the Afrikaner Weerstandsbeweging and the Boeremag, plagued the planning of the Slagtersnek rebels: they talked too much about their plans, and their own people ran to the authorities. Kasteel Prinsloo wrote a letter to Jacobus Kruger to recruit him, but the messenger took the letter straight to the magistrate. Four days later Kasteel was arrested.

It was time for action. On 14 November 1815, some fifty-five men drove up to Vanaardtspos, where Kasteel was detained. They took up their positions and sent an emissary with the ultimatum that Kasteel should be released, or else. For four days there was a stand-off, and on 18 November the soldiers attacked. After a few shots were fired, negotiations resumed. The rebels were waiting for Faber and his Xhosa posse to come to their aid, but he arrived alone.

First thirteen and then eighteen rebels decided that it was a lost cause and gave themselves up. The rest of the rebels fled, with the soldiers in pursuit. Hans Bezuidenhout was killed when he didn't want to surrender, and one after the other the rebels were caught. The Slagtersnek rebellion was a huge flop.

Their trial started on 15 December. On 19 February 1816, the Council of Justice sentenced five rebel leaders to death: Cornelis Faber, Stephanus Bothma, Hendrik 'Kasteel' Prinsloo, Theunis de Klerk and Abraham Bothma. The others were fined or sentenced to hard labour. All were told by the court to witness the execution as part of their sentence.

On Monday 4 March 1816, the condemned men were brought to the Slagtersnek area. One by one the men walked onto the hastily built scaffolding. The hangman and his assistant put the nooses around their necks. The crowd, all the other rebels and the condemned men's wives and family went absolutely quiet. Then magistrate Cuyler gave the sign that the trapdoor be dropped on which they stood. A terrible sight followed. Only one noose held, the others broke and the four men fell on the ground, choking. Stunned, they crawled to Cuyler and begged him to spare them. The wailing families and friends joined in.

Cuyler did not spare them. The hangman took the noose of the dead man, and one by one the other four were hanged.

The story of the Slagtersnek rebellion was milked for its anti-British value and as a symbol of Afrikaner nationalism until after 1948. It only stopped when Afrikaner historians rewrote history in the 1970s and illuminated the fact that not only did the rebels consort with black women, but they made common cause with the Xhosa, even asking them to rise up against fellow whites.

By this time, black South Africans had replaced the British as Afrikaner nationalism's enemy number one. The Slagtersnek story lost all its propaganda value.

5

A barrel of gunpowder

AT SOME POINT in the history of my ancestors, they stopped being European colonists or settlers – but at what point? It clearly wasn't enough to simply call themselves by a name that indicated they were of Africa – Afrikaanders, as Hendrik Biebouw called himself in 1707.

My feeling is that this point occurred around the mid-nineteenth century, two centuries after Van Riebeeck. The white farmers outside Cape Town, especially those in the southern Cape, the Klein Karoo and the Eastern Cape, came from many generations of people who had no intention of ever returning to Europe. They were of mixed blood – not only mixed in terms of Dutch, German and French blood, but mixed with slaves and even Khoikhoi. And they stopped speaking Dutch, French or German, developing instead a new language derived mostly from Dutch.

Now they were ready to leave the colony and trek into the interior.

Twenty years after Slagtersnek, around 1835, many of the white farmers on the eastern frontier decided to escape the jurisdiction of the British and to seek greener pastures. They trekked north and east, into the land of the Zulu, the Sotho, the Tswana, the Pedi and the Venda, conquering and occupying land as far as they went.

They did not see themselves as colonists, but as indigenous people expanding their sphere of influence and economic activity. The black groups saw them simply as foreign invaders.

Many books and learned articles have been written in an attempt to pin down the causes, nature and effect of the Great Trek. Lately the favourite activity of history academics is to debunk the myths surrounding the Great Trek created after the event by Afrikaner nationalists and their loyal historians. There was nothing great about the Trek, the thinking goes; it was simply a migration of a violent, boorish group of white supremacists who refused to accept the efforts of the British colonial authorities to curtail their abuse of the indigenous people. They stole land as far as they went and subjugated every tribe they came across, in the process destabilising ancient cultures and populations.

However oversimplified that is, and however offensive that may sound to my Afrikaner ears, there is some truth to it. The men who planned the Trek certainly did not have any grand ideas about nationalism or the founding of a new nation.

They were indeed an inbred, rough bunch of people, and became more so as they moved into the interior. (Ox wagon trash?) There were very few teachers and ministers of religion among them, no mobile libraries, no clothes shops or ablution blocks on the way.

They were indeed racist: they saw themselves as the carriers of a superior, Western Christian culture and the local people as primitive heathens. And yes, they did despise the British, believing that they favoured the Khoikhoi, the slaves and the Xhosa over the trekboers. They were angry that slavery had been abolished. And yes, they stole all the land they could get their hands on.

A footnote in Paul Kruger's 1902 autobiography puts it bluntly: 'South Africa has room for only one form of civilization, and that is the white man's civilization; and, where there was only a handful of white men to keep hundreds of thousands of black natives in order, severity was essential. The black man had to be taught that he came second, that he belonged to the inferior class which must obey and learn.'

(In 1882, President Kruger, in a more lucid moment, referred to the 'native problem' in an address to his *volksraad* [national council]: 'All who know the difficulties of this problem will most certainly agree with me when I say that the greatest benefactor of South Africa would be the man who could provide a completely satisfactory solution to this problem. That man is perhaps as yet unborn.' Some would say that man was born thirty-six years later: Nelson Rolihlahla Mandela.)

As an Afrikaner, I have to face all these facts about my forefathers. At this point in history, I cannot merely justify their actions as the behaviour of a strange group of pale-faced people who came from Europe. Their sins are being visited upon me still today.

Perhaps, in mitigation, I should plead that this was the mid-nineteenth century, not the twenty-first. Shaka and Mzilikazi and other African chiefs and kings of the time were an equally rough bunch; tribes and chiefdoms saw themselves as superior to others; armed aggression, land grabbing and cattle theft were the order of the day.

Unless, of course, we state that the European culture from which the trekkers came was superior to African culture, and that they should have known to behave better. That's just so much nonsense. There is no such thing as a superior culture. And I have learnt too much about the richness and sophistication of African civilisations going back millennia to even entertain any notion of Western culture being 'more advanced'.

The Voortrekkers' real sin, of course, was not that they attacked other tribes or occupied their land. It was that they had white skins, originated in Europe and had no business being in Africa. This argument implies that the peoples of the world should all have stayed where they were born: Europeans in Europe, Asians in Asia, Arabs in the Middle East.

Only the aboriginal people would today populate North and South America,

Australia and New Zealand, and there would be no Arabs in North Africa. If the Irish had never migrated, Ireland today would have been a vastly overpopulated, impoverished slum.

But it is simply against human nature not to migrate. Our very survival as a species rested upon our instinct to trek, to seek out new corners of the planet. That is why we are spending billions on space exploration. Who knows if we wouldn't have gone the way of the other humans, the Neanderthals, if we had all stayed in Africa, where we originated; to colonise is in our genes.

It was inevitable that Europeans would have found Africa and tried to conquer it, just as they found and conquered the Americas. The only reason why Africans, native Americans and other aboriginal groups did not colonise other continents, is that they had no need to: their own continent was vast and offered them enough land and food.

It was equally inevitable that the trekboers, who found themselves in the Eastern Cape in the early nineteenth century, would at some time have tried to expand their land. It would have been against human nature for them to know that there was a vast interior with good grazing, fertile soil and abundant game, and not at some point try to go there.

In a nasty quirk of history, the *Lifacane* – the massive upheaval among chiefdoms in eastern and central South Africa – took place just a few years before the Voortrekkers moved into these areas. The social and economic structures of the Bantu-speaking farming communities were fundamentally disrupted. There couldn't have been anybody in these communities who was untouched by death, displacement, destruction, disease or hunger. The hardship was so extreme that it even gave rise to bands of cannibals roaming the plains of the Highveld.*

The Voortrekkers moved into Natal and the central Highveld in the aftermath of the *Lifacane*, before the black communities had regained their social and economic equilibrium. This gave rise to the myth, still believed by many, that most of the Free State and old Transvaal were unoccupied and thus unclaimed when the whites arrived.

On 19 August 1953, for instance, the South African high commissioner to the United Kingdom, Dr AL Geyer, declared: 'South Africa is no more the original home of its black Africans, the Bantu, than of its white Africans. Both races went there as colonists and, what is more, as practically contemporary colonists. In some parts the Bantu arrived first, in other parts the Europeans were the first comers.'

---

* In 1824, Moshesh's beloved grandfather, Peete, was killed and eaten by a group of cannibals. Instead of killing Peete's murderers, Moshesh performed a ritual purification on the killers, as their bodies had become Peete's tomb – to kill them would be to desecrate his grave. These and many other groups of cannibals would later find a home and rehabilitation at Thaba Bosiu.

The other myth is that it was simply the sudden appearance on the scene of murderous tyrants such as Shaka and Mzilikazi that led to the *Lifacane*. The reality is far more complex, and involves the militarisation of the societies as a result of the booming ivory trade in Mozambique, the destabilisation of societies further north on the east coast because of the slave trade, and a reaction to white colonisation of the Cape up to the eastern frontiers.

However one understands the Great Trek, the fact remains that this became a migration that fundamentally changed the future of the subcontinent and contributed to the birth of Afrikaner nationalism. The Voortrekkers formed their own sovereign republics in the Free State and the old Transvaal. They were eventually defeated in war when the British Empire suddenly developed a new interest in the area after the discovery of diamonds and gold.

Again, allow me to tell a little story that will demonstrate that everything during this time wasn't what it appeared to be.

Josias Hoffman was a talented accordion player, a lover of history and someone who spoke Afrikaans, English and Sesotho. He walked with the help of crutches after a childhood accident.

Hoffman was one of the first Voortrekkers who crossed the Orange River and claimed a big piece of land to farm. He called it Jammerbergdrift. In 1854, Hoffman was chosen as the first president of the Republic of the Orange Free State. He was a good man for the job: as a youngster accompanying his trader father, he had met the Zulu king, Shaka. He had also met King Moshesh of the Basotho while doing building work at a mission station near Thaba Bosiu. One source believes he built Moshesh's house on Thaba Bosiu.

Hoffman's first diplomatic act as president was to invite King Moshesh to Bloemfontein for a state visit. The king praised the president at the state banquet, saying he was a man of peace and a friend of the Basotho because he respected them and the authority of their king. 'I have noticed that Mr Hoffman has feeble limbs and must use crutches, but when all persons who are blessed with sound limbs kept running backwards and forwards in time of disturbance, that gentleman stood his ground, stuck to his farm, and honestly adhering to the truth, fearlessly admonished and reproved at one time even myself, and at other times the British Government, and though many, both black and white, envied, hated and persecuted him, he continued with his family to enjoy safety in the midst of all changes and tumults.'

Hoffman responded and talked about his deep respect for the Basotho king as a man of peace and integrity. The only way forward would be a road of cooperation, partnership and respect between the Boers and Basotho.

But all was not well inside the ramshackle new republic. The son of Voortrekker leader Andries Pretorius, Marthinus Wessel Pretorius, disliked Hoffman for his lenient attitude towards the Basotho and the Griqua, and believed he should have been president. He lobbied for people to rise up against Hoffman, and his 'Hoffman is soft on the *kaffirs*' argument fell on many a susceptible ear. Even the senior British colonial officials agreed with him. Sir George Cathcart privately called Moshesh a fraud and a violent man who should be subdued.

A while later, Hoffman was invited on a state visit to Thaba Bosiu. He was welcomed by three hours of musketry salutes, and for four days he was treated like a guest of honour, Moshesh's many wives personally tending to his needs (let's not go too deeply into that). The Free State president and the Basotho king became good friends. Hoffman's son Daniel later recorded that his father told him '*Moshesh is 'n swart koning met 'n wit hart*' [Moshesh is a black king with a white heart].

When Hoffman was leaving Thaba Bosiu, he asked Moshesh if he could do something for him. Yes, the king said, gunpowder was very scarce and they had used up quite a bit of their supply when they welcomed him with the salute. Hoffman consulted with his *veldkornets* and then promised to send Moshesh a '*klein vaatjie*' [small barrel] of gunpowder.

Soon afterwards, Moshesh sent a messenger to Bloemfontein to collect the gunpowder. Hoffman wrote a note to go with the *vaatjie*: 'It is hereby made known to all whom it may concern that the bearer has under his charge a little barrel containing 50 lbs of powder that is being sent by the Orange Free State to the Chief Moshesh as a token of friendship. Everybody is commanded to let this pass unhindered. JP Hoffman, President.'

News of the *vaatjie* and the note spread quickly. One of Hoffman's bitter enemies, a member of the *volksraad* named F Linde, actually laid a charge of 'gunpowder smuggling' against the president with the Bloemfontein magistrate.

In January 1855, Hoffman opened the session of the *volksraad*. He said: 'With the Chief Moshesh, I have continuous friendship, and I think of speedily having another meeting with him in order to make, if possible, such arrangements as shall best lead to the establishment of a permanent peace.'

This was fuel to the fire. On 9 February 1855, a simple majority of the *volksraad*, without hearing evidence, found the president guilty of a 'high crime' – giving gunpowder to an enemy of the republic. The anti-Hoffman members rushed out to meet a crowd of their supporters outside. They stormed the Fort and trained the cannon at the president's house.

A two-thirds majority was needed to properly impeach the president, but the next morning Hoffman's resignation as president was read to the *volksraad*.

Jacobus Boshoff, who saw Moshesh as cunning, primitive and violent, replaced Hoffman as president. The result of the change of power was that relations between the Basotho and the Free State deteriorated quickly, and not long afterwards they were at war.

The British sided with the Boers, and not only did they wage war against Moshesh themselves, but gave a large chunk of his land to the Free State. The bitterness that created among the Basotho is still simmering in the Lesotho kingdom.

Imagine if Hoffman had continued as president for another few years, establishing a long-term, structured relationship between the Free State and the Basotho – the 'permanent peace' he spoke about. Moshesh's stabilising influence in central South Africa would have blossomed even more, and relations between the races could have developed in a much healthier way. In fact, perhaps the Basotho army would have fought on the side of the Boers in the Anglo-Boer War forty-five years after this incident, and perhaps the British would have been defeated. Imagine that.

But the British did defeat the Boers. Just as the two Boer republics had swallowed up the black chiefdoms, they were now swallowed up by the British Empire. It was a chance to end the fragmentation of the country, until the war involving the British colonies at the Cape and Natal, Basutoland, Bechuanaland, Swaziland and the two republics. It was also a chance to fulfil the dream of imperialists like Lord Alfred Milner, who stated in November 1899: 'The ultimate end [of British policy] is a self-governing white Community, supported by well-treated and justly governed black labour from Cape Town to the Zambesi.'

In 1910 the British called for a national convention. Their solution was a system of rigid racial separation and bantustans. Not a single black, coloured or Indian person was present at the convention. The two republics and the two colonies would form the self-governing Union of South Africa. Except for a very limited franchise in the Cape, black South Africans were completely excluded from any political decision-making. Basutoland, Bechuanaland and Swaziland would remain outside the new union as black protectorates of the British. These three black 'homelands' later became independent: Basutoland became Lesotho, Bechuanaland became Botswana and Swaziland kept its name.

The die was cast. It was the twentieth century, and the mighty, enlightened United Kingdom put its seal of approval on the concept that South Africa was white man's land. In 1959 the limited black franchise, and in 1968 the coloured franchise, were finally abolished. Did anyone really expect the Afrikaners to turn around in the years after 1910 and say, wait a minute, we want equal political representation for our black compatriots? If it was going to be good enough for the coloniser, it was going to suit the Afrikaner just fine.

The circle that had started in 1652 was now closed. The people who had lived in South Africa before the arrival of the Europeans – the San, the Khoikhoi and the Bantu-speaking groups – now had no say in the government of their land. By this time it was also true of most of the rest of Africa – colonies of the British, the Portuguese, the Belgians and the French.

Colonialism had a devastating effect on Africa. It is the only reason why we constantly see references to 'Chinese civilisation' or 'Indian' and 'European' civilisation, but nobody ever talks about the 'African civilisation'. The slave trade and colonialism disrupted Africa before its civilisation could blossom and become known on other continents.

African civilisation is indeed the mother of all civilisations. This is where humans developed language, culture, art and religion; where they tamed fire and water; where they domesticated animals; where they planted crops for the first time; where they learnt to understand the stars and the seasons.

Yet the popular view outside Africa was expressed succinctly by the writer PJ O'Rourke: 'Man developed in Africa. He has not continued to do so there.' This is dumb, racist nonsense. Mr O'Rourke clearly knows nothing about the Egyptian civilisation, their sphinxes and pyramids and their intricate knowledge of the stars; or of the royal court of Timbuktu, which was as sophisticated and learned as any other kingdom in the world in the fifteenth and sixteenth centuries; or of the ancient universities in Morocco, Mali and Egypt; of the advanced cities of Carthage and Great Zimbabwe millennia ago.

But I don't think one should measure the 'development of man' according to the development of technology or the building of sophisticated cities or universities. Spirituality, artistic creativity and the fine art of living in harmony with the planet are more important.

An example of someone who was uninfluenced by anyone outside the indigenous black people of southern Africa was the eighteenth-century sage Mohlomi, yet as a philosopher and spiritualist he had an understanding of the human psyche on a par or above those of his peers in the 'developed' world of the time. King Moshesh's extraordinary diplomatic skills were unparalleled among statesmen and military leaders in the mid-nineteenth century. (King Napoleon of France recognised this and sent Moshesh a set of ornamental pistols as a diplomatic gift.)

But let's go even further back. The San or Bushman of southern Africa are, according to biogeneticists, the oldest human stock in the world; that is, they are genetically closest to our ancestral Eve. Today they are widely described as the most primitive people left in the world, stuck in the Stone Age. Yet they created, for tens of thousands of years until about 200 years ago, the most magnificent art. Not pretty pictures of animals and people (although that, too), but deeply spiritual art with many layers of meaning. We can still not reproduce the material they used to make paintings that lasted for a thousand years or more, exposed to the elements. I believe southern African rock art is the most underestimated art treasure in the world today.

The Bushmen had, for thousands of years, an egalitarian society with a gender equality and religious tolerance that were only reached by pockets of Western society in recent decades. There were no great chiefs; leaders came forward where their skills were best. The shaman was the spiritual leader of the group, but a group could have several shamans, each preaching a different view of the spiritual world. Women became shamans as easily as men.

Let me give you one example of the Bushman's extraordinary ability to live in harmony with their world. (It is the only society ever studied in the history of mankind where the concept of suicide never existed.)

Around the end of the fifteenth century, a community that was part of the civilisation at Great Zimbabwe decided to leave and move south under the chief Ghoya. These people, called the Leghoya, eventually came to rest in the northern and eastern Free State, where they built their stone villages on hilltops bordering the Vals, Renoster, Wilge and Sand Rivers. The ruins of some of these settlements are still to be seen near Kroonstad, Heilbron, Lindley, Edenville, Senekal, Paul Roux, Winburg and Rosendal.

I discovered the remains of such a village on my farm some years ago after the tall grass had burned, and spent months researching their builders. The last of the Leghoya were eventually wiped out during the *Lifacane*, although it is known that some of them settled under the protection of Moshesh and became Basotho.

In the areas where they settled, they came across the hunters of the San or Bushman. Unlike later Bantu-speaking groups, the Leghoya coexisted in peace with the Bushman – according to some oral sources, even teaching the hunters to cultivate crops on occasion.

This was lion country. The Leghoya built formidable stone kraals to keep the lion out, but the human toll was high. The Leghoya started noticing that, while lion ate many of their number, including young cattle herders, the Bushman never lost anyone. Eventually they figured it out, and it remained a famous fireside story for many generations.

The Bushman knew every single lion in the specific area where they lived at the time. They knew and understood the social structures of every pride in the region. They could sense when the alpha male was nearing the end of his reign, and kept a close watch. On the day the new alpha male ousted the old one, they would wait until he slept. They would creep up on him as soundlessly as only Bushmen could, and then jump on him, shouting and screaming at the top of their lungs, beating the lion with sticks. But they would never kill him.

This was their way of arranging a truce between lion and Bushman: we leave you alone, you leave us alone. Of course, when that alpha male was successfully challenged, the process had to be repeated.

Modern society can only dream of understanding nature in this way. How's that for 'human development', Mr O'Rourke? Isn't the ultimate success of human development the ability to understand our environment and to survive happily and prosperously in it? The Bushman, the Khoikhoi, the Bantu-speaking farmers of millennia ago understood 'sustainable development' a whole lot better than anyone alive today.

I suspect what O'Rourke and others mean when they make derogatory remarks about Africa is that Africa has been a mess in recent decades when one measures it according to democracy, good governance, human rights and economic development. And that is a simple statement of fact.

A lot of Africa's failures can be attributed to the destructive effects of three centuries of colonialism. But most of Africa was given its independence in the 1960s. Why has the progress to democracy and economic sustainability been so slow?

I believe the answer is that the psychological damage of colonialism was worse than the physical oppression. The psychological damage has still not been repaired, not even in the more progressive societies like South Africa and Zimbabwe.

The human beings who left Africa some 100 000 years ago and eventually settled in Europe, looked no different from their African cousins who remained on the continent. But through natural selection and adaptation to the very different environment, including diet, within 20 000 years or so they looked very different.

Scientists have established that melanin, of which black skins have a lot and white skins virtually nothing, is the most efficient protection available against the sun's harmful ultra-violet rays. Very black people cannot suffer from sunburn. To have lots of melanin is obviously very good in hot, sunny climates. But the skin is our factory for Vitamin D, and it needs sunlight to produce it. So when you live in a cooler climate, your skin has to have less melanin to produce sufficient Vitamin D, which means you will be paler. Therefore we find that the people who live along the equator have very dark skins, and the further one goes towards the poles, the lighter people's skins are. It's as simple as that.

Underneath the skin we are the same. In fact, biogeneticists have found that there is less variation in the mitochondrial DNA of the six billion human beings in the world today than in that of a small population of chimpanzees or gorillas found in one region. That is mind-boggling. It supports the theory of most modern scientists that we all come from one genetic 'Eve' some 200 000 years ago.

I digress. The Europeans were not blessed with the same tropical and subtropical climates, unending savannahs and abundant wildlife as those who stayed behind. They became more settled in stable communities and developed a different culture. They started sailing around the world to discover whether the grass on the other side was greener. And then they discovered that they did not have to do all the manual labour themselves: they could capture the dark peoples of Africa and India and make them do the work. Slaves were almost by definition black.

Thus it became a popular belief, even in ancient times, that black people's role in life is to work for white people. African kings and chiefs who helped capture their fellow Africans and sold them to European or Arab slave traders strengthened this perception. In the Americas, especially, the patterns of class and race were firmly established 400 years ago: black/poor, white/rich. Blacks' destiny in life was to be the hewers of wood and carriers of water. After four centuries, this mentality is still alive in the world: intellectually, Africans do not actually measure up to the white races; they cannot rule themselves properly; they don't understand democracy.

Africans were confronted with this view since the earliest days of colonialism. Eventually, a large number of them started wondering if there was actually some truth in it. They started neglecting their own cultures, languages and customs; parents stopped telling their children the glorious stories of the past. That's serious damage to the soul.

It was a slow process, and it is taking a long time to repair that damage. Intellectually, Africans know that they're the equals of anybody anywhere. But the insecurity keeps on gnawing deep inside. It is something black Africans share with Afrikaner Africans. And the way they overcome it is by being defensive and over-accentuating self-pride.

That is, I believe, how we should read Kwame Nkrumah of Ghana's defeatist maxim: 'We would rather misgovern ourselves than be governed properly by others.' This has been the attitude in many mismanaged African countries. It is the mentality Zimbabwe's Robert Mugabe has exploited to the full towards the end of his reign. He has destroyed his country's economy and violated his people's human rights like Ian Smith never did, but Africa, including progressive, democratic South Africa, has never stood up to him because he has successfully painted his opposition as consisting of 'white colonials' and 'puppets of British imperialism'.

The man whose views on Africanism influenced me the most was the president of the impoverished Burkina Faso in West Africa, Thomas Sankara. I met him at his residence in Ouagadougou in 1987, with a group of South Africans who went to West Africa for a meeting with the exiled ANC leadership.

Sankara was only thirty-seven years old when we met him. He had assumed power through a coup, and changed his country's name from Upper Volta to Burkina Faso, meaning Country of Free and Dignified People. He was very critical of other African leaders who, he said, were more interested in enriching themselves than serving their people. His official limousine was a beaten-up Peugeot 404 with a cracked windshield. He once presented a gift on behalf of his nation to the ANC as the primary liberation movement of South Africa: a rusting old AK-47 rifle without a magazine – all the Burkinabe could afford, he said.

Sankara told us that the 'problem with Africa' was that Africans had gained formal political power, but their minds were still colonised. They are Africans, but they really want to be like their former colonial masters, the French, British and Portuguese. Too many Africans suffer from self-loathing, he said. They are in perpetual conflict: they know and honour their own culture and ancestors, but part of them agrees with the European view that perhaps these are inferior and primitive. That was, Sankara said, why there were so many corrupt and power-crazy African dictators.

Just over a month after we met him, on 15 October 1987, Sankara was assassinated by troops loyal to his deputy and lifelong comrade, Blaise Compoare. Compoare became president the same day.

I often wonder if South African president Thabo Mbeki suffers from the inner conflict Sankara talked about. It is hard for me to think now of any world leader who is a match for Mbeki's intellect. Yet he is ultra-sensitive to criticism, blaming it on racism and colonialist attitudes whenever he can. His condoning of Zimbabwean president Robert Mugabe's erratic and despotic behaviour and his bizarre views on HIV/AIDS are based on the premise that the whole world sees Africans as primitive beasts.

One of Mbeki's worst slips of the tongue was when he called white South Africans 'colonialists of a special kind'. That must be how he sees them. It is ludicrous to brand Afrikaners as colonialists in the twenty-first century. Condemn them as an arrogant, violent tribe, perhaps, but not as colonialists – not after their history of the last 350 years.

In July 2003, the chief executive of the South African National Parks Board, Mavuso Msimang, announced that he and his board had decided to remove the statue of Paul Kruger from the gate of the Kruger National Park.

On 3 August, I wrote a column in the Afrikaans Sunday paper *Rapport* on this decision:

> Why don't ordinary Afrikaners complain when the statues of DF Malan or Hendrik Verwoerd are removed or the names of towns and streets named after them are changed, but they are upset when Paul Kruger's statue is removed from the Kruger Park?
>
> This is a good debate: of which parts of the Afrikaner's history can we be proud, and which parts should we simply try to understand and learn from? Every people and nation ask this question about their own history – the proud Russians don't like to boast about Joseph Stalin, the Germans not with Adolf Hitler, the Serbs not with Slobodan Milosevic, the Ugandans not with Idi Amin.
>
> Am I proud of my history? Well, I am proud of figures such as Louw Wepener, Jan Brand, Marthinus Steyn and Josias Hoffman. I even have a soft spot for the Slagtersnek thugs, the Prinsloos, Fabers, Bothmas and Bezuidenhouts. I'm definitely proud of Christiaan de Wet, Koos de la Rey, Jopie Fourie and the combatants who fought the British Empire.
>
> I am not proud of the bloated, hypocritical, self-important and mostly

corrupt fathers of the volk who had dominated the Afrikaner's politics and culture the last fifty years. I am not proud of Hendrik Verwoerd, John Vorster and their governments who oppressed black South Africans and damaged them psychologically for generations, whose sins are now being put at my door.

And I am bitterly ashamed – revolted, to be honest – of what had been done in my people name by men such as Magnus Malan, Wouter Basson, Lothar Neethling and the bloodthirsty cowboys of Koevoet, Vlakplaas and the CCB.

I am offended when I come across apartheid premiers in place and street names. I would like to see an end to all public glorification of white leaders since Union – and while we're at it, also the statues of Cecil John Rhodes, Queen Victoria and Sir George Grey. They belong somewhere in a museum. We dare not forget them, but we shouldn't honour them. I would like to see the big names from our common history getting recognition; people like Autshomao, Adam Kok, Moshesh, Sol Plaatje, Clements Kadalie and Albert Luthuli.

Why do I want to remove Rhodes and Verwoerd to a museum, but not Kruger? Because there is an important time in the history of my ancestors that I believe can be honoured without guilt or shame: the time after colonialism, but before apartheid.

My earliest ancestors on this soil of ours were colonial occupiers; slave owners who treated the Khoikhoi and Bushman like animals. But then they accepted the country as their own and forgot Europe; the Dutch, Germans and French intermarried, also with slave and Khoi women.

This new bastard nation later called themselves and their new language after the continent of Africa.

I don't think anyone should feel offended by Oom Paul. President Thabo Mbeki will increase his own stature if he intervened now and said wait, we have to talk about this first. You may not touch one group of South Africans' symbols without listening to them first. That's what Nelson Mandela would have done.

6

May God punish England

WITH THE BLACKS in their place, the Afrikaners' real task began: to regain political dominance and to repossess the economy. This fight wasn't against black South Africans, but against 'the English'.

That great South African liberal icon, Alan Paton, told a story that illustrates the flavour of the single-mindedness of this anti-English fervour. He spoke Afrikaans fluently and developed a deep sympathy for the resurgence of Afrikaner nationalism, which expressed itself during the symbolic reenactment of the Great Trek in 1938. Ox wagons trekked from various points in the country to Pretoria, where, on 16 December – Dingane's Day – the foundation stone would be laid for the Voortrekker Monument.

In an essay on Afrikanerdom written in the late 1970s, Paton wrote:

In 1938 I decided to go to the laying of the foundation stone of the Memorial, and grew a beard and bought Voortrekker dress. The Education Department gave us permission to take out two ox-wagons to the ceremony and, flying the Vierkleur flag of the defeated Transvaal Republic, we went rolling to Pretoria.

We arrived on a hot day, and I went straight to the showers. Here I was greeted by a naked and bearded Afrikaner patriot who said to me, 'Have you seen the great crowds?' I said 'yes' (there were a quarter of a million people there). He said to me, with the greatest affability, '*Nou gaan ons die Engelse opdonder*' [now we are going to give the English hell].

The great day was full of speeches, and the theme of every meeting was Afrikanerdom, its glories, its struggles, its grief, its achievements. The speaker only had to shout *vryheid* [freedom] to set the vast crowd roaring, just as today a black speaker who shouts *Amandla* [power], can set a black crowd roaring. A descendant of the British 1820 Settlers who gave Jacobus Uys a Bible when he set out on the Great Trek was shouted down because he gave his greetings in English as his forebear had done.

It was a lonely and terrible occasion for any English-speaking South African who had gone there to rejoice in this Afrikaner festival … After the laying of the stone I left the celebrations and went home. I said to my wife, 'I'm taking this beard off and I'll never wear another.' That was the end of my love affair with Nationalism. I saw it for what it was, self-centred, intolerant, exclusive.

I grew up in a community of fierce anti-English sentiment. I was told many stories about my grandmother and her sisters' terrible time in a British concentration camp, while my grandfather was sent to Ceylon as a prisoner of war. A saying I remember hearing many times was, 'It is true that the sun never sets on the British Empire, because God cannot trust the English in the dark.' I knew an uncle who never swore, but when he was really angry, like when he hit his finger with a hammer, he would mutter '*God straf Engeland*' [may God punish England].

I never really got to hate the English. I took Latin in high school, which put me in the English class of our dual medium school because most Afrikaans kids studied German. I do remember that they sometimes referred to Afrikaners as 'hairy-backs' or 'rock spiders', but I didn't take it very seriously – after all, we called them *souties* or *rooinekke*. In any case, in my home town of Kroonstad, the majority of English-speakers were not English at all, they were Jewish or Lebanese.

I have on occasion experienced, as has every Afrikaner, English-speaking white South Africans treating me like someone not so cultured and sophisticated. When in the company of English-speakers such as these, Afrikaners become very nervous about their pronunciation and table manners. The English attitude sometimes annoyed me, but mostly I just thought less of them.

What irritated me the most was the suspicion among white English-speakers on the left that Afrikaners who supported the struggle against apartheid had to be spies of the regime. I once had a relationship with a woman from an activist family, and it took them more than a few years to really believe that I wasn't secretly working for the security police. When I was a correspondent in Namibia, my friends in SWAPO regularly gave me good stories. Some of my English-speaking colleagues quickly spread the rumour that I got my information from the police.

My old Kroonstad friend Antjie Krog gave me an old copy of M Streak's *The Afrikaner as Viewed by the English* for my fiftieth birthday. It made for interesting reading.

An example: Sir John Barrow, writer, academic and at one time Auditor-General at the Cape (he married Anna Maria Truter), wrote of the typical trekboer in the Graaff-Reinet district.

His pipe scarcely ever quits his mouth, from the moment he rises till he retires to rest, except to give him time to swallow his sopie, or a glass of strong ardent spirit, to eat his meals, and to take a nap after dinner. Unwilling to work, and unable to think; with a mind disengaged from every sort of care and reflection; indulging to excess in the gratification of every sensual appetite, the African peasant grows to an unwieldy size, and is carried off stage by the first inflammatory disease that attacks him.

Of the Boer woman he wrote:

The good lady, born in the wilds of Africa, and educated among slaves and Hottentots, has little idea of what, in a state of society, constitutes female delicacy … Most of them can neither read nor write, so that they have no mental resources whatsoever. Luckily, perhaps, for them, the paucity of ideas prevents time from hanging on their hands.

Offensive, yes, but racism was rampant in those years and not the monopoly of the Afrikaners. Even the angels, the icons of tolerance and brotherly love, practised it. Like the great Mahatma Gandhi.

A quick browse through some of the copies of his newspaper while he was in South Africa, the *Indian Opinion* (accessible at the South African National Library), and the website devoted to his work, www.mkgandhi.org, reveals some of his shockingly racist statements.

In September 1896, Gandhi said this about the struggle of Indian South Africans: 'Ours is one continued struggle against degradation sought to be inflicted upon us by the European, who desire to degrade us to the level of the raw Kaffir, whose occupation is hunting and whose sole ambition is to collect a certain number of cattle to buy a wife with, and then pass his life in indolence and nakedness.'

Commenting on a piece of legislation planned by the white Natal Municipal authority, called the Natal Municipal Corporation bill, Gandhi wrote in the *Indian Opinion* of 18 March 1905: 'Clause 200 makes provision for registration of persons belonging to uncivilized races, resident and employed within the Borough. One can understand the necessity of registration of Kaffirs who will not work, but why should registration be required for indentured Indians who have become free, and for their descendants about whom the general complaint is that they work too much?'

On 15 February 1905, Gandhi protested against the fact that blacks had been allowed to settle in an Indian residential area: 'Why, of all places in Johannesburg, the Indian location should be chosen for dumping down all Kaffirs of the town, passes my comprehension. Of course, under my suggestion, the Town Council must withdraw the Kaffirs from the Location. About this mixing of the Kaffirs with the Indians I must confess I feel most strongly. I think it is very unfair to the Indian population, and it is an undue tax on even the proverbial patience of my countrymen.'

Referring to the racial policies of the whites, Gandhi wrote on 24 September 1903: 'We believe as much in the purity of race as we think they do, only we believe that they would best serve these interests, which are as dear to us as to them, by advocating the purity of all races, and not one alone. We believe also that the white race of South Africa should be the predominating race.'

Perhaps Gandhi would have approved of this editorial in the *Natal Mercury* of 20 December 1860: 'The Coolies, though not so physically strong as the Kaffirs, do on the whole a better day's work, as they are not only diligent and regular, but they economise their strength and finish their appointed task in a much more satisfactory manner ... Their capacities for devouring food are happily much less than the Zulus'.'

Don't be too harsh on the Mahatma. Black African views on whites and Indians in those days were equally racist and equally crudely expressed. That was the way of the world.

I have a sense that Afrikaners were no more racist in the nineteenth and early twentieth centuries than any other group of people in the world, including the Americans and the British, Germans, Belgians, Portuguese and Italians, who had vast colonies in Africa.

Afrikaner society had a dire shortage of academics and educated intellectuals in the period after the Boer War, so a small number of intellectuals had a dispro-portionate influence on Afrikaner thinking. With the anti-British sentiment so high, a number of bright students chose to study in Germany and the Netherlands in the first three decades after the Boer War. The new way of looking at humanity, through racial analysis, was taught in these countries in the 1920s and 1930s. Genetics, not culture or personal achievement, determined the value of a human being. This was the intellectual premise of Adolf Hitler's National Socialism.

Two of the students who studied in Germany and came back with this sort of thinking, Nico Diederichs and Piet Meyer, became very influential in Afrikanerdom: Diederichs eventually became state president, Meyer the chairman of both the influential Afrikaner Broederbond and of the state broadcaster, the South African Broadcasting Corporation (SABC). Dr Hendrik Verwoerd, the most influential thinker in Afrikanerdom between the 1940s and the 1960s, refused an Abe Bailey bursary to study at Oxford; instead he studied at Leipzig, Hamburg and Berlin. He became editor of the Johannesburg newspaper *Die Transvaler*, the Minister of Native Affairs in 1950, and prime minister in 1958.

I don't look at my tribe with twenty-first-century eyes and then condemn their racism. But during my lifetime, in the last five decades or so, most of the rest of humanity came to understand that practising racism was fighting against the continuous evolution of the human species. Being 'modern' and 'civilised' meant one had the ability to overcome one's most basic urges and prejudices. Christians started realising that Christ's dictum in Matthew 1:12, 'All things whatsoever ye would that men should do to you, do ye even so to them', meant respecting everybody's human rights and dignity. Most of the African countries colonised by the Europeans were given back their freedom in 1960 and thereafter.

Afrikaners like me can legitimately use the argument that their forefathers were simply the products of their time, circumstances and history until the period after the Anglo-Boer War. They can be very proud of the way Afrikaners fought poverty among their own ranks and regained their dignity and self-esteem in the decades after the war.

But halfway through the twentieth century, they gained absolute power over their land and its peoples. And then they started behaving worse than all of the imperialist and despotic colonial rulers and tribal chiefs before that.

This was more or less the time I was born: three years after the National Party came into power in 1948. I never knew any other government until the ANC assumed power in 1994.

And that's my excuse for being so screwed up.

PART II

Serving the mouthpiece

7

Influences

THE QUESTION I have been asked most often in my life is why I became so different from the majority of Afrikaners. I often answered that perhaps I was one of the few who remained true to their original *hardegat* [stubborn] Afrikaner roots, and that those who had become arrogant and fat under apartheid were the aberrations.

But I have often wondered about it myself. I did not become a *dominee* or a lawyer or a respected Afrikaans journalist or a pillar of society, as my family background suggested I would. I have been in conflict with my immediate society for most of my adult life. Surely I would have had a more comfortable life if I had been able to conform, go with the flow, benefit from being white and Afrikaans – while it lasted?

Most people expect me to tell them of some dramatic Damascus experience that changed me from a barefoot Kroonstad boy into a left-wing maverick. I have no such tale to tell.

It is not due to any inherent nobility on my part that I did not become an apartheid assassin, a Broederbonder or corpulent apartheid beneficiary. I think I'm merely the product of my circumstances: the personality I was born with, including an intense dislike of all authority; my family's basic sense of decency, justice and fairness; my obsessive love of reading since I was very young; my exposure to the real world when I became a journalist. But I suppose somewhere along the line there were some serious decisions made also.

My interest in political affairs started during my early teenage years. The first political figure I remember having a keen interest in was Bram Fischer, the Afrikaner communist. Fischer to Afrikanerdom was like having an uncle in jail; it was considered a family scandal that one of us could go so horribly wrong and join the enemy. So either you don't talk about him, or you deny your family connection.

Fischer came from a prominent Free State Afrikaner family – his grandfather, Abraham, was elected prime minister of the Free State in 1907, represented the province at the National Convention in 1910, and was appointed Minister of Land Affairs in the first cabinet of the Union of South Africa. Bram's father was a judge in the Supreme Court.

I first took notice of Fischer when he acted as counsel for Nelson Mandela, Walter Sisulu and others at the Rivonia Trial – and I only took notice because the people in my town said it was scandalous that an Afrikaner from such a good Free State family would help defend the communist enemies of South Africa. I even remember a rumour at the time – I was about fourteen years old – that Fischer had a black girlfriend. You would expect that from a traitor, wouldn't you?

But then Fischer himself was arrested in 1964 as a member of the Communist Party of South Africa – actually, the chairman of the party. Sleeping with a black woman was one thing – we all have our weaknesses – but to be a communist was to be the right-hand man of the anti-Christ. Fischer skipped bail and was on the run, often dressed as a woman, until he was rearrested late in 1965 and sentenced to life imprisonment. He was released shortly before his death of cancer in 1975.

I cannot say I saw Fischer as a role model. I did not know for sure what communism really was. I was bombarded at home, in school and in the church with the message that communism was hell-bent on destroying Christianity, and in South Africa on chasing the white man into the sea. They would then take his farm, his house and his car to give to the black workers. Soon your farm worker and your black gardener would be in government. And during this process there would be a lot of raping of mothers and daughters, slaughtering of animals, looting, and wild singing and dancing.

Now all this, it appeared to me, would not exactly be in my interest. But was it really what communism meant? I did not know. I had no access to sources of information other than the local newspaper, *Die Volksblad*, the radio news of the state-run SABC, and my father, the *dominee* and the teachers at school. I knew I really disliked the *dominee* and my teachers, and viewed what they told me with great suspicion. To my childish mind, communism became a forbidden fruit, like my fantasies about having sex with Mrs Botha, my English teacher.

But I did romanticise Fischer. I secretly read everything I could about him. He was from a good Afrikaner Free State family. So was I. But he wasn't really *one of them*. I was beginning to think I wasn't either. He was prepared to defy them, to stand alone and live his life according to his own truths. I found that fascinating.

Later in my life, when I did in fact defy Afrikaner nationalism and came into conflict with the white establishment, Bram Fischer became an inspiration to me. I met his daughter a few years ago and told her this story. She really appreciated it.

A very important day in my early political consciousness was Tuesday 6 September 1966. We had just had our normal family lunch, during which no one was allowed to say a word while my father listened to the radio news at fifteen minutes past one. (The Afrikaans news bulletin was not at one o'clock, because people needed a few minutes to get home for lunch. Things were different then.)

After lunch, us children had to do our homework. I was sitting in my room, probably reading a book, because I had little interest in my schoolwork, when I heard a loud wail coming from my father's study.

I rushed out and saw my parents in front of the yellow banana wood radio and record player cabinet. My mother was crying and my father's face was like stone. He was sitting on the edge of the chair, his ear close to the radio.

Then it came again: a number of beeps, and the sombre voice: '*Hier volg 'n noodberig* [This is an emergency message]. The prime minister, Dr Hendrik Verwoerd, was assassinated in parliament this afternoon.' It was followed by solemn music.

I remember that afternoon as if it happened yesterday, probably like Americans remember where they were and what they were doing when President Kennedy was assassinated. The big impression it made on me was not because I loved or even had an opinion of Verwoerd, but because of the effect it had on my parents and the community in which I lived.

We all wore black armbands for the rest of that week. At home and at school nobody talked about anything else. For the first few days, the stories were wild. The parliamentary messenger who stabbed Verwoerd in the neck and chest in his bench in parliament, Dimitri Tsafendas, was a highly trained Russian agent. He was part of a conspiracy hatched in Moscow aimed at overthrowing the government and replacing it with a black communist regime.

As the days went by, the rumours changed. Tsafendas was not a white man, but the son of a Greek man and a coloured woman. That was the source of his bitterness. The conspiracy reached right into the public service, because he was given a work permit although his record stated that he was a member of the Communist Party. And so on.

That Saturday, the tenth of September, we were all sitting around the radio (television only came to South Africa ten years later) to listen to commentary of the huge state funeral. At 2.15 pm cars and buses stopped all over South Africa, and everyone stood to attention for a minute: it was the same time of day as four days earlier when the prime minister had died.

We heard months later, when Tsafendas's court case started, that he wasn't an evil communist agent, but a sad, lonely and seriously disturbed individual. He told psychiatrists that a worm inside his body had told him to murder Verwoerd.

It was a time of great fear. I was only fifteen years old, but I sensed that the community in which I lived felt lost, rudderless and scared. They had blindly placed all their trust and hopes in the hands of their Leader. Suddenly, their Moses was gone. That was the mentality of Afrikaners in the time after the Anglo-Boer War: find a strong leader and follow him without question.

Verwoerd, more so than anyone before or after him, was not a man who consulted others in defining policy. He was like a fatherly genius; no need to think and ponder when 'Doktor' could do that for you. All was well with Afrikanerdom under his rule. He finally 'liberated' them from British imperialism by withdrawing

South Africa from the Commonwealth and changing the country's status to that of a republic in 1961. Between 1960 and his death, South Africa experienced extraordinary economic growth. His cocksure rationalisations of apartheid on moral and religious grounds stayed with many Afrikaners long after his death.

They got another strong leader to replace Verwoerd: John Vorster. But where Verwoerd earned the reverence he enjoyed through his (rather twisted) intellect, Vorster had to get it through pure *kragdadigheid* [forceful and uncompromising tactics] and an aggressive leadership style and body language. It was easier to discard him in the end, and even easier in the case of his successor, PW Botha.

It was more or less at this time, around 1967, that I read a book that stimulated my political awareness even more: *Rivonia: Masker Af!* [Rivonia unmasked], a book on the trial of Nelson Mandela and his comrades, arrested at Lilliesleaf farm in Rivonia, the headquarters of the ANC's military wing, in July 1963. I can't even remember who wrote it. Two admirable figures emerged from the book: Nelson Mandela and Percy Yutar, the state prosecutor.

I didn't see Mandela as a political hero, because he scared me; he was the enemy. But he impressed me because so many people were so scared of him, and because he defied all authority and risked his own life for his ideals.

I quite fancied Yutar, who was hero-worshipped in the book because he was so clever and could sway the court with his intellect. Or perhaps I was looking for affirmation from my father, who spoke highly of Yutar and said I could become like him if I studied law.

I followed my father's advice and studied law at university. It was a bad decision. The law interested me, and it still does, but the lecturers were pompous and over-bearing. They bored me to death. There was no room for debate or discussion or imaginative thinking; it was learn by heart and repeat verbatim. Yet I was apparently the only one in the class who thought like that: the rest of the poor sods thought the lecturers were gods and studying law was the highest calling in the universe.

I did not go the University of the Free State like the rest of my family. My brothers were there at the time I had to decide where to study and it sounded far too much like an extension of high school. I told my father I did not want his money; I was going to pay my own university fees, so he had no say in where I went.

I wanted to go to a university where I would be free to think and do what I wanted, to get this retarded adolescence thing behind me. But I did not for one second consider going to an English language university, although I could speak English fluently by then. Going to Stellenbosch University was a big enough jump for me.

I was in awe when I arrived in Stellenbosch. It was the *bakermat* [cradle] of Afrikanerdom and the nursery of prime ministers, cabinet ministers, cultural and financial leaders. I am now among the elite, I thought.

The awe did not last very long. I rubbed shoulders with the sons of the prime minister, cabinet ministers and prominent Afrikaner industrialists. The rich kids and those with powerful fathers ruled. But I came from a virtually classless background: my family always had more than enough money, but it never meant that we were better than the kids whose fathers worked as labourers on the railways. I found the elitism and rampant materialism at Stellenbosch vulgar and boring.

The fact that I worked on the railways for four months a year to pay for my studies throughout my university years perhaps contributed to my low tolerance for snobbery. The shunters, stokers, drivers and loading masters with whom I worked were all working-class Afrikaners, salt of the earth types. And I worked very hard and very long hours.

All in all, Stellenbosch was a huge disappointment. Most of my lecturers were *Boere-ooms* [uncles] with grey shoes and grey minds. In my first year, I had to wear a tie to class. It was a bit of a glorified high school. For years I thought this was going to be the liberation of my mind, but it was just more of the same. The late-night discussions in the pub were far more interesting, and at least I had the opportunity to experiment with sex, drugs and rock 'n roll. That was a real education.

My student life confirmed my family's worst fears about me. One Saturday night, I went with friends 'to do' Cape Town's nightclubs. By the time we reached a club called Catacoombes, I was very tired and emotional. I must have passed out in the club's foyer, because the next thing I knew I woke up with my elder brother sitting over me. He was a senior theology student, and part of a Christian group who worked the Cape Town nightclubs on weekends – to help sinners like me.

In my third year I switched to political science, because I realised I couldn't become what my father wanted me to be. I wanted to be a journalist. When I was about twelve, I won an essay competition, and was astonished that I could be successful at something that didn't feel like hard work.

I enjoyed the freedom from discipline and restraints at university, but I had great difficulty in finding some form of personal identity. I tried very hard to conform, to be like the other white Afrikaans students. In fact, for a while I tried to be a good Afrikaner nationalist.

But new influences came to play a role in my life. I discovered Bob Dylan, Donovan, Joan Baez and John Lennon. And Jimi Hendrix. I spent many a boozy night singing along with Dylan: 'Blowin' in the Wind', 'The Times They Are A-Changin'', 'Masters of War'. I loved protest songs, but I'm not sure I always grasped what they really meant.

I wanted to be a hippy, but I did not know how. I grew my hair long and tried to grow a beard, but real grooviness escaped me – it lost an ongoing battle against my Calvinist genes. I did take to wearing a black hat with a gold chain around it, but one night it was eaten by a monstrous black-and-white cow at a picnic spot in the bush outside Stellenbosch. It might have been the first night I experimented with marijuana.

An odd thing happened in 1970. I read in *Time* magazine about the four students at Kent State University who were shot by the National Guard on 4 May. They were protesting against the United States' adventures in Cambodia and were killed in cold blood. The story hardly featured in the South African media, but I suddenly felt a strong empathy with the students and a rage against Richard Nixon and his armed goons. I could not talk about it to anyone, because at Stellenbosch in 1970 nobody would have had sympathy with anti-war protestors.

It was almost as if I had a dark secret. I was fascinated by the French-German student revolutionary leader Daniel 'Red Danny' Cohn-Bendit. I felt a deep bond with the students who rebelled against the war in Vietnam and against the conservative governments in Germany and France. They fought for peace and the dignity of all people, and I thought that was noble. And yet I could not talk to my fellow students about it.

I find it interesting now that I associated so deeply with the anti-war and civil rights movements in the Unites States, but showed very little interest in the South African anti-apartheid struggle. Perhaps it was because there was more information available about the civil rights movement than about the resistance inside South Africa. Perhaps it was just easier to associate with a noble struggle for human rights in a place far away. To get involved in the local struggle would have been dangerous and would have alienated me even more from white society.

But is also possible that deep down I had the uncomfortable knowledge that the struggle against apartheid also threatened my privileged white life. Anyway, I did not know any black person other than farm workers, gardeners and domestic workers.

I lived in a world very far removed from black people.

8

The volk calls

IT IS TELLING of the state of my mind at the time that when I reached the point of seeking employment after university, I had no hesitation in applying for a job at the Afrikaans newspaper in the Cape, *Die Burger*. Not the *Cape Times* or the *Rand Daily Mail*, but *Die Burger*, the archconservative mouthpiece of the National Party.

I wasn't feeling completely at home in my Afrikaner skin, but it was unthinkable to even contemplate working for an English language paper. Self-respecting Afrikaners didn't work for English institutions.

From the first week in my job as a reporter, I knew that's what I was meant to do, wanted to do and would keep on doing. I never had one second's doubt about it. As my two brothers had a calling to be ministers in the Dutch Reformed Church, so I had a calling to be a journalist. Only, in the old school you called yourself a reporter – 'journalist' was a term reserved for experienced reporters who had thoroughly earned their spurs. As a young reporter at *Die Burger*, I dreamt about calling myself a journalist one day.

I had good training at *Die Burger*: how to get a story, how to check and double-check your facts, how to keep your opinion separate from the facts, how to write an intro and construct a readable story. And in 1974, the next year, I was seconded to Johannesburg as a member of the editorial team who was to launch a new Afrikaans newspaper in the north, *Beeld*.

It was exciting, pioneering work. I was in my element. Most of my younger colleagues were sharp, unorthodox and adventurous people. I was a hard newsman trying my best to live up to the romantic image of a macho news hound: worked all hours, played hard, drank hard and went for the scoops. I found a new role model: Hunter S Thompson, the American gonzo journalist.

For the first time, I felt at home in my environment. I was even quite happy to run the newspaper's campaign in support of the National Party in a by-election against the right-wing Herstigte Nasionale Party (HNP) in Alberton. I think it was in 1975.

At the time, I felt proud of how we rubbished the HNP and how we secured an overwhelming victory for the National Party. It was a trap I got out of quickly enough, but one that most Afrikaans journalists stayed in right until 1994, believing you're on the side of the righteous because you oppose the white right.

I've had several arguments with Afrikaans journalists over the years about this issue. The thinking was that the more vicious you were with the HNP, the Afrikaner Weerstandsbeweging (AWB) or the Conservative Party (CP), the more licence you had to support the National Party. It fooled many people: you redefine the extremes and place yourself in the middle, and thus your position appears reasonable and responsible. You ridicule the AWB, you cut down the CP, you slaughter everybody to the left of government, and that gives you the right to support the government, because they're then in the middle.

Of course that was nonsense. The AWB and CP were always on the lunatic fringe, the NP on the right, the white opposition on the centre right, the United Democratic Front and African National Congress in the centre left, the Communist Party, Pan Africanist Congress and others on the extreme left.

My one-time news editor at *Beeld*, Hennie van Deventer, later editor of *Die Volksblad* and head of all the Nasionale Pers newspapers before he retired, even wrote an entire book, *Kroniek van 'n Koerantman*, to praise himself for bravely opposing the AWB and CP.

My argument was always that the Afrikaans newspapers' most important role was to show their readers the true face of the right wing, and what the end result of their policies would be. But more important was showing them, in a way that would be palatable to most Afrikaners, the real face and consequences of apartheid; the real culture in the police and army; to always give them a true glimpse of what the black majority felt.

My first editor at *Beeld*, Schalk Pienaar, was seen as the bravest and most reformist of all senior Afrikaans journalists. Yet he deeply believed in grand apartheid and waged war against all liberals and other opponents of the National Party government – even campaigning viciously against the highly respected Afrikaner rebel, theologian Beyers Naudé. According to his best friend, Piet Cillié (who was my first editor at *Die Burger*), he and Pienaar believed in apartheid 'like the Marxists of the Soviet Union believed in communism'. In 1978, Prime Minister PW Botha awarded the National Party's highest honour, the DF Malan Medal, to Pienaar.

Pienaar achieved his iconic status in Afrikaans journalism by being the HNP's most vociferous critic, and by occasionally criticising petty apartheid – separate benches, toilets, lifts and beaches.

Early in 2003, I wrote a review of a biography on Pienaar, *Voorloper – Die lewe van Schalk Pienaar* by Alex Mouton, for *Die Burger*. I said Pienaar did not deserve his reputation as a leading critic of the apartheid government and that he should merely be seen as a reformist inside Afrikaner nationalism. He did very little to help the country make progress on the road to an open and just democracy, I wrote.

My review was met by angry reaction in the letters column. The assistant editor of the paper, Leopold Scholtz, wrote in a column on the editorial page that I was judging Pienaar without recognising the political reality of his time. And he presented the most trusted argument of his ilk: Pienaar had to remain 'within hearing distance of his people', otherwise he would have had no influence.

I responded:

I did not criticise Pienaar because he did not demand Nelson Mandela's freedom or the unbanning of the ANC. I did not question his 'forerunner' status because he did not ask for a full democracy in a unitary state in the 1970s. It would have seen him branded as a communist and a traitor thirty years ago.

I also did not expect him to embrace Beyers Naudé. But by being in the forefront of the witch-hunt on Naudé and similar Afrikaans dissidents and to discredit all criticism of apartheid as '*Boerehaat*, unpatriotic and steeped in communism', he showed that he wasn't the prophet many thought he was.

Scholtz says people like Pienaar prepared Afrikaners for democracy by 'remaining within hearing distance of their own people'. Of course the argument of 'staying within hearing distance' is a legitimate one. Herein lies the actual debate. Does 'remaining within hearing distance' mean people shouldn't be confronted with the reality of their society?

In the last years of PW Botha and FW de Klerk, Afrikaners suddenly realised that the world was a very different place to the one their leaders had painted for so long. After 1994, especially with the revelations before the Truth Commission, the most popular Afrikaner tune was: We did not know. Well, if they did not know, it was because opinion formers and journalists like Pienaar did not tell them – they were too busy 'staying within hearing distance'. They supported the pass laws, the large-scale violation of human rights and the homelands policies: policies for which the National Party and most Afrikaners humbly asked for forgiveness after 1994.

But I did not hold these views as a young reporter in 1974 and 1975. I was too happy playing the role of a Boere Hunter Thompson.

In 1975, I attended a compulsory three-week military camp at Tempe outside Bloemfontein. (I did my initial military training in 1969 at the Army Gymnasium in Heidelberg. It was a fun time: long before the South African state got engaged in war in neighbouring countries.) Very early one morning, I switched on my radio in my tent out in the veld to listen to the news. I was stunned: Breyten Breytenbach, the prince of Afrikaans poetry, had been arrested a short while after he arrived in South Africa from France, and charged with terrorism.

I had not met Breyten at that point, but he had already become a symbol of resistance against apartheid and narrow-minded Afrikaner nationalism. He was living in France with his Vietnamese wife, Yolande, whom he wasn't allowed to bring to South Africa – because she was considered not white. South Africans were barred by the Immorality Act from marrying (or having sex) 'across the colour line'.

I remember how the news of Breyten's arrest stirred a deep anger in me. Was this the Vorster regime's answer to dissent? What kind of future would I have as a young Afrikaner if this was how the *volk* was going to treat one of the most talented voices in our midst? What kind of people put their poets in jail?

I was so angry that I declared a go-slow for the day and informed my officers of my reasons. It was not a clever thing to do. I suffered extra duty and punitive marches with full pack for the rest of my camp.

I did not know at the time that Breyten had been the co-founder of an organisation called Okhela with close ties to the ANC, which sought to undermine the apartheid government. Still, it did not seem to warrant his nine-year jail sentence.

It later became clear that Breyten was followed from the moment he arrived at Johannesburg airport in disguise and with a false passport. It had nasty consequences for some of the people he contacted inside the country. Breyten maintained afterwards that he was sold out by the ANC itself, or rather some communist elements within it. I tried for years to find out if this were true, but everybody I spoke to in the ANC and Communist Party vehemently denied it – they blamed his own sloppiness. Perhaps it was the work of one or two security police moles in the ANC.

I eventually met Breyten thirteen years after his jailing. It was after a conversation with him, Van Zyl Slabbert and Beyers Naudé that I decided to launch an anti-apartheid newspaper in Afrikaans.

Breyten and I later had a serious falling-out after I criticised his political style. It became quite acrimonious and we had no contact after that. I still think he is the greatest Afrikaans poet ever, but I really don't think he is much of a politician.

9

Soweto

THE FROST WAS lying white and crisp on Johannesburg's suburban lawns early on the morning of Wednesday 16 June 1976. Our old Peugeot 404 was reluctant in the cold, but by the time we started seeing the brown haze that always hung over Soweto in winter, it became more willing.

I was mildly irritated to be on this mission. I did not like working in Soweto. I always felt like an unwanted alien; I sensed the hostile stares of people on the street. No doubt many of them wondered if I was a security policeman. The dirty, dusty streets and extreme poverty made me very uncomfortable. I did not want to know about this side of my society.

But there was also a hint of excitement on this winter's morning. Soweto school pupils had been demonstrating and striking against tuition in Afrikaans for two weeks. A week earlier, police detectives had been stoned and their car burnt when they tried to arrest a pupil at Naledi High School. A sign went up at Morris Isaacson High School ordering the security police to stay off the premises. The police told me that on Sunday youth leaders had decided to stage a protest march for this day – and dropped a juicy hint that made my ears prick up: Winnie Mandela, they said, was behind the troubles.

The *Beeld* photographer and I were apprehensive as we drove past the Baragwanath Hospital into Soweto, but we felt better when the first group of pupils we encountered gave us peace signs. We went straight to the Protea Police Station. At that stage, *Beeld* had no black reporters, and white reporters like me had no contacts inside the township. We relied on the police to give us information.

At the police station we were told that all the pupils were on their way to Orlando West. There could be trouble, the police said, but they seemed very relaxed, smoking and talking in the sun next to their vehicles. A young policeman walked up to us standing at our car, smiled and said: '*Julle wit outjies gaan op julle moer kry. Die klonkies hou nie van wit gesigte in Soweto nie*' [You white guys will get into trouble. The children don't like white faces in Soweto].

Suddenly an order was shouted, and all the men jumped into their vehicles and drove off. We followed. They stopped near the Orlando West School. Policemen were standing in a half circle facing a large group of pupils, shouting and milling about. 'Down with Afrikaans' read one of the placards I could see. I heard shots being fired.

I was quite sure that the pupils would run once the police started shooting. They did not budge. Instead, they threw stones and screamed and yelled. In the distance I could see two youngsters being carried away. Eventually the crowd split, just to regroup and confront the police once again.

By noon, Soweto was in chaos. Pupils burned down beerhalls and state-owned vehicles; they ran around the township in groups with their placards and their stones.

I knew then, deep in my heart, that South Africa would never be the same again. A youngster of fourteen who steps to the front of the crowd with the police just metres away must know that he could be the next one to die. When I was fourteen, I had not even been in a fight in the schoolyard. I was dreaming of becoming a lawyer or a journalist; I was dreaming about seeing Paris and London following the stories my parents had told me; my mind was occupied with girls and rugby. I could not imagine two human lives further apart.

What drove this lad with his burning eyes to put his body in the line of fire? How did he overcome every normal person's fear of mortal danger? My answer at the time was that one could only act in this way if there was an absolute absence of hope. But I also considered that this small body stored the pent-up frustration and resentment of his parents and grandparents, perhaps of generations of proud ancestors who were forced to wear the white man's pass book, who were treated like perpetual servants in the country of their birth and forced to live in the slums that surrounded me in Soweto.

What was to become of this boy if he wasn't killed in the riots? It was unthinkable to me that he would eventually be pacified to settle down as an obedient black man in an apartheid society – a mineworker, or perhaps a gardener. These were unsettling thoughts for a young Afrikaner reporter. For the first time in my life, I fully understood that there was something fundamentally wrong in my society, and that it would have to change drastically and soon.

But if you'd asked me then what change that should be, I'm not sure if I would have said South Africa should become a democracy with simple majority rule. I probably would have cooked up some plan that would better the lives of black people, but I think I believed quite firmly that black people were not ready for democracy. I think I might have shared some of the prevalent white fear at the time that 'they would do to us what we did to them'.

Our car was stoned by youths three times in the days following 16 June, shattering the windscreen and side windows. Two of these were very close encounters. It was frightening. On both occasions, I was quite sure that the pupils would have killed us if the car had stalled or overturned. I saw it in their eyes in those frantic, scary moments.

But it was more than just a scare. It was a fundamental shock to my system. Every time I saw these angry youths up close, it got hammered into my brain: it was *me* they hated! I wasn't merely an uninvolved bystander. It was my language I saw on those angry placards. If you had asked them whom they hated the most, they would no doubt have said, 'white Afrikaner males'. I was all three of those. The policemen who shot at these youths were men who looked and talked like me and had similar family backgrounds. The three men these youngsters hated the most were the leaders of my tribe: John Vorster, Andries Treurnicht and Jimmy Kruger (I only found out much later that Kruger was a Welsh orphan brought up by an Afrikaans family).

The next day, 17 June, was much worse. The youths' anger had deepened because the police had shot and killed several of them without really being threatened. The police clearly had orders that the uprising had to be put down quickly and violently. Both sides were more violent on the second day. Fires were burning all over Soweto, and gangs of youths were roaming the streets, stoning vehicles, setting up roadblocks, taunting the police. On the Friday, the photographer and I rushed to Alexandra, a township inside the borders of 'white' Johannesburg. It was the same story.

I tasted tear gas for the first time on 16 June – something I became quite used to during the next few months. The police soon progressed from ordinary gas canisters to monster 'sneeze machines', trucks with a huge funnel on top from which clouds of tear gas could be blasted onto the crowds of youngsters. Every time I had a whiff of tear gas in later years, I remembered the morning of 16 June.

The 'unrest' (it's like calling war 'unpeace') became my beat for the rest of that year. From Soweto and Alexandra, the riots quickly spread to most of the townships on the Witwatersrand, and then beyond. My *Beeld* colleagues and I kept our contacts in the police and the black Education Department in Soweto and other townships, but we quickly learnt that not only did they put their own spin on things – most of the time they did not understand what was happening. It was an education to start developing contacts in the black community – to overcome the suspicion that we were spies or police agents, but also to deal with radical young black people who only had one thing on their minds: to overthrow the white state, of which we were a part.

The 'unrest beat' was never a nice once, but it suited my view of myself as a macho, hard-nosed reporter, as at home drinking hard with the cops as I was facing the dangers on the township streets. We could not compete with the black reporters of *The World*, many of whom lived in Soweto, but keenly competed with the *Rand Daily Mail*. We were smug that the 'left-wing liberals' had a custom-built 'riot car' with bullet-proof windows and spikes under the sides to prevent rioters from overturning it, while we as Boere did our jobs in our Peugeots and VW Beetles – and still sometimes scooped them.

I formed a good friendship with the director of black education in Soweto, a big, friendly man named Jaap Strydom, brother of a senior *Sunday Times* journalist I admired, Hans Strydom. Jaap didn't seem like an ideologue to me, and was very critical, in private conversation, of the police and politicians such as Treurnicht and Kruger.

Jaap Strydom had an unfortunate influence on my analysis of events. He often sympathised with the black youth – 'Would you not have rioted if you were in their shoes?' he once asked me. He said it was short-sighted and counterproductive to enforce Afrikaans as a language of tuition. Instead, he believed it should have been made attractive and easy for the black youth to study and speak Afrikaans.

Strydom did insist, however, that a large number of the school pupils were only taking part in the riots because they were egged on and exploited by 'agitators' – adults with ulterior political motives, probably communists. The only strategy, according to Jaap, was to undermine the revolution by removing the most obvious sources of frustration: better classrooms, better teachers, downscaling Afrikaans and improving living standards in the townships. Make the youth feel better, give them a sense that they have a future, and they will stop rioting. Of course, this strategy also meant that one had to deal harshly with the 'ringleaders' and those adults 'exploiting the pupils'.

It was comfortable for me to buy into Jaap's approach. I could recognise that the nasty police and government were wrong, I could sympathise with the angry youths, and yet I did not have to believe in anything that would really threaten my white way of life.

Jaap later tried to get me involved in a newspaper he wanted to publish among the youth in the townships. He was going to call it the *Golden City Times* or something like that, and the idea was to have a voice critical of the government, but at the same time undermining the revolutionary elements. Years later, I discovered that the notorious Department of Information had funded the project. Thankfully, I never had anything to do with it.

Jaap's thinking had one big flaw, which I realised soon enough. The uprising was not organised by adults or outsiders or agitators. It served the interests of both the Vorster government and the ANC to state that the ANC had been behind the revolt. They were not; they only became involved in the days and weeks after 16 June. Despite what the cops had told me earlier, not even Winnie Mandela was involved; some of the student leaders merely approached her for advice.

Most of the prominent student leaders were not ANC supporters, but followers of the Black Consciousness movement. It was as close as one can ever get to a spontaneous uprising. Spontaneous, yet not out of the blue: the psychological impact of Frelimo's takeover of power in neighbouring Mozambique in 1975 and the growing influence of Black Consciousness leaders such as Steve Biko had created a new urgency in young leaders' minds to liberate themselves.

The 'ringleaders' were in fact seventeen- and eighteen-year-old pupils. I never met any of them during the uprising or its immediate aftermath, but I was fascinated by these secretive, charismatic young leaders: Tsietsi Mashinini, the first president of the Soweto Students' Representative Council, and his successors, Khotso Seathlolo, Dan Sechaba Montsitsi, Trofomo Sono. Mashinini and Seathlolo left the country in the months after June 1976. Mashinini lived the high life for a while in West Africa, but died a lonely and sick man in Guinea-Bissau in 1991. Montsitsi became an ANC member of parliament in 1994.

And then there was the quiet young man, the tactician behind Mashinini, Murphy Morobe.

I eventually met Morobe nine years after the Soweto uprising, when he became the publicity secretary for the United Democratic Front. He was arrested near the end of 1976, held and tortured in Leeuwkop Prison not far from Soweto, and eventually sentenced to three years in jail for sedition. He served his jail term on Robben Island, where he completed his matric, and was released in 1982. I interviewed him in his jail cell twenty years later for a television documentary on the island.

Morobe became a trade unionist after his release, and was an active force from the first day in the new internal liberation movement, the United Democratic Front, in 1983. In 1987 he was again jailed, this time for fourteen months, but during a visit to hospital he escaped and sought refuge in the American Consulate in Johannesburg with Mohammed Valli Moosa, later an ANC cabinet minister, and Vusi Khanyile. They walked to freedom after five weeks.

Morobe, as one of the foremost voices of the Mass Democratic Movement, earned the deep respect of many South Africans when he jeopardised his political career in the late 1980s by publicly condemning the behaviour of Winnie Mandela, one of his biggest heroes when he was a student leader, and that of her so-called Mandela United Football Club.

He went on to study in the United States, and on his return became a member of the ANC's team that negotiated with the National Party government. He was later appointed chairperson of the Financial and Fiscal Commission.

I got to know Morobe fairly well over the years. In my book, he is senior cabinet minister material. If the politics inside the ANC worked differently, I have no doubt that he could have been in line for the top leadership position. But perhaps he is just too much of a straight shooter. He is a special man.

It is interesting how many of the other characters who had played a role in the 1976 uprisings were prominent in post-1994 South Africa. South Africa's top black industrialist and former premier of Gauteng, Tokyo Sexwale, gave Morobe and other student leaders crash-weapons training in 1976. A young student leader, Billy Masethla, who had a top intelligence job in the first democratic government, recruited Morobe for training and later became Director-General of Home Affairs.

Jackie Selebi, who was fired as a teacher at Orlando West High School a year before the uprisings for 'politicising' pupils, became a key ANC underground organiser in the June 1976 aftermath, recruiting youths for underground cells or for training outside the country. He is today South Africa's Commissioner of Police.

The violence in South Africa's townships continued unabated for the whole of 1976. Late that year, I think it was around October, there was a lull of a few days with no incidents of violence. White South Africa breathed a sigh of relief. I phoned the Minister of Police, Jimmy Kruger, late one evening at his home. The riots are over, he told me – the police had broken the back of the revolutionary onslaught.

The story appeared in *Beeld* as the front-page lead under my byline the next morning: 'The violence is over'. It was not a good day for me. Between going to print around midnight and the time the newspaper vendors started selling the paper in the streets, serious violence had broken out in several townships. *Beeld*'s readers had breakfast with my news on the front page, with the radio in the background announcing the 'serious unrest' all over the country.

We still don't know exactly how many people died in Soweto in June 1976 and in the months that followed. The police announced that 21 blacks and 2 whites died in Soweto on 16 June and 1 005 were injured, including 11 policemen. On 21 June, Jimmy Kruger told parliament that 130 people had died during the first five days of violence in Soweto, and 1 118 were injured.

Tsietsi Mashinini later said that he and his comrades had gone into the mortuaries every day from 16 June, and counted 353 bodies during the first three days. The Black Parents' Association collated figures learnt from eyewitnesses, hospital and mortuary reports, and announced that more than 500 people had died during the first five days.

In May 1976, the South African Institute of Race Relations said they had verified the deaths of at least 618 people. At the hearings of the Cillié Commission into the riots, the police said some 450 people were killed between June and October, not all by police bullets. In later years, some researchers claimed that more than a 1000 people were killed during the countrywide uprisings in 1976, and more than 5 000 injured.

The notorious Colonel 'Rooi Rus' Swanepoel, a police riot squad commander with a taste for violence, told the Cillié Commission that it was hard to tell how many people had died, because of 'an old Bantu custom to remove the dead and injured from the battlefield'.

John Vorster delivered his New Year's message to the nation at midnight on 31 December 1976. He warned South Africans to 'fasten your seatbelts', because 'the storm has not struck yet. We are only experiencing the whirlwinds that go before it.'

He got that right.

I O

Wine in the swimming pool

IN THE JOURNALISM of the 1970s and 1980s, the quickest way to make progress in one's career was to become a political reporter. I was very ambitious when I was young, so I was pleased when the editor of *Beeld* asked me in 1978, at the relatively young age of twenty-six, to join the parliamentary reporting team of the Nasionale Pers group.

In the language of the time, I was promoted from covering extra-parliamentary politics – the stuff blacks were up to – to parliamentary politics, the stuff that was really important. I was, so I thought, going up in the world.

Parliament is the most seductive place for a journalist to work. Working journalists (as opposed to editors and other desk jockeys) earn very little money and have a low social status in society. (I was still earning a lot less than R1 000 a month when I was sent to parliament.) Suddenly one is right in the heart of the ruling elite, strolling the corridors of power. Cabinet ministers call you by your first name; you share jokes and drinks and confidences with MPs; occasionally, you even shake hands with the prime minister. As a lowly reporter, your first instinct is not to do anything to jeopardise your position in this cosy and privileged environment. Journalists as a species love to be close to the rich and powerful, probably in the subconscious hope that some of it will rub off on them.

The white parliament of the late 1970s was a very strange place. Most of the members of parliament, the cabinet itself and the senior civil servants behaved as if they were the centre of the universe. Parliament was an island in a sea of hostility: internally the black resistance was still smouldering and building up new steam; internationally the apartheid regime was increasingly isolated. After the Soweto uprising in 1976 and the killing of Black Consciousness leader Steve Biko in a police cell by members of the security police in 1977, the anti-apartheid movement grew in strength worldwide. President Jimmy Carter and Prime Minister Jim Callaghan were much more hostile than their successors, Ronald Reagan and Margaret Thatcher.

My first big shock as parliamentary reporter came when I was invited, as a member of the trusted Nasionale Pers team, to some of the parties thrown by cabinet ministers and deputy ministers early in the session. I was no stranger to a decadent lifestyle with far too much alcohol and other types of rowdiness – on the contrary. But I was a young, gung-ho reporter, in no position of authority, and I never pretended to anyone that I was an upstanding member of society and a pious Christian.

The late-night parties of some of the top Nats were truly something nobody had prepared me for, and a serious indication of my extreme naivety. I might not have liked them much, but I seriously thought the leaders of the *volk* were staunch men of good conscience who adhered to a sober Christian lifestyle. Instead, they made our journalistic parties in Johannesburg look like high school fun. Several times I saw pillars of my society grope any available girl, or fall down drunk. One night, for everybody's entertainment, a cabinet minister threw an expensive bottle of KWV red wine into a swimming pool, then pulled out a pistol and shot it to pieces, the wine slowly staining the crystal clear water, like blood.

I can handle decadence, but there was something very sick and sad about the behaviour of these men.

A high point was at the after-party of a ministerial reception when only a few of my Nasionale Pers colleagues had remained with the hosts. The wife of a very senior colleague, who was the prime minister's confidante, had had too much to drink. She proclaimed in a shrill voice from the top of the stairs of the ministerial reception room: 'Did you know that the prime minister has serious problems with piles, but they can't operate on him because they fear they will cut off my husband's head?' I thought she had a point.

In our reporting team, we took turns going into the House of Assembly to report on debates. After a month or three, I was trusted to report on a slightly more important debate. I took copious notes, then went back to the office to type my story and send it off to the different newspapers in the group. As I was about to send it off, the head of our team, *Die Burger*'s political correspondent Alf Ries, asked to see my copy.

I gave it to him to read, but he started walking out the door with it. I asked him where he was going. He said the minister (in this case it was Fanie Botha) wanted to 'have a quick look' at the story before it went out. And if he doesn't like it the way I have written it, you would change it, I asked. Yes, Ries replied, surprised at this young upstart's arrogance. So our newspapers could actually state something that was different from *Hansard*, I asked him. Deeply annoyed, he answered with dripping sarcasm: 'Who will the people believe, *Die Burger* or *Hansard*?'

I lost my enthusiasm for parliamentary reporting after that, and was never trusted again with important stories. I spent the rest of that parliamentary session having serious fun around Cape Town. I also knew that I was gaining a reputation in the group I worked for as 'not a team player'. I heard later that my habit of sometimes having lunch or a drink in the press gallery restaurant with some of the journalists from the English-language newspapers also raised questions about where my real loyalties lay.

It was from these colleagues that I first heard the rumours of a huge scandal brewing in government. It involved the Department of Information, secret funds and the newspaper that was founded in late 1976 in opposition to the liberal *Rand Daily Mail*, *The Citizen*. I asked our senior political correspondents and other colleagues about it, but they dismissed it as 'opposition propaganda'.

In May 1978, an opposition MP, Harry Schwarz, asked the Minister of Information, Connie Mulder, directly in parliament whether his department had funded *The Citizen*. Mulder denied it categorically.

In the weeks and months after that, the rumours grew stronger: that the Department of Information had spent millions on front companies all over the world, on trying to buy a US newspaper, and on other projects meant to improve the apartheid government's image. Stories started appearing in the *Rand Daily Mail*, the *Sunday Express* and the *Financial Mail*, but not in the Afrikaans papers.

Prime Minister Vorster was by now a shadow of his former self, and his health was also deteriorating. The jockeying for his successor started in all earnest, with PW Botha and Connie Mulder the front-runners. One day I was invited to lunch by a surgeon, who was closely associated with the multinational corporation Lonrho, a company with huge mining interests in southern Africa and elsewhere.

I'm still not sure why he approached me, because I was in no way a big player on the political scene. I had met him once before through my interest in the Angolan story. Perhaps he thought, as did most of my Afrikaans colleagues by now, that I was a 'loose cannon'. The man told me that they regarded Mulder as the favourite to win the race for prime minister, and they thought that this would be a disaster for South Africa. He asked me to help them spread a scandalous story – a true story, according to him – involving Mulder's private life. They would supply me with photographs and help me wherever they could, he said, because their resources were virtually limitless.

I knew that the newspapers I worked for would never break such a story. Why didn't he give the story to the opposition papers, I asked. Because, he said, it would then be seen as a ploy by the enemies of the National Party and have no effect. And there, I felt, ended my possible interest in it, because my business was in reporting facts, not distributing rumours to other journalists.

I was also nervous. For a start, I seriously doubted whether the story could possibly be true. But by then I also had enough sense to know that being the source of a story that could seriously harm the National Party government could have dangerous consequences for my health – I remembered my encounter with General 'Lang Hendrik' van den Bergh, a close friend of Mulder's.

I don't know whether the Lonrho man gave the story to other journalists, but it never surfaced anywhere. The whole episode remains a mystery to me to this day.

Vorster resigned on 20 September 1978, and was appointed state president, a ceremonial position. Botha was elected as his successor: he received 98 of the National Party caucus votes to Mulder's 74. PW Botha became South Africa's prime minister in October 1978.

A month later, Judge Anton Mostert, who led an inquiry into exchange control violations, confirmed that *The Citizen* was indeed a Department of Information project funded with state money through industrialist Louis Luyt. A commission of inquiry under Judge Roelof Erasmus later confirmed all the other rumours about the department.

It was the biggest scandal to hit the National Party since it came to power in 1948. PW Botha and his political allies used it very cleverly to get rid of John Vorster and Connie Mulder, and to my utter disillusionment, my political colleagues at Nasionale Pers played along with their game. Not at any point did the political correspondents or investigative reporters of *Die Burger* and *Beeld* break any of the Info Scandal stories – they merely reported the government's reaction to the stories in the English press. And yet they had known most of the basic facts since July or August 1978 – probably as much or even more than those reporters who did write on the topic. That was what Afrikaans journalism was like in the 1970s and 1980s.

Looking back, the Info Scandal was a very important moment in the history of South Africa and of Afrikaner nationalism. The apartheid government came under severe pressure after 1976, internally and internationally. Their only response, apart from suppressing all internal resistance, was to 'spin-doctor' their way out of it. That's why they spent many millions on *The Citizen* and on trying to buy the *Washington Times*, on lobby groups all over the West and on projects aimed at enhancing Pretoria's image.

As a friend of mine would say, you can't polish a turd. The Info Scandal put an end to that foolishness and forced the government to turn to reforming their apartheid policies as a more appropriate response to pressure.

But, more importantly, the old myth that the leaders of Afrikaner nationalism were honest, straightforward and God-fearing men who had to be followed blindly and trusted because they knew the way forward was blown sky-high in the eyes of their once loyal followers. They were exposed for what they were: bloated, self-important, morally corrupt, incompetent charlatans.

Thus, in the years after the Info Scandal, ordinary Afrikaners – and certainly journalists – found it much easier to criticise and even ridicule their leaders. PW Botha, not the brightest bulb in the socket, could never understand why he wasn't treated with the same reverence as Vorster and Verwoerd.

The discovery that the Great Leaders had feet of clay also hastened the departure of the National Party's right wing, in the form of Andries Treurnicht's Conservative Party. If Treurnicht and his men had stayed in the NP for another three or four years, the National Party would probably not have embarked upon the road of faltering constitutional reform when they did – reforms that in the end snowballed into talks with the ANC.

But reporting on the intricacies of white political games was not the road I was to follow.

Towards the end of the 1978 parliamentary session, my then editor, Ton Vosloo, asked me to have lunch at a private club around the corner from parliament. Also present was the editor of *Die Burger*, Piet Cillié. They informed me that I was to open an office for the group in Windhoek, the capital of Namibia. Namibia, with the acceptance by South Africa of the Western Five's settlement plan, had become a very important story for South Africa. In very diplomatic terms, they made me understand that the positioning of their newspapers on the story at that point was undesirable. My brief was to go to Namibia and report truthfully and objectively, without getting sidetracked by the different political factions.

I took their brief literally. Vosloo and Cillié didn't bargain on that.

PART III

Mr Foreign Correspondent

11

Boetie gaan border toe

'IF YOU WANT to experience high drama, get into that chopper very quickly,' the media officer of the South African Army told me. I was in Ruacana, in the 'operational area' on the border between Namibia and Angola, trying to get a feel for the state of the war between the South African army and the South West African People's Organisation (SWAPO).

I got into the military helicopter with a few other journalists, and we took off, flying higher and higher, a lot higher than helicopters normally fly. Down below we could see the Cunene River, which formed the border between the two countries. We drifted over the border and a few kilometres to the west. A small village came into view: Chitado. I had been there a few years earlier; it was a typical Portuguese colonial hamlet. The houses and offices had wide verandahs and red-tiled roofs – a sweet little place.

We craned our necks to see down below. Smoke was coming from the town, and then we could see a building being blown up: the roof shattered into a thousand pieces spiralling upwards. We had a bird's eye view of the destruction of an Angolan town. 'We are wiping out a SWAPO forward base,' the media officer told us.

A few minutes later the helicopter descended, then landed right next to the town. A few South African soldiers in camouflage were still hanging around, assault rifles over the shoulder, faces dirty and sweaty. The village was devastated. I even saw two dead chickens.

The intelligence officers came towards us with arms full of documents and posters: a commander's notebook, a few crude maps of the area, a picture of SWAPO leader Sam Nujoma, a SWAPO poster. This was to prove that it was in fact a SWAPO base and not another attack on Angola.

I started wandering away from the group. Then I saw bodies in the grass on the outskirts of the village. I walked closer. I saw three young black men in grey-green camouflage uniforms. They had grotesque wounds to their faces and bodies. I took photographs.

Then I stepped over another body to take a picture with the sun from behind. The body moved. I went closer. The young man was lying on his back, one arm clutching his chest, the other folded in under his body.

He looked at me and whispered: '*Het die baas vir my water?*' [Can the boss give me some water?]

I froze completely. This was too much to take in. When I came to my senses and looked around for a source of water, he was dead.

I had seen people die before, in Soweto and other townships, in Mozambique, in Angola and northern Namibia. I had stepped over dozens of dead bodies in my life as a journalist. Eventually one develops a defence mechanism that cuts in and there's no damage to one's psyche. No damage that could not be washed away with a few bottles of beer. Quite a few.

This was different. This young man's death and his words to me would haunt me forever.

It was different not only because of the macabre view we had of the destruction of the village and the people occupying it. It was different because here was a soldier, probably just a few years younger than me, two countries away from my own, talking to me in my own language, Afrikaans. (Afrikaans is Nambia's lingua franca.) He was a freedom fighter fighting for his country's independence against the mighty army of my country, yet he called me by the form of address enforced by whites on black people for centuries: *baas*.

I was in a daze. There was something very wrong with what I had just experienced. Six words from a dying man that cast a dark shadow over everything I was and represented. How could I be the same after that?

I went to one of the senior officers and told him that one of the SWAPO guerrillas was still alive when I got to him. He denied it absolutely, saying his men had made sure all the wounded were evacuated. He even told a colleague of mine later that I had made up the story. I wish I had. I wish that it hadn't really happened to me. There's a pockmark on my soul from that day.

When I look back on my life today, two young black men stand out as beacons in my fast-changing consciousness: the fourteen-year-old Soweto boy who stepped forward to face the police bullets in 1976, and this young Namibian soldier.

It seemed as if a higher force was propelling me from one life-changing experience to the next, hell-bent on forcing me to start walking on a road that would lead to conflict with my employers and my *volk*. After covering the township uprisings in 1976 and 1977, I was sent to cover the white parliament in 1978. And now I was based in Windhoek, covering the unfolding events in Namibia and Angola.

To fully understand the drama that played itself out in Chitado on that day, I have to take you back a few years.

* * * * *

The 16th of June 1976 was without doubt a turning point in South Africa's history. But two years earlier, events in a country far away had prepared the ground for 16 June, and the ripple effect of these events would affect the whole subcontinent.

It would also indirectly push me into inevitable conflict with my community.

That country was Portugal, colonial master of Mozambique, Angola and Guinea-Bissau. In August 1973, a number of young career officers in the Portuguese army formed the Movement of the Armed Forces (MFA). They were weary of the protracted bush wars they had to fight against liberation movements in the three colonies and angry with their fat-cat generals. Ironically, many of their young leaders were influenced by the textbooks they had to study to understand their enemy: the revolutionary theories of Amilcar Cabral, Ché Guevara and Mao Zedong.

The MFA quickly grew in numbers and revolutionary fervour. One of their heroes, General António de Spínola, published a book, *Portugal e o Futuro*, in February 1974, arguing that no military solution was possible in the colonies, and that Portugal could not afford these wars. This was grist to the MFA's mill, and on 25 April 1974 they staged a military coup.

It was a moment as significant to southern Africa as the fall of the Berlin Wall would be to Europe fourteen years later.

Spínola, the leader of the military junta, was sworn in as president of Portugal. After negotiations with the liberation movements PAIGC in Guinea and Frelimo in Mozambique, he quickly agreed that Guinea should be given its independence on 10 September 1974 and Mozambique on 25 June 1975.

Angola was more complicated with its three liberation movements: the MPLA, FNLA and UNITA. The three groups signed a deal with Portugal to govern together until elections could be held. Instead, the MPLA grabbed the seat of power. Already feuding for some time, the three liberation movements started fighting each other instead of the Portuguese.

The fact that Marxist liberation movements that had good relations with the Soviet Union were ruling in two states in southern Africa sent shivers down the spine of South Africa's white rulers and generals. The 'white south' was being encircled. Could Rhodesia and South West Africa be next – and then South Africa?

With a communist movement in control of Angola, it would be very difficult to contain the Namibian liberation movement, SWAPO. Namibia, treated by South Africa as its own colony, was the buffer state between itself and black-ruled Africa. The Marxist governments in Angola and Mozambique would surely also afford the guerrillas of the African National Congress training and operational bases, until then restricted to Zambia, Tanzania and Uganda.

Two countries rushed their military forces to Angola during the course of 1975 to bolster the MPLA and UNITA respectively: Cuba and South Africa. For more than a decade, these two countries insisted that the other was there first and was the reason for its intervention. I have little doubt that South Africa would have rushed to the aid of UNITA and the FNLA even if the Cubans never got involved, and the Cubans would have assisted the MPLA whether South African forces intervened or not.

A very senior SADF officer told me much later that defence minister PW Botha visited the border between Angola and Namibia early in August 1975. The officer told me Botha was 'shocked to his core' and 'red in his face with anger' when he saw the white Portuguese, who had fled Angola with only their clothes, now living in the veld. He rushed back to Pretoria to advise Vorster that South Africa had to get its hands dirty in this 'fight against communism'.

By August 1975, both countries had a military presence in Angola. On 24 September 1975, PW Botha signed off on an operational plan aimed at driving the MPLA out of southern Angola. On the same day, Commandant Kaas van der Waals, code-named Fox, arrived at Silva Porto as permanent liaison with UNITA leader Jonas Savimbi, whose code name was *Spyker* – it means 'nail', but is also Afrikaans slang for the sexual act.

At the end of September 1975, Task Force Zulu started its ambitious invasion of Angola. The South African soldiers were complemented by fighters from the FNLA and UNITA, and by Bushman soldiers who fought with the Portuguese. The war for Angola was called Operation Savannah.

Behind the scenes, South Africa was egged on by the CIA and elements in the administration of President Gerald Ford, as well as by Zambian president Kenneth Kaunda and Zairean president Mobuto Sese Seko, who had a good relationship with UNITA and the FNLA. (FNLA leader Holden Roberto was married to Mobuto's sister.)

The South African strike force was initially very successful and moved with astonishing speed up the Angolan coast, conquering first Sá da Bandeira and Moçamedes, and then Benguela, Lobito and Novo Redondo.

On 4 October, FNLA leader Roberto told SADF chief General Magnus Malan at a meeting in Ambriz, north of Luanda, that he aimed to capture the Angolan capital before independence day on the 11th, after his first attempt on 25 October had failed. Botha and Malan decided South Africa should help him this time. It became one of the jokes of the war.

The South Africans flew their 5.5-inch cannons with C130 freight planes to Ambriz. The SADF personnel were issued with Russian uniforms and rifles. The artillery attack on the MPLA forces on the outskirts of Luanda started just after 6 am on 10 November. But the ground attack only started two hours later – the South Africans told me Roberto slept late and had a hearty breakfast first while his soldiers were waiting for his command. The enemy had ample time to regroup after the initial bombardment. The MPLA soldiers quickly identified the South African artillery pieces, and they had to withdraw.

The South African Air Force sent three warplanes from Rundu in Namibia, 1 300 kilometres away, each with three 1 000-pound bombs to be dropped on the soldiers defending Luanda. The first fell in the sea, the second on the beach, the third far south from any troop presence. Not one of the six bombs used fell near the target, and the bombers returned to Rundu.

The attack on Luanda was a disaster. The South African soldiers were now stranded north of Luanda, and a navy frigate, the SAS *President Steyn*, had to rescue them at the fishing harbour of Ambrizete, 150 kilometres north of Luanda, on 27 November.

At midnight on 10 November 1975, the Portuguese flag was lowered in Luanda and the last Portuguese soldiers got on a ship and left. The MPLA of Agostinho Neto was the recognised government of the independent People's Republic of Angola. And they were there to stay: after the abortive attack on Luanda, more and more Cuban soldiers were sent to Angola.

The South African public – and parliament – had no inkling that their troops were involved in a foreign adventure. But on 1 November, a Reuters correspondent, Fred Bridgland, landed at Serpa Pinto airport and noticed young blond men hanging around armoured cars who could not speak Portuguese. When he asked one of the men where he was from, he said, according to Bridgland: 'From Inger-land.' Bridgland also met Van der Waals there and was sure he had an Afrikaans accent.

After gathering more evidence, Bridgland wrote on 14 November 1975 that he had proof that South Africa was involved in the war in Angola. It was front-page news all over the world. It cost UNITA most of its friends in Africa and Europe – the South African apartheid regime was regarded as the most unsavoury in the world at the time. It also led to the CIA cutting off all aid to UNITA.

The Vorster government felt betrayed by the US. Vorster later said that US secretary of state Henry Kissinger had personally urged South Africa to get involved in the war, but when it became controversial, the Americans abandoned South Africa.

Of course, John Vorster and PW Botha denied vehemently that South Africa had any troops in Angola. For about four months after Bridgland's first reports, the whole world knew South African troops were fighting with UNITA, but thanks to strict legislation, not a word of it was allowed in the South African media. One could read about it in international magazines and newspapers sold in South Africa and hear daily reports on BBC World and Voice of America, but not in our own media.

It was absurd, and it was very disturbing being a journalist and not being able to report what I knew to be true. It must have been even more disturbing for the families of the number of young South African men who died in Angola, but were officially reported by the Defence Force as having died in Namibia or even in 'accidents' in the operational area.

Defence minister PW Botha admitted for the first time on 26 January 1976 that the South African Defence Force was engaged in a war in Angola, although he gave the impression it was only to protect the hydroelectric scheme at Calueque.

Operation Savannah, the source of many legends and myths of South African military prowess, ended with the South African withdrawal on 27 March 1976 – fifty days before Soweto erupted. But South Africa would be involved with Jonas Savimbi's war for two more decades, often using units such as 32 and 34 Battalions, consisting of former FNLA fighters, Angolan Bushmen and mercenary types, who paraded as UNITA soldiers.

Internationally, the South African withdrawal was perceived as a major victory by the MPLA and their Cuban allies and a bloody nose for the white army. I had many arguments with a number of senior SADF officers in later years about this perception. They maintain to this day that Operation Savannah was a dramatic military success, and that they would have handed the country to UNITA and the FNLA if America had not abandoned them.

They also felt they had to convince the white South African public that it had been a success, and in 1976 re-enacted a battle for television cameras that took place on 10 December 1975 near Quibala in central-west Angola: the Battle for Bridge 14. The propaganda film was broadcast and rebroadcast on the SABC. It was one of the most expensive public relations exercises ever in South Africa, but it did the job. Most white South Africans truly believed what they saw: death-defying white soldiers making mincemeat of bungling black fighters and cowardly Cuban soldiers.

My personal view is that Operation Savannah was a colossal blunder, and massively expensive in both financial terms and in terms of lives lost. Some of the SADF units did indeed prove that they were among the most formidable soldiers in the world, but the whole exercise was ill conceived and badly executed. It had 'PW Botha' stamped all over it: a very poor understanding of the geopolitics of southern Africa; a total misreading of the international climate; an arrogant attitude that white might is right. Outside white party-political street fighting, Botha was no strategist. In fact, he was a buffoon – he proved it even more after he became prime minister.

But ultimately the responsible person was Prime Minister John Vorster. He never seemed to have a good grasp on what this foreign military adventure would mean in political, military and diplomatic terms. He left the decision-making on the Angolan war to Botha and to his closest confidante, Bureau of State Security General 'Lang Hendrik' van den Bergh. His Minister of Foreign Affairs, Hilgard Muller, was completely out of his depth and his input was close to zero.

Van den Bergh was an unstable megalomaniac who openly boasted that he was 'the most powerful man' in South Africa after the prime minister. He had been close to Vorster since the 1930s, when they were both senior officers in the military wing of the pro-Nazi Ossewa Brandwag movement.

I had only one personal confrontation with Lang Hendrik. A year before the Angolan war, a police officer told me about a South African policeman fighting in Rhodesia who was captured by Zimbabwean guerrillas. A group of his colleagues, so the story went, crossed the Limpopo River one night, wiped out the guerrilla base and brought their comrade back. According to my source, he was so badly tortured that he was close to being a vegetable.

I quietly started digging into the story, even finding the place in the Magaliesburg where the tortured policeman was being treated. The story seemed to be true, but I needed confirmation.

Out of the blue I got a phone call: 'Lang Hendrik' van den Bergh wants to see you in his office tomorrow at eight. Interesting, I thought, and arrived at his office in Pretoria the next morning. After waiting for twenty minutes, his aide opened his door and said: 'The general will see you now.'

It was a huge, dark, wood-panelled room. Van den Bergh was sitting behind a formidable desk, and at first did not look up as I walked towards him. I stood in front of his desk for what must have been a minute, and when he looked up, I said, 'Good morning General' and extended my hand to greet him. He ignored my hand, looked at me with what he probably wanted to portray as disdain, and then said, '*Ja, mannetjie*' [Yes, little man].

He told me that he knew I was working on a story that would 'compromise state security'. 'It's all a lot of shit, man. You are far too lightweight [*lig in die broek*] to start messing in affairs like this.' I replied that I was merely investigating a story that could be of interest to our readers. 'The hell with your readers,' he said, leaning over his desk, and with his most scary face said, 'I'm not interested in your fiction. All I want to know is, who told you.'

I told him that I gave my source a solemn undertaking never to reveal his identity. This was not a good answer. Lang Hendrik became agitated: 'Listen you little snot nose, I will lock you up for eighty days, and when you come out, I will ask you again. If you tell me you can't reveal your source, I will lock you up again for eighty days. And when you come out, I'll ask you again …' He repeated the scenario another few times for effect.

I told him that I would talk to my editor and give a response later the same day. He chased me out of his office. My editor asked the chief reporter, Jack Viviers, to 'smooth things over' with Van den Bergh, with whom he had a good relationship, in exchange for not writing the story. I only found out much later that Viviers' 'good relationship' with Van den Bergh was an understatement, and that it was Viviers who had reported my interest in the police rescue to Van den Bergh in the first place.

My impression of Van den Bergh was that he was quite mad and dangerous. Nobody could ever prove it, but along with several other investigative journalists, I believe he had something to do with the brutal murder of the brilliant young economist Robert Smit, because Smit was threatening to spill the story on huge underhand deals by senior government figures.

Operation Savannah was really the beginning of a huge cultural and political phenomenon among white South Africans that lasted for more than a decade: the 'border war' mentality. During this time, hundreds of thousands of young white men were called on to do compulsory military service, most of them for two years full time, followed by a number of 'camps'. We will never know exactly how many of them died or were maimed for life in Namibia and Angola. Nor will we know how many of them came back seriously disturbed human beings – the Defence Force never recognised the existence of the psychological condition, post-traumatic stress disorder.

But the damage to South Africa was much greater than the number of lives lost. White South Africa quickly developed a culture in which military might was glorified. We're the best soldiers in the world, and we'll fix our problems through the barrel of the gun. Shoot first, talk later.

The macho 'border' mentality permeated every level of society, even affecting daily language with newly created words and sayings. Young men, most often seventeen-, eighteen- and nineteen-year-olds, were told that this was the noblest calling any human could have: to fight for your country in the name of Christianity and civilisation against the forces of darkness, against communism. Most of them believed it, especially after having been fired on once by the 'enemy'.

Through this indoctrination, the youngsters started seeing all black people opposed to South Africa's white government as communists – which, of course, technically they were: the MPLA, SWAPO and the ANC were all Marxist movements, at least on paper. But it was a gross oversimplification of what these movements really were and what they were fighting for.

In 1985, I was at a party in Cape Town, mostly attended by yuppies and young professional Afrikaners. A young lawyer, who was a prominent member of the Progressive Federal Party, asked me whether I really regarded myself as someone without racism, without prejudice against black people. I replied that one constantly has to examine oneself for signs of hidden prejudice, but yes, I certainly did not regard myself as a racist.

The man lifted his trouser leg, exposing a badly maimed calf. He became very agitated, angrily shouting in my face, 'Then you have never looked a *kaffir* with a gun in the eye. Killing whites is the only thing that makes them happy.' He said he was wounded during the Angolan war. When I asked him why he went there in the first place, he physically attacked me and had to be led away by his friends.

In the era after 1976, the military culture among white South Africans prepared the ground for the ascension of two men who would eventually nearly drive South Africa over the edge. They were defence minister PW Botha, who became prime minister in 1978, and General Magnus Malan, Chief of the Defence Force, who became Botha's defence minister.

Botha and Malan not only militarised white South African society, but also militarised their own government. Soon the country was effectively governed not by parliament or even the cabinet, but by the State Security Council, consisting of key ministers, the military and other securocrats.

Under their leadership, the ideology of the 'Total Strategy' against communism's 'Total Onslaught' would lead to increasingly violent repression and carte blanche to military and police death squads, as well as biological and chemical warfare projects. Under their leadership, a dangerous policy of clandestine destabilisation of neighbouring states would be followed, and eventually white military conscripts would be employed to crush uprisings in black townships.

Under the leadership of PW Botha and Magnus Malan, South Africa spent billions on the manufacturing of several nuclear bombs.

Prime Minister Vorster did not allow further incursions into Angola after Operation Savannah, but once Botha had taken over as prime minister, several big cross-border operations were again launched: Operation Protea in 1981, Operation Askari late in 1983, and Operation Reindeer in 1984.

During Operation Reindeer, an airborne attack was launched on Cassinga deep in southern Angola on 4 May 1978 – Ascension Day, a religious public holiday in South Africa. SWAPO said it was a refugee camp, the SADF called it a military camp. SWAPO said more than 700 people were killed, mostly women, children and old people. The SADF said it was a fraction of that, and most of the dead were guerrillas.

I interviewed several senior SADF officers, including the later head of the Defence Force, General Constand Viljoen, who took part in the battle, as well as two senior SWAPO military commanders, trying to get to the truth of what had happened at Cassinga. Years later, I got hold of secret video footage of the aftermath of the attack, shot by the SADF. It showed dozens of bodies being shoved into a huge ditch with a caterpillar. Most of them did not look like fighting men to me.

The truth, I concluded, lay somewhere in the middle: it was a refugee camp where some SWAPO guerrillas were stationed. I accept that Viljoen and his men did not know that there were so many civilians. I do not accept that they keep on denying that they killed refugees and refuse steadfastly to ask the forgiveness of the Namibian people. No other single event in the protracted war made Namibians hate white South Africans as much as the massacre at Cassinga. The day is still honoured every year in Namibia.

The conflict in Angola and Namibia made it more urgent for the international community to find a peaceful settlement for Namibia. The US, Britain, Germany, France and Canada – the 'Western Five' – devised a plan for Namibia's independence after a full democratic election under UN supervision. It was accepted by South Africa in April 1978, and became Resolution 435 of the UN Security Council.

In July 1978, I left for Nambia as the correspondent of the newspapers in the Nasionale Pers stable, *Die Burger, Beeld* and *Die Volksblad,* to report on these new developments and the arrival of the UN Special Representative for Namibia, Martti Ahtisaari.

12

In the colony

SOMEONE, SOMEWHERE CALLED NAMIBIA 'the land God made in anger', and it later became the title of a book. I think that person must have a grim view of God. It is a country as spectacular as one can imagine: the wide, arid south, the generous north, in the west the most beautiful desert, a coastline that sets one's imagination racing, the unique Etosha Pans, the subtropical Kavango and the Caprivi Strip.

I own a part of that soil. I spilled my blood there and very nearly died twice. Namibia changed my life, and I have a special place for it in my heart.

Since 1915, when the German forces surrendered to the South African Army, white South Africans viewed Namibia as part of South Africa, almost as a fifth province. They called it South West Africa. The fact that the United Nations merely gave South Africa a mandate to administer the territory did not matter to them.

South Africa applied their apartheid policies to Namibia: they gave white Namibians direct representation in parliament in Cape Town; and in 1968 they even divided the country into bantustans, as they did in South Africa.

But after the decolonisation of Africa started in the early 1960s, the international community began applying pressure on South Africa: the UN Mandate was rescinded by the Security Council in 1969, and the International Court declared in 1971 that South Africa was occupying Namibia illegally.

But after Angola's independence and the coming to power of the Marxist MPLA, Namibia's liberation movement, the South West African People's Organisation, started escalating the armed struggle in northern Namibia. South Africa's military incursions into Angola increased the pressure, and in 1978 an isolated South African government had no choice but to accept a Western-negotiated plan for Namibia's independence, sanctioned by Resolution 435 of the Security Council.

When it became clear that independence for Namibia was inevitable, Botha and his government and military obsessed about influencing events in Namibia in such a way that SWAPO would not be allowed an election victory. By 1980, liberation movements South Africa had fought against were in government in three southern African states: Frelimo in Mozambique, the MPLA in Angola and ZANU-PF in Zimbabwe. In Pretoria, the nightmare was that if there were a SWAPO government in Namibia, an ANC government in South Africa would be next.

PW Botha's biographers, Dirk and Johanna de Villiers, explained the mindset. Referring to information given to Botha, when he was defence minister, about SWAPO's strong anti-South African stance, they state in their book *PW*: 'With this the Communist plans to conquer Southern Africa became clearer. The southward pincer movement that had already been started by the Marxist terrorist organisations in Angola and Mozambique, were aimed at also taking South West Africa and Rhodesia, and then expose the Republic of South Africa.'

But there was another consideration. In 1978 the ruling National Party split when the right-wing faction under Dr Andries Treurnicht formed the Conservative Party. There were some 80 000 white people, mostly Afrikaners, living in South West Africa. After Pretoria accepted Resolution 435, a good number of them were already blaming Botha for selling out the whites – a message that could only assist the Conservative Party in its rapid growth.

South Africa's strategy was twofold: to destabilise SWAPO as much as possible, crushing their armed wing operating in the north and over the border in Angola; and to bolster ethnic political forces inside the country into an alternative to SWAPO.

On 1 September 1975, the leaders of white Namibians and representatives of all the ethnic groups (coloureds, Basters, Ovambos, Kavangos, Caprivians, Namas, Damaras, Bushmen, Tswanas, Hereros) gathered in a refurbished old gymnastics hall in Windhoek called the Turnhalle. With two or three exceptions, these tribal leaders were seen as the puppets of the whites. But they were preparing a constitution for an independent Namibia without homelands and without apartheid. That meant there was no turning back for South Africa.

The Turnhalle forum set the stage for a charismatic Afrikaner farmer, Dirk Mudge, to start dominating the internal politics for the next few years.

Mudge's conversion from a staunch Afrikaner nationalist and apartheid disciple to a liberated Namibian patriot fighting against racial discrimination happened within a span of three, four years. It was not a dramatic exchange from one ideology to another. It was simply brought about by the fact that he got to know black people from up close.

As one of the leaders of the National Party of South West Africa, he was responsible for persuading the different tribal leaders to participate in the Turnhalle exercise. One of these, Herero leader Clemens Kapuuo, was a strong and stubborn leader and no one's puppet. During their first two meetings, Kapuuo was suspicious and not very cooperative. During a visit by internal Namibian leaders to the UN in New York in September 1973, Mudge visited Kapuuo in his hotel room.

This time Kapuuo opened up. He spoke of his people's history, how thousands of Herero were killed by German soldiers, others chased all the way into Botswana. And now, because they were not part of SWAPO, the international community was shunning them, the first petitioners to the UN against South African occupation.

'This was the first time in my life I could see myself in the shoes of a black Namibian,' Mudge declared.

Mudge said later that he felt liberated by this conversation and fully realised what a special privilege it would be for him to work with black Namibian leaders for their freedom and recognition.

This and similar meetings with black Namibians pushed Mudge in a direction his own party – and often the South African government – did not like. In October 1976, his fellow NP leader Eben van Zijl attacked the Damara delegation in the Turnhalle for saying whites were responsible for the mess Namibia was in. Van Zijl said: 'Who picked you up from the mud? The whites. The whites of this country and the whites of South Africa. Who fetched you from the mountains and put clothes on your backs? The whites.'

That was the real face of the National Party of South West Africa. A year later, on 27 September 1977, Mudge challenged AH du Plessis, a former South African cabinet minister, for the leadership of the party. Mudge lost by six votes, 141 to 135, and walked out of the party. A week later he formed the Republican Party, and a month later joined ten black ethnic parties in forming the Democratic Turnhalle Alliance (DTA). In directly translated English, this would read the Democratic Gymnastics Hall Alliance, and that would actually not have been inappropriate.

This was the Namibia in which I arrived in mid-1978.

When my editors Vosloo and Cillié advised me to steer carefully between the different factions, they did not mean I should refrain from writing propaganda against the liberation movement, SWAPO – they meant I should repair their newspapers' tarnished reputation. Since 1977, their Namibian specialist, Ebbe Dommisse (later editor of *Die Burger*), sided with the apartheid dinosaurs in Namibia and demonised Mudge as a dishonest megalomaniac sell-out. The DTA, built around Mudge's charisma and organisational skills, had become the only political grouping that could possibly take on SWAPO at the polls, and that became the primary focus of South Africa's foreign policy.

Mudge embarked upon his new political career with an energy and tenaciousness I have never seen in a politician anywhere before or since. In the early years, he flew to virtually every hamlet in the country in his own small aircraft, sometimes holding two meetings a day. His Herero friends in the party called him 'the white horse that never tires'.

Many white Namibians hated Mudge with a passion. Horrible stories about him, his wife and his children were made up and spread by right-wingers. He was cursed in public, and once even spat on by whites.

The DTA had the clear majority support among the Herero under Clemens Kapuuo, a credible claim to the support of most of the coloureds, Tswanas and Bushmen, and good support among the whites, Damaras, Namas and Basters. They even had substantial pockets of support among the Caprivians and Kavangos. But their problem was the Ovambo in the north, by far the biggest ethnic group in the country. They were solidly behind SWAPO, and most of the senior leadership of SWAPO and its army, the People's Liberation Army of Namibia (PLAN), was drawn from their ranks.

This was the reality of Namibia in the 1970s and 1980s. The country was rigidly divided along ethnic lines. The division was also regional. The vast majority of the citizens lived in a narrow band of land on the northern border of the country: the Ovambo, Kavango and the Caprivians.

The resentment was at its strongest between the Herero and the Ovambo. In his biography of Mudge, *Dirk Mudge, Reënmaker van die Namib*, historian At van Wyk quotes Kapuuo as saying: 'Those people in the north made babies while we were murdered in the south, that's why there are so many of them.'

SWAPO itself, while paying lip service to non-ethnic politics, played the tribal game like everybody else.

Ethnicity became the big issue in Namibia. Tribalism was the big taboo in progressive African politics, and to the modernising urban elite, ethnic politics smacked of colonialism and apartheid. Yet ethnicity was playing a very real role in Namibia, far more so than in South Africa.

The urban elite in all groups in South West Africa, except the whites and Hereros, was mostly pro-SWAPO. So the target groups for Mudge and his DTA had to be the whites, the Hereros, the more traditional people and the peasant farmers in the country. The DTA was therefore an alliance of eleven ethnically based parties. Their strength became their biggest weakness, because their opponents successfully hung the tribal apartheid tag around their necks.

Without the whites, the DTA would not have existed. Mudge's party for whites, the Republican Party, had all the money and organisational skills. The whole exercise was Mudge's initiative, and without him it would never have taken off. He was not only the strategist and strongest, most charismatic leader, but also the glue that kept the different factions together. At the same time, the fact that the DTA was led by a white Afrikaner, who had been part of the apartheid system for so long, counted heavily against the DTA. Mudge knew it, always trying to push one of the black leaders to the forefront.

Mudge also had to play peacemaker. In March 1978, Clemens Kapuuo was assassinated by SWAPO at his home in Katutura, Windhoek's black township. It took all Mudge's human skills to stop young Hereros from launching revenge attacks on Ovambos in Katutura. Mudge's genuine and deeply felt grief at Kapuuo's death endeared him even more to his black colleagues.

Mudge had a bigger albatross around his neck. South Africa was still running Namibia through an administrator-general. Most of the considerable amount of money needed to run the DTA and its campaigns came from the South African government. SWAPO was conducting a strong military campaign and would simply have overrun the territory and seized power if the South African Defence Force had not stopped them.

So not only could his opponents claim with some legitimacy that Mudge was doing apartheid South Africa's work for them, it also meant that he did not have a free hand in practising the kind of politics he believed would succeed in Namibia at the time.

The South African government, through arrogance and ignorance, was playing a very silly game in Namibia. They saw Namibia both as an experiment in strategies that could later be followed in South Africa, and as their private backyard where they could swagger about and call the shots. And they were paranoid at all times about the effect their actions or non-action in Namibia could have on white politics back in South Africa.

The South African security forces regarded themselves as the kings of the north, Ovambo, Kavango and Caprivi, where they were fighting the SWAPO insurgents. They were very proud of their clever senior officers, who thought they knew everything about 'revolutionary war', the '10 per cent military and 90 per cent political' doctrine and 'hearts and minds' campaigns.

They didn't understand a thing. They suffered from the same disease their political masters in Pretoria did: they had no idea what was going on in the minds of the black majority or of the dynamics of liberation politics. Deep down they believed a black man understands only one thing: power. I heard it so many times from officers: 'Hearts and minds are important, but remember, Africa only respects the strong man.'

In practice it mostly meant that they tried to 'out-terrorise the terrorists'. I was witness at more than one occasion when members of Koevoet, a police anti-insurgency unit, paraded through the villages of the north with dead guerrillas or SWAPO sympathisers strapped to the mudguards of their armoured vehicles. When the police or army had a suspicion that a kraal or village was pro-SWAPO, they often flattened all the huts with their vehicles, shooting or detaining the occupants. Torture of captured guerrillas or suspected sympathisers was common.

Mudge's son-in-law, Paul van Schalkwyk, told the story of how he accompanied Mudge on a visit to the north. While they were there, there was a firefight between the SADF and SWAPO guerrillas. A soldier approached them afterwards and said: 'Mr Mudge, do you want to see the *kaffirs* we shot?'

The SADF also tried their hand at politics. When the DTA did not make progress fast enough to their liking, they formed a political movement called Etango [the rising sun] in Ovambo. Its membership never grew beyond a few dozen black military officers and their families.

The military persuaded an utterly mediocre and vain man, the senior Ovambo speaker in the DTA, Peter Kalangula, to quit, and then tried to boost him into the new leader who would tackle SWAPO. It was a joke.

The only thing the old SADF and SA Police could do properly, was wage war.

Still, they were not all bad. The commander of the forces in Namibia while I was there, General Jannie Geldenhuys, was a thoroughly decent man. Politically we were on different planets, but I appreciated his company then and afterwards in South Africa.

And then there was dear old Pik Botha, South Africa's foreign minister. He saw Namibia as a backward little colony and treated everybody outside SWAPO as his minions. He was the great chess player that would outsmart the international community and fix Namibia's problems himself.

Botha and Mudge were like two bulls in one kraal. Mudge knew the country, its people and its politics; Botha did not. But, more importantly, Namibia was Mudge's first priority, whereas Botha only wanted what was in his own and his party's interest. Both men were used to getting their own way and did not like being criticised.

Mudge was at a huge disadvantage: Namibia and the DTA needed South Africa's money, and Botha never allowed him to forget it.

In 1982, Prime Minister PW Botha said that the white Namibians (referring to Mudge and the right-wingers from the National Party) should stop quarrelling and remember that the Namibian administration cost South Africa R600 million every year. Mudge reacted by quite correctly stating that the R600 million included the large chunk of customs and excise revenue that was due to Namibia anyway.

PW was livid, and during his next visit to Namibia summoned Mudge to the administrator-general's official residence. He read from newspaper clippings that Mudge had repudiated him. Mudge responded that he merely explained that some of the money was Namibia's anyway.

At this point Pik, who clearly saw this as a good opportunity to not only please his own leader but also put Mudge in his place, wrote on the back of his cigarette pack: 'Is it too much to say you're sorry?' and pushed it over the table to Mudge. Mudge wrote back: 'Sorry for what?'

Pik jumped up and accused Mudge of being ungrateful for all PW had done for him. According to Mudge, who couldn't take it after a while, he stood up and said, 'Pik, I'm not a child. I'm older than you are. I'm not your junior, I've been in politics longer than you.' He walked out and slammed the door behind him. A few policemen witnessed the scene, and the story spread like wildfire. I was told about it the same night. It was regarded as a bit of a sensation, because nobody had ever slammed the door in PW Botha's face before.

In December 1978, an election for all Namibians was held to elect a constituent assembly, but SWAPO did not take part and it was not recognised by the international community. The DTA got more than 80 per cent of the vote, with the National Party's attempt at a coalition, Aktur (Action Front for the Preservation of the Turnhalle Principles) a dismal second.

I will remember forever that Saturday morning in December 1978 in Kaiserstrasse, Windhoek's main street. A DTA parade was coming down the street with a band on the back of a truck. They were playing a pop hit of the time, 'Love is in the air'. It was very jolly.

The next moment a bomb exploded right behind me in one of the arcades. The band was oblivious, and while panicked and injured shoppers scuttled about, one could still hear them further down the street: *Love is in the air.*

During that same period I again happened to be in the city centre on a Saturday morning when I heard a great commotion and saw people running. I hurried towards the Model Supermarket about fifty metres away, where the people were running from. At the door I met a reporter of the SWA Broadcasting Corporation, who told me a bomb had been found in the parcels shelves. A few minutes later the police arrived and cordoned off the area. I asked the reporter how he knew there was a bomb. He said the 'security forces' had phoned them about ten minutes earlier. There had long been a suspicion that the police or army sometimes planted bombs in order to put the blame on SWAPO. This was the first time I had proof of it. Of course, my newspaper would never have printed the story, and if they did, it would have had serious legal, and possibly physical, consequences. I did publish reports on this kind of 'false flag' operation years later as editor of a newspaper, and that did get me into trouble.

The DTA's election meetings were something I had never experienced before or since. It was usually held in large marquee tents, because it would be too dangerous to hold it out in the open: most of the DTA leadership were on SWAPO's hit list. Namibia is a very hot country, and sometimes the temperature inside the tent came close to 50°C. And it took hours.

The meetings normally started late, because people had to come from afar and not everybody had transport. At meetings held outside a particular language area, speeches were interpreted into seven languages: Nama, Ovambo, Kavango, Bushman, Herero, Afrikaans and English. It took several minutes for every sentence to be translated. But the people sat there patiently, and they sang and they danced. And always, right in front, was Dirk Mudge.

It was a real experience in areas like the Kaokoveld to see hundreds of Ovahimba people, almost naked but with red clay smeared on their bodies and with elaborate hairstyles, come to these meetings. Or in the Okahandja area, to see the graceful Herero women in their magnificent colourful traditional dresses, each consisting of some fifteen metres of material, at the rallies.

I remember sitting there thinking: this is real, and this is important, even if it was an exercise only recognised by South Africa. For most of these people it was their first taste of proper democracy, and they experienced it in their own language. I thought to myself: if only my own country could have this kind of exercise, and soon.

I can't think of any other country in Africa south of the Sahara where politics was conducted so inclusively and non-racially. To see conservative Afrikaner aunties and farmers sit among the masses of supporters, men in suits from the north mixing with half-naked Bushmen, all cheering and giving the DTA's V-sign, gave me hope for Namibia and for my own ethnic group.

Of course, it wasn't real. Two-thirds of the people of Namibia supported SWAPO, and they were not part of this process. Most of the senior SWAPO leaders were still in exile in Angola or Zambia.

Mudge and his DTA never had a chance. Even aside from the ethnic majority support SWAPO had, the DTA's inevitable links with apartheid South Africa, the presence and conduct of the South African army and police, and the fact that the DTA had so much visible white support, simply meant that the majority of black Namibians detested them.

Moreover, black Namibians needed the psychological release of 'revolution'. Or if they couldn't have a proper revolution, at least have as their first government the liberation movement that had fought an armed struggle against the occupier and white domination. The suffering and humiliation had simply gone on for too long for them to accept that their liberators could include white Afrikaners with strong links with South Africa.

Still, the South African government did Namibia a disservice by limiting the DTA's options, because it could have developed into a much stronger opposition party than it did in the end. It would have been in South Africa and Namibia's long-term interest if the DTA had been given the leeway to distance itself from apartheid South Africa; even to express the strong animosity felt towards South Africa by most Namibians, including the DTA leadership.

As the political dynamics in Namibia changed during the 1980s, the DTA declared itself a 'liberation movement' as well, and tried to move away from the overemphasis on ethnicity. But Mudge could not even get the South Africans so far as to abolish the Day of the Covenant (more commonly known as Dingane's Day) in Namibia, an Afrikaner nationalist day of remembrance. He had to fight them tooth and nail to downscale the ethnic second-tier powers of the interim administration, because it was a sensitive issue to Afrikaners in South Africa.

At the base of the South African government's complete misunderstanding of the political dynamics in Namibia – and even in Angola – was the fact that most white South African politicians' only experience of black people was the contact they had with a gardener or domestic worker, or the sycophantic puppets they had installed in the black homelands – people such as Ciskei leader Oupa Gcozo or Bophuthatswana's Lucas Mangope.

People such as PW Botha and Magnus Malan, and even the more progressive Pik Botha, could simply not rise above the inherent racism that had driven them through the ranks of the National Party over the decades. Deep down they believed that black politicians and leaders could be bamboozled and bribed and blackmailed by clever white people.

The first black South African leader they met face to face who stood his ground and was more than a match for them in every way was Nelson Mandela, and that was only in the late 1980s.

I developed a soft spot and a lot of respect for Dirk Mudge, although after a few months in Namibia I knew in my heart that SWAPO deserved to be the winners of the first Namibian election. It was not the most mature liberation movement in Africa's history, and was dominated by one tribe, but it had fought long and hard and bravely to get Namibia to the point where independence was being discussed.

I have told senior SWAPO leaders on more than one occasion that they ought to erect a statue of Dirk Mudge somewhere in Windhoek, because he did more than anyone else to prepare the whites and other minorities in Namibia for freedom and independence. He has to get at least some of the credit for the stability Namibia enjoyed before, during and immediately after independence. SWAPO leaders such as Hage Geingob, Mose Tjitendero and Theo-Ben Gurirab reluctantly acknowledged Mudge's positive role, but would probably never express it publicly.

Mudge had the potential to be a great leader of Namibia. But I could have told him then: *History is against you, my brother.*

Once, not long after Namibia's independence, I had a long conversation with a top official in Pik Botha's office about the way they had sabotaged Mudge. The DTA never really stood a chance of winning an election against SWAPO, he responded. His department always had a bigger picture in mind: to secure the best possible deal for South Africa and Namibia in the negotiations with the UN and the international community, and to get the Cubans out of Angola.

'Cuba out of Angola' did become the theme of the negotiations after 1982. South Africa's new demand was supported by the new administration in the US under Ronald Reagan and his very resourceful point man in southern Africa, Chester Crocker.

It did happen, but not only through negotiations. PW Botha and Fidel Castro were too much alike for that to have happened easily. It took the biggest military confrontation Africa had ever seen. Between late 1987 and July 1988, a series of ferocious clashes between Cuban and Angolan government forces (FAPLA) on the one side, and the SADF and UNITA forces on the other, took place in south-east

Angola. It ended with a final confrontation at Cuito Cuanavale and the retreat of both sides on 27 June 1988.

The South Africans were overextended so far from home, and were vulnerable with their long lines of support. On top of that, their Mirage F1s were no match for the new Russian MiG-23s used by the Cubans and Angolans. But the South African secret weapon was the G5 howitzer, an artillery piece developed after Operation Savannah, which the Cubans could not match in terms of range.

When the Cubans agreed to withdraw, they did so claiming victory over South Africa. South Africa denied this, but never really publicly claimed victory themselves – for diplomatic reasons, they later asserted.

Eight years after Cuito Cuanavale, I was standing in the Museum of the Revolution in Havana, Cuba. There was a huge model of the battle areas mounted on one wall. The government representative who briefed me had no doubt whatsoever in her mind that it represented a 'massive victory' for the Cubans over the 'apartheid forces' and 'a glorious day for Cuba'.

The head of the SADF at the time, General Jannie Geldenhuys, is equally certain that his men had won. They never wanted to capture Cuito Cuanavale, because they would have had to defend it afterwards, and that made no military sense. Their main purpose was to prevent the Cubans and FAPLA capturing the strategic town of Mavinga, and UNITA's headquarters, Jamba. In that they were successful. Geldenhuys says the Cubans and FAPLA suffered severe blows at the hands of the SADF on the Lomba River, and that seriously undermined their morale.

So who did win the battle of Cuito Cuanavale? I have listened to many arguments from both the South African and the Cuban side. I have read the British foreign correspondent Fred Bridgland's book about the war, *The War for Africa – Twelve Months that Transformed a Continent*, very carefully. My personal analysis is that both sides got to a point where they knew they were simply wasting human lives and ammunition, and stopped. Both sides were also under pressure from the Soviet Union and the United States, who at this stage were beginning to agree that the Angolan and Namibian conflicts should be stopped.

But I do have a suspicion that the SADF probably fared a lot better than the Cubans expected or were later prepared to admit.

Many men died during these battles, but it represented an important turning point in the fortunes of southern Africa. Shortly after the final battles, the Cubans agreed to withdraw from Angola, and South Africa agreed to the swift implementation of the Namibian independence process.

13

Bleeding in the sand

A SOCIETY IN FLUX, which Namibia was in the last few years before independence, is always a magnet for cowboys, crooks and freaks. Instability and insecurity often lead to great decadence.

I had a great life in Namibia, where I lived for four years – a rather decadent life. I loved living among the cowboys, the crooks and the freaks. In fact, I think I became a bit of a cowboy myself.

The worst cowboys in Namibia were the pilots. They were mostly young white South African males with crew cuts and teardrop sunglasses. It was heaven for them: a vast country with lots of foreigners who had to fly all over the place, and little control over air traffic.

Going up to the north, where a war was being fought, was their idea of fun. SWAPO guerrillas with missiles occasionally took potshots at aircraft flying near the Angolan border, so pilots had to fly very low, as in twenty, thirty metres above ground. This often meant swerving the aircraft violently to and fro to miss high palm trees and landing fast and hard. Macho stuff, and after a few trips I started enjoying it.

It was no different on 24 August 1978, when a few press colleagues and I got into a chartered fourteen-seater to fly to Ondangwa in Ovamboland. The United Nations' special representative for Namibia, Martti Ahtisaari, had arrived in the country and was meeting leaders of communities all over the country. We followed him.

From Ondangwa we flew to Opuwa in Kaokoveld in the desolate north-west of the country. The landing strip was a dirt track going over a slight hill. Before you land, you phone the local police and they chase the goats off the landing strip.

It was very hot, and it was very boring. We were not allowed in the meetings that Ahtisaari held with the chiefs, so we mostly just waited to see if something unexpected was going to happen. The heat and the boredom drove us to drink a lot of beer.

Around noon on 25 August, my colleagues and I decided to leave the Ahtisaari party behind and fly to the next stop. I think it was supposed to be Rundu in Kavango, where we had access to telephones and could file our stories. We chased the goats off the landing strip and got into the Cessna.

Now I have to dig deep into a very fuzzy memory to recall how things happened. The way I remember it, there was no wind, so it didn't matter in which direction we were going to take off. But Ahtisaari's Dakota was parked at the one end of the runway with the crew sitting in the shade under the wing. Our pilot decided that he had to take off from the other side, or his propellers would kick up a lot of dust in the aircrew's eyes.

I was sitting behind the co-pilot, but I remember that I turned in my seat to look at the runway through the front windshield between the pilot and co-pilot. I saw the pilot pulling back the throttle and we raced forward, the nose of the Dakota looming larger and larger. I saw the pilot hesitate for a second, pushing the throttle forward, as he probably thought we weren't going to make it, but then he pulled it back again as it dawned on him that we would not be able to stop in time.

I sensed trouble in that instant, and shouted to my friends to fasten their seatbelts – we had become so blasé flying every day that we never bothered to use safety belts. That probably saved lives.

The aircraft cleared the nose of the Dakota. I don't really have a recollection of what happened next. I remember thinking with relief that we made it. But the next moment we flew straight into the ground, nose first, and tumbled head over tail several times. The impact was so fierce I thought my whole body would break into pieces.

Then there was absolute silence for what felt like a minute. Those who were in one piece crawled out of the crunched-up wreck, which now lay on its fuselage. I was still strapped in my seat, but it had been torn from the floor and I was lying half on my side. The aircraft started burning, and it became very dark inside because of the black smoke.

I knew for certain that I was going to burn to death. My mind was filled with absolute, overwhelming terror. So this was my life, then. I was overcome with a deep sadness that my life so far had amounted to so little, and now I was going to die. Irrationally, that moment of intense sadness stayed with me for many years. If I close my eyes now, twenty-five years later, I can immediately bring back that dark moment of extreme anguish.

I tried to release the buckle of the seatbelt, but my arm would not follow instructions. The next moment *Rand Daily Mail* photographer Stefan Sonderling, bloodied but in one piece, popped his head through the opening in the wreck and said: 'Your arm is gone, use your right hand.' Then he was gone.

I managed to free myself, crawled out and fell flat on my face in the dirt. I could not see much, because there was blood all over my face and body. I did notice Stefan coming closer to take pictures. Someone picked me up and dragged me away from the burning aircraft. Only then did I remember that I hadn't been alone, and I looked around for my mates. They were all there: Stefan, the SABC's

Ossie Gibson, Argus Africa News Service's Lester Venter and the *Rand Daily Mail's* Dave Forret, bloodied, dirty and in severe shock. No – Con Crous, the veteran among us who worked for Sapa, was missing, as was the pilot.

Then I saw people struggling to free the two men from the pilot and co-pilot seats. Their faces were pulp, their arms and legs badly broken. But they were alive. (Crous and Forret died some months later. I never found out how directly their deaths related to their injuries from the crash. I also have no idea what happened to the pilot; my memory had blocked out his name, because I knew he was responsible.)

My left arm above the elbow was crushed into many splinters. The metal of the aircraft's bodywork had cut the side of my face, leaving an indent even on my teeth, which were slightly loose. There was a deep cut under my chin. I was bleeding profusely.

Pushing the loose flap that was my cheek onto my teeth with my right hand, my left arm dangling, I was helped into Ahtisaari's Dakota, the only other aircraft available. Con, the pilot and I needed very urgent medical attention. A huge man with a friendly full-moon face assisted me into a seat and helped me to lie down with my head in his lap. He dabbed my face with a wet, white handkerchief and said soothing things to me that I could not hear. It was Martti Ahtisaari himself, I noticed later. (That, perhaps, became my biggest claim to fame: I could say that I once lay in the lap of the president of Finland, which was what Ahtisaari later became.)

We flew very quickly to Ondangwa, where a team of army doctors waited for us. A very young doctor roughly stitched up my face, right there at the air base under the wing of an Air Force aircraft. From there, Con, the pilot and I were flown to Windhoek Hospital. My first visitor, with a bunch of flowers, was Martti Ahtisaari. He was a very special human being.

A few days later, upper body in a cast and with plasters all over my face, I flew with an SAA Boeing 737 from Windhoek to Johannesburg. About ten minutes after take-off, the pilot announced that the aircraft was experiencing technical difficulties and he was going to have to make an emergency landing.

I was so freaked out I could not speak. Why was this happening to me? After what felt like an hour of excruciating anguish, flying very low, we landed, later getting into another aircraft to Johannesburg. I nearly lost my mind.

I went to the Eugene Marais Hospital in Pretoria, where the first of two bone transplants were done to fix my arm. The wound on my face had healed, but my right eye pulled down slightly, and that had to be fixed.

I was estranged from my family and in the middle of a divorce. I lay in a white bed in a white hospital room all on my own. Those weeks of anger, helplessness and loneliness, and the fear that I was going to lose my left arm, were like severe torture. The after-effects of this trauma troubled me for years afterwards.

When I got out of hospital, I was frantic to live a full life. But my arm would not heal, and it took two more operations – and a crater in my hip from where they took all the bone – to get the bone to knit, and then only with the help of plates and pins. For some two years I drove a car, took photographs and lived a fast and furious life with my arm in a cast, along with all kinds of contraptions to keep my wrist and fingers from getting stiff and unusable.

On occasion, I used my dead arm as a drunken party trick: I could put a cigarette out on my arm or set it alight without feeling a thing. It is unpleasant to remember that.

But the universe was trying to tell me something. Six months after the crash, still in a cast but back on the job, I was in a forty-seater aircraft with a runaway propeller forced to make a crash landing at Eros Airport in Windhoek. Four months after that, still in a cast, I was in a military helicopter crash in Caprivi, and actually broke my elbow on the cast. A few months later, a six-seater aircraft in which I was travelling to the Skeleton Coast crash-landed on a dirt track in the desert. I broke my nose and injured my knee. Cosmic payback. Bad, bad karma. I must have been a serial killer in my previous life. Or perhaps a sinful, gung-ho journalist.

These experiences left me with an intense fear of flying. I can only fly if I sit on the aisle, and I prefer to sit as far back in the aircraft as possible: in our crash, the guys sitting at the back were injured the least.

It also left me with claustrophobia so extreme that I cannot get into a lift with more than one other person. Last year I had to go for a neck scan, a related injury. I was fearful of being pushed into the scanner's low tunnel, just a few inches above my face, but I knew I had to have the scan. Then everything went blank, and the next thing I knew a doctor and two nurses were holding me down in the room next door. I had given one nurse a bloody nose and knocked down another in a blind panic. I eventually had to get the scan done completely anaesthetised.

But strangely enough, while I still have a fear of being maimed or crippled, the aircraft accident liberated me to a large degree from a normal person's fear of death. One only fears the unknown, and I feel that at that moment in Opuwa I stared death in the eye. I think I know what a human being's last few moments of life feel like. The crash and the several painful operations have also raised my tolerance for physical pain quite remarkably.

The accident led to the first of my many bad experiences with lawyers. A lawyer from the most prominent Afrikaans firm in Johannesburg advised me to settle a claim against the insurance company for R16 000. He appointed a specialist to certify that my arm had healed completely, and told me that I'd got a very good deal. I thought it odd, but it did not even cross my mind that it might be a swindle: they were all such good, prominent Afrikaners.

To this day I have about 50 per cent use of my arm, with no feeling in the part below where it was crushed. It has led to serious back and neck problems, which I fight on a continuous basis with exercise and physiotherapy. I have spent at least R100 000 in medical bills over the last twenty years.

About ten years later, I related this story to a friend of mine, who was a judge. He phoned me a week later to tell me that the lawyer who had handled my case actually worked for the law firm that represented the insurance company from which I had claimed. But it was too late to do anything about it.

Well, I didn't hate all lawyers. One of my good friends during my stay in Namibia was Anton Lubowski, a tall, handsome Namibian lawyer with a zest for life. One Friday night, Anton and I, both recently divorced, sat drinking in the Kaiser Krone Hotel in Windhoek with a few friends. By midnight everyone else had left, except for Anton, a mutual friend and myself. And we did not feel like going to bed just yet.

We got into Anton's sports car and raced at high speed to the coastal town of Swakopmund, some 300 kilometres away. We booked into an A-frame chalet in the town's beach resort and continued drinking. At one point Anton and I got annoyed with our friend's incessant talking, and half in jest tied him to a chair. He fell asleep, still upright and tied up.

Well, we were playing all kinds of games when we suddenly noticed a lot of smoke. The chalet was on fire. We rushed out, and only when the police and the fire brigade arrived, did we remember our friend was still tied to a chair inside. He was fortunately not hurt, just badly shaken.

Anton and I were arrested. We knew that a court case – the charges would probably have been arson and attempted murder – and the publicity would kill our careers. We really panicked, very sober by this time.

We persuaded the policeman on duty, in the early hours of the morning, to allow us to use the phone. Anton called a man in a senior position in the Namibian judiciary whom we both knew well, and I called a top official in the South African administration, explaining what had happened and begging for them to intervene.

They did. We were released without charge the same morning, with only an undertaking to pay for the damages. It was a close shave.

I was always surprised that the police did not use this incident against Anton later, when he became a senior SWAPO leader. Perhaps the local Swakopmund police did not realise it was the same man.

But they got to him a few years later.

14

Holding court

IT TOOK ME just a couple of weeks in Namibia to realise that the life of a correspondent far away from head office suited me very well. You determine your own schedule, pick your own stories, and when there is a lull you don't have to sit in the office pretending to work. I was like a duck in water – some would say like a pig in shit.

I had done proper homework before I arrived in Windhoek and I quickly got my head around the essence of the story. For a young journalist, this was a sweet combination of stories: the political manoeuvring; the military conflict in the north and across the border in Angola; the international intrigue involving the United Nations, South Africa, Cuba and the Western Five (the US, Canada, Britain, France and Germany), who took the regional initiatives.

My newspaper group's previous Namibian expert, Ebbe Dommisse, had painted himself into a corner in Namibia by siding with the white right wing. I was welcomed with open arms by the DTA, the South African administration in Namibia and diplomats concerned with events, because I quickly made it clear that I was going to be a journalist without an ideological agenda. I represented the four most influential Afrikaans newspapers in South Africa, and all the concerned parties knew that the view portrayed by those papers could have a significant influence on white South African public opinion.

Two parties did not welcome me: the white National Party, who actively gossiped and wrote smear stories about me in their newspaper, *Die Suidwester* (they referred to me as 'Mad Max'); and SWAPO, who thought I was just another apartheid Boer who would disseminate the army and the DTA's propaganda.

My relationship with the white conservatives never improved and they complained bitterly about me to my superiors. But it took me just a few months to start building a relationship with the internal leadership of SWAPO.

It was actually quite easy. I had a good basic understanding of the South African government's agenda in Namibia, of the political dynamics in white South Africa, and of the nature and strategies of the DTA and other internal political parties. Yet I belonged to no side; I had no interest in favouring any specific grouping or country. Thus I became the first port of call for parachute foreign correspondents, quicky diplomats, and all kinds of spooks and agents who wanted a quick briefing on what was really going on in Namibia. I always got something back from these people – that is, besides a free lunch. Everyone had a bit of information or a point to push or some information to plant. (My good relationship with diplomats had another nice spin-off: I went on month-long, all-expenses-paid tours of the US, Canada, Germany and later Australia.)

My office was in the main arcade in the centre of Windhoek. There was a lovely restaurant and coffee place called Café Schneider on the ground floor. My routine would be to check in at my head office in the early morning, then move straight down to a table outside Schneider's. Sometimes I would stay there all day.

On average, it took about ten minutes for the first diplomat, politician, fellow journalist, businessman or shady agent from somewhere on the globe to walk past and join me for coffee, because the arcade was at the heart of Windhoek. By lunchtime, I either had a new story, a new insight or the idea for a story. Or, of course, a juicy bit of gossip I could use to impress someone from whom I wanted information.

I held court at Schneider's. The art of trading information that I learnt there stood me in good stead later.

The gathering at Schneider's coffee tables became a bit of an institution. More than once, politicians, even diplomats and officials of South Africa's foreign affairs department, used the place to make contact with someone who would otherwise have been difficult to approach. Staunch political enemies often sat down around my table. I once even had the leader of the Herstigte Nasionale Party, Sarel Becker, drinking coffee at my table with two prominent black revolutionaries. Sarel was so right wing that he refused to use the Turnhalle's toilets, because blacks were also allowed – he got in his car and drove to his office every time he wanted to pee.

Whenever silly season arrived, it was time to travel in search of a story or a 'colour piece'. I once heard that UNITA forces were on their way to attack towns on the southern border with Namibia that had been taken by MPLA forces. I climbed the SABC transmitter tower outside the Kavango town of Rundu to check if anything was going on across the border. To my amazement, I saw UNITA forces sneaking up on the town on the other side, Calais. I stayed up there for about four hours, witnessing the battle for Calais, which UNITA won.

A few months later, when Calais was deserted, I crossed the river and wandered through the town. It was once a quaint little Portuguese colonial village where Namibians loved to go for peri-peri chicken and Angolan beer. Now it was devastated. It was like a scene from a Spike Lee gangster movie: 'Viva MPLA' painted on the wall was crossed out and replaced with 'Viva UNITA'. That, in turn, was crossed out, and 'Viva MPLA' written below. And so on. I stood there, pondering the utter senselessness and sadness of war.

Back on the Namibian side, angry SADF soldiers awaited me. I did not have permission to go to Calais, they said. What is more, *they* hadn't even been, because the whole town was one big minefield. Well, I thought, it was about time my luck turned.

Another time I took a walk with a friend, a foreign correspondent, along the Kavango River east of Rundu. A man in camouflage uniform and an AK-47 over his shoulder appeared on the Angolan side and shouted at me in Afrikaans: '*Wat maak jy?*' [What are you doing?]. He jokingly asked if I could chuck a couple of beers over the river. I had little doubt that he was a SWAPO guerrilla, because UNITA and the MPLA did not speak Afrikaans. We were about five kilometres from an SADF base. It was rather bizarre.

I did have a bit of a death wish after my series of aircraft accidents and operations. I once drove up to Oshakati, right in the war zone, where I met up with a South African colleague. Late at night in the pub we decided to drive to Ruacana the next day. Problem was, it was a dirt road – and it was mined virtually every night. Early the next morning, soldiers stopped us where the dirt road started. They were amazed that civilians with ordinary cars wanted to drive on the road. We said we were journalists, and we had to go. They advised us to wait until after the road had been cleared of landmines, as was done every morning with specialised vehicles.

We dared each other like schoolboys, and neither of us wanted to back out. So we drove all the way to Ruacana. It was very scary, but we arrived without incident. Later that day, soldiers told us that their minesweeper had set off five landmines on that road just after we had been on it. It was one of the most stupid things I have ever done.

White society in Namibia at the time was very conservative. I could count the number of like-minded white progressives on the fingers of my two hands. Naturally, we were drawn together. But this social group, consisting mostly of journalists, academics and lawyers, was terribly small and incestuous, so it naturally happened that my social circle broadened to include the black progressives in Windhoek, especially those who had returned from exile.

Andreas Shipanga was a founder, with Sam Nujoma and a few others, of the South West Africa People's Organisation in 1960. He clashed with Sam Nujoma, who was SWAPO's leader, on policy and personal issues, and left the organisation to form the SWAPO-Democrats. Shipanga returned to Namibia after the arrival of the United Nations, when it was clear that the country was going to get its independence.

I became very fond of Andreas (I called him Tovarech, Russian for comrade), and spent many hours listening to the stories he had to tell about SWAPO and the other liberation movements of the region, whose leaders he had met in various African capitals.

His most entertaining story was about when he was a waiter in Cape Town in the late 1950s and early 1960s. Being a Namibian, he did not have a *dompas* [pass], which every black South African had to carry. His only way out was to try to pass as a coloured, because they weren't compelled to carry passbooks. His problem was that he was very black, and, of course, that he wasn't the first black man to pull this trick. But he knew how the policemen decided whether someone was a 'legitimate' coloured. They would pinch the person; if he responded with anything but *eina*, he would be suspect. To make doubly sure, they would ask him to pronounce the Afrikaans word for a jackal. 'Jahkahls' would indicate that he was coloured, 'yakalas' would mean that he was black.

I also got to know former exiles such as Kenneth and Ottilié Abrahams, Norah Chase, Zed Ngavirue and Moses Katjiuongua quite well. Kenneth was a medical doctor and former Capetonian, and Ottilié was from the prominent Schimming family of Rehoboth. They were among the first SWAPO activists, and even had to flee Namibia in disguise (Kenny was dressed like a Herero woman, if I remember correctly) to escape the South African security police. They also became disillusioned with SWAPO. Norah was Ottilié's sister.

Moses Katjiuongua was a flamboyant, jovial man and leading activist of the other, much smaller liberation movement, the South West Africa National Union (SWANU). He had also just returned from exile. We really enjoyed each other's company. Dr Zed Ngavirue, one of the finest gentlemen I have ever met, had just returned from Papua New Guinea, where he was a university professor. I also got to know two of SWAPO's most senior internal leaders, Danny Tjongarero and Niko Bessinger.

All these friends inevitably influenced the way I perceived Namibia and the subcontinent's liberation politics. It was a great privilege for me as a young Afrikaner to be allowed an insight into a world and a political culture alien to me. They accepted me without reservation.

This also meant that I was in a corner. How could I possibly go back to South Africa and continue my career with a newspaper group that supported the apartheid government?

I knew by then that SWAPO not only had the greatest support among Namibians, but that it would be historically correct for them, as the group who had fought a bitter war against occupation, to become the first government of an independent Namibia. I had excellent contacts in SWAPO, and always included their points of view in my reports. Whenever the DTA or the SADF fed me anti-SWAPO propaganda, I always checked it with SWAPO sources first. Not only did I believe that it was the correct thing to do professionally, but I thought it was important to slowly prepare the white South African public for the inevitability that SWAPO was going to be the next government. But this stance, not surprisingly, did not go down well with some of the editors I worked for.

Contrary to what my Afrikaans colleagues thought at the time, I never really felt comfortable with SWAPO. I knew that the movement was run by a Kwanyama (a sub-group of the Ovambo) mafia. I believed Andreas Shipanga and others when they told me that Sam Nujoma had them thrown in harsh detention camps because he felt threatened by them. I was getting too many bits of information that torture and beatings, even executions, were taking place in some of SWAPO's camps in Angola.

I thought Sam Nujoma was a bit of an embarrassment. Two of my fellow South African correspondents and I ran a little satirical magazine (circulation about fifty) from Windhoek, called *The Spike*. Once SWAPO sent me the full script of an important speech Nujoma had made in Luanda. Every second sentence was 'the South African racist military junta' or 'the Pretoria murderers' or 'the fascist white regime' – a first-year student radical would have been ashamed.

I published the speech verbatim in *The Spike*, simply presented as an address delivered by the leader of SWAPO. One of my SWAPO contacts phoned me after he'd seen it. He was livid. It was cruel and racist, he said. How could I mock his great leader with drivel like that? He was deeply embarrassed when I showed him that I had not changed one word of Nujoma's original speech.

Yet I was widely seen as being pro-SWAPO. My son John was taunted at his primary school because his father was a 'terrorist'. Once, while we were on holiday on the Namibian coast, I went with my kids to Swakopmund on a Saturday morning to eat breakfast in a famous place called Treffpunkt. We were about 100 metres from the entrance when we saw the whole facade of the restaurant being blown up by a massive bomb. Several people were badly injured.

With the kids safe, I rushed to the scene. A white man whom I did not know pushed me in the chest, hissing, 'This is your work, you SWAPO people did this. Are you happy now, you bloody terrorist?'

SWAPO's head office was in Luanda, and its senior leadership mostly operated from there and from Lusaka in Zambia. I decided that it was important to get a view on SWAPO and its policies and plans from the horse's mouth, and asked for an interview with Nujoma. The SWAPO information officer organised an interview in Lusaka.

I arrived in Lusaka and went to State House, President Kenneth Kaunda's residence, where Nujoma always stayed when in the city, and where I was to meet him. Kaunda's press secretary was an extremely friendly and helpful man, and became even more so when he learnt that I was an Afrikaner. He explained that Nujoma's plane was still stuck in Luanda, and it wasn't clear when he would arrive.

I explained my problem: I was booked on the last flight out the same day and had not brought money to pay for a hotel room. One of the men disappeared into a back office, and re-emerged with a big smile: 'You are now the guest of the president of Zambia.' They gave me a room in a cottage on the grounds of State House.

I woke up the next morning at about six from a banging on my door. A young woman stood there with a broad smile: 'The president wants you to join him for breakfast.' I took a quick shower and rushed over to the main residence.

'KK' was sitting all on his own at the breakfast table in a large dining room, reading a newspaper. He was dressed in a grey-brown safari suit with a white handkerchief in his top pocket. 'Ah, my Afrikaner friend,' he said with a huge smile as he stood up and walked towards me. 'Mr President,' I said, extending my hand to greet him. He took it, but drew me closer and gave me a bear hug.

I joined him at the table. He said he was told that there was an Afrikaner journalist staying at one of the State House cottages waiting for Nujoma, and decided he had to meet me.

In good Afrikaner/African style, he asked me about my father, my children and whether we had had good rains. We were eating porridge and fruit salad. He spent about fifteen minutes lecturing me on the importance of eating enough fresh fruit and vegetables and not too much meat – and another ten on the evils of smoking when I confessed that I was indeed a smoker.

He then lectured me on Afrikaner history, saying that all Africans were proud of the way in which the Afrikaners fought the British during the Anglo-Boer War. 'But your people were misled by despots after that,' he said, explaining that the whole subcontinent would be drawn into a bloody conflict if the apartheid government did not release Nelson Mandela soon and start talks with the black political parties.

'You should not be afraid of the ANC,' the president told me. 'I know them; Tambo [Oliver Tambo, president of the ANC] is a dear friend of mine. They are as keen as the rest of us in southern Africa to accept you Afrikaners as fellow Africans. Apartheid [he pronounced it appart-height] is your enemy, not Tambo.'

He started to tell me what he thought of PW Botha, but then one of his aides called him and my meeting was over. It was a moment I still cherish, and I've had a soft spot for Kaunda ever since. He played a facilitating role during the final Namibian negotiations, and hosted some of the earliest contacts between the South African business sector and the exiled ANC. His long reign did not do the Zambian economy and civil administration much good, but he handed over power to his successor, Frederick Chiluba, apparently without much reluctance.

Oh, and the next day I had my interview with Nujoma. He was a pleasant surprise – warm and grandfatherly – but the interview was not much different from the speech I had printed in *The Spike*. I thought he was a bit like PW Botha: very good at the cut and thrust of party politics, but without the intellect, vision or understanding of the world that would be prerequisites for a national leader. But it was also very clear to me that there wasn't a communist bone in Nujoma's body.

The day after my Nujoma interview, I tried to get on an aircraft, but was told that there were no seats available for four days. I mentioned this to the member of Kaunda's staff who had helped me before. He took me straight to the airport, flashed his credentials and we walked right through customs. He spoke to someone in an office, and the next moment I was taken to the waiting aircraft. As I walked up the steps, an elderly white guy in a suit carrying an attaché case was getting off, cursing loudly. Only when I sat down in the completely full aircraft did I realise they had kicked him off to make space for me.

The SWAPO leadership's most criminal act came after they were already assured of the free and fair election they had fought for, for so long. On 1 April 1989, D-Day for the independence process, they broke all agreements and sent several thousand of their guerrillas over the border into Angola. It gave the South African security forces the last chance to kill, and 312 of the guerrillas were mowed down before peace was restored.

In 1991, when I was the editor of a weekly newspaper in South Africa, I published the stories of several people who testified how they were tortured and kept for months in underground dungeons in SWAPO camps in Angola. They claimed that some eighty people had died in these camps. Solomon Jesus Auala was SWAPO's chief of intelligence, but was widely referred to by his victims as the Butcher of Lubango, where SWAPO had its most notorious camps. Bizarrely, Auala even jailed Nujoma's wife, Kovambo, and her brother, Aaron Mushimba, on suspicion of being South African spies.

Auala and his thugs came back to Namibia in 1989 and paraded the streets shamelessly as heroes. There was no independent investigation launched into these gross human rights violations, no truth commission.

On 7 November, Namibia went to the polls. SWAPO received 57 per cent of the votes, and the DTA 28 per cent.

I went back to Namibia for the independence ceremony. On the stroke of midnight on 20 March 1990, the South African flag was lowered and the new Namibian flag raised. South Africa was represented by its new state president, FW de Klerk, who had just released Nelson Mandela from jail. But I'm getting ahead of my story; that was still years away.

15

Catholics and communists

WORKING IN NAMIBIA, mixing with stalwarts of the liberation movements and striking up good friendships with senior United Nations officials such as Ahtisaari's deputy, the urbane and resourceful Cedric Thornberry, expanded my mind and my horizons. For the first time I was beginning to feel that I wasn't just a little parochial reporter working for an ethnic newspaper.

Still, working for a South African newspaper meant there was little opportunity to work outside southern Africa. If I wanted to taste journalism elsewhere in the world, I would have to make it happen myself.

In 1980 I got divorced, and felt it was a good time to spread my wings. My employers, in the meantime, had sent a senior journalist to join me in Namibia. I liked him and thought he was doing a good job. So I took all the leave due to me – and then some – and went to where the biggest news story was happening at the time: Northern Ireland.

I had long been fascinated by the ongoing conflict in Northern Ireland, but found it very difficult to get my head around the essence of the 'troubles'. When I heard that a Republican activist just three years younger than me, Bobby Sands, had started a hunger strike and vowed not to start eating until his demands were met, I went to Belfast.

I was intrigued by the similarities between the Irish conflict and the struggle in South Africa. The Irish in the north of the island were conquered by the English, and after 1610, just less than fifty years before Jan van Riebeeck set foot on Cape soil, the English started giving the land to the English Protestants and dispossessed the Irish Catholics. They revolted in 1641, but were quashed. More and more English Protestants and Scots arrived, and soon the Catholics were in the minority. The fighting between Catholic and Protestant has continued on and off since then. The southern counties were given dominion status in 1921, but the north, Ulster, was ruled as part of Britain. Irish Catholics were treated as second-class citizens in their own country.

The parallels with South Africa are obvious: oppression, land grabbing, marginalisation, and the political divide coinciding with a class divide. Of particular interest to me was the position of the Protestants: they were mostly descendants of the colonisers, yet they, too, were now Irish – as my European ancestors had become Africans. Of course, the differences were also vast: the South African conflict was both racial and cultural but religion played no role.

I had done a lot of homework, but I wanted to hear from the people themselves. I did not register as a journalist, but arrived in Belfast early in 1981 as a tourist. At the airport, I followed one of the men who offered taxi rides, and when he asked me where I wanted to go to, I said I would prefer a bed and breakfast belonging to a local family.

He delivered me to the door of the Flynn family, who had two spare rooms for guests at a very reasonable price. Breakfast was eaten with the rest of the family; supper, too, for a little bit extra.

They were Catholics, and as friendly and welcoming as a Free State farming family. At first I told them that I was a writer, and just wanted to soak up the local atmosphere and meet some locals. Almost the first thing they told me was that they were working class and proud of it – even their eldest son, who was a junior lecturer at a Belfast college.

The first night I went to the local pub was like an experience out of a movie. The moment I walked through the doors, a hush fell over the place. I walked up to the counter, greeted the barman and ordered a beer. Suddenly everyone was talking again. A few minutes later, a man came over to where I was sitting all on my own. So where are you from, he asked me. I noticed that the guys at the nearest table were pricking up their ears for my answer. Oh, you noticed my accent, did you, I said, so where do you think I'm from? At this stage they invited me to join them at their table. New Zealand, said the one. Australia, said another.

South Africa, I said, and noticed a slight change in their openness. So, what do you think of your country's situation, one asked me, and it dawned on me that they would not welcome me if they thought I was a supporter of apartheid. Well, I wasn't, and told them so. And I told them that I was an Afrikaner. This was the magic key to their friendship: someone who's against apartheid, but whose ancestors had also given the English hell – they knew as much about the Anglo-Boer War as I did, and knew the Irish heroes who had fought on the side of the Boers by name. In my heart I quietly apologised to my English-speaking South African friends, and took part in their Pom bashing.

I stayed very late that night and learnt many things. It was the beginning of a good friendship with several Belfast Republicans. I even had a visit one night in my room from a man I later suspected could have been a local IRA leader, who believed it was his job to educate me about Northern Ireland.

I was brought up to regard the *Roomse Gevaar* [Roman Catholic threat] to be as dangerous as the *Rooi Gevaar* [red threat] and the *Swart Gevaar* [black threat].

Yet here I was, not only feeling completely at home among the Catholic Nationalists, but also feeling a deep sympathy with their cause.

Part of it was my natural instinct to side with the underdog, as well as a genuine disgust at the way the Republicans were treated by the Loyalists and by Britain. The demand for one Ireland seemed to me to be reasonable and historically fair and correct. And I suppose part of it was my tendency to romanticise revolutionaries.

Another part was recognising Afrikaner patriarchal figures in Protestant leaders such as Reverend Ian Paisley. He even looked like the head of the NG Kerk when I was a student, Koot Vorster, brother of prime minister John. Paisley had a long history of opposing marriages between Catholics and Protestants and the allocation of council houses to Catholics. His actions had led directly to some of the worst rioting in decades.

The Protestants' arrogance and prejudice reminded me of my own community. I had a heated exchange with a young Protestant lawyer about this at a reception in a fancy Belfast hotel. He told me with great enjoyment how his little brother and his friends had written 'Feed Bobby Sands' all over walls in Belfast. I told him his people reminded me of Nationalist Afrikaners, but his retort put me on the spot: 'So what are you doing here? Why do you want to save the Catholics if your own people are oppressing the blacks?' Good question.

Northern Ireland in 1981 was a depressing place. The hatred and resentment between the two communities ran much deeper than anything I had experienced in South Africa or Namibia. I saw hope and potential in South Africa and Namibia; I saw only bitterness in Northern Ireland.

I had a feeling that the Irish had become the victims of their history. I grew up with stories of the British atrocities in the Boer War concentration camps where my own grandmother had suffered. But my generation did not harbour these resentments. The Irish talked about the 'Potato Famine' as if it had happened during their lifetime – it happened in 1846. All the symbols used by the two sides were symbols of conflict from the past. The Irish were stuck in their history.

A particularly depressing experience was visiting a crèche in Derry, or London-derry, as the Loyalists call it. I walked down a road towards a part of the city regarded as the heart of Catholic resistance. When I saw children playing in a small garden, I went in. The teachers could not actually believe that a non-Catholic insider dared to walk that road, apparently one of the most dangerous in the whole country. I pretended to be brave, but the truth was that I simply did not know any better.

But the teachers were friendly and talked to me openly. I was astonished that the lively young women who so clearly loved the children they were looking after could be filled with so much bitterness and deep-seated hatred. It meant that those children would grow up harbouring the same resentments.

Bobby Sands and his fellow hunger strikers in the H-Block prison were in the background of all the conversations and news reports during my stay. Bobby's stature as a hero grew each day he refused food, and the Republican community was abuzz with stories of how he had become a breathing skeleton. In April, he became the member of parliament for Fermanagh and South Tyrone. His election agent was allowed to see him, and he reported that Sands was indeed reduced to a pitiful, blind bag of bones.

Bobby Sands, MP, died on 5 May 1981 in the H-Block hospital at Long Kesh. He had not eaten for sixty-five days.

A man prepared to die the most horrible death imaginable for a political ideal left in me a deep impression of human beings' irrepressible thirst for freedom. It took my mind back to the youngsters in Soweto, and to Robben Island, where a number of black liberation fighters were patiently sitting out the apartheid regime.

During my stay in Belfast and Derry, I had picked up lots of macho talk from Republicans about the Irish Republican Army's military exploits. I was sympathetic to their cause, but I have always had a deep-seated revulsion to physical violence. I made contact with some of the Belfast journalists to get a more balanced view.

They told me many stories, showed me reports and photographs, and gave me the names of survivors, some of whom I then visited. A disturbing picture unfolded of a culture of violence, a glorification of bloodshed on both sides of the Irish divide. Reluctantly, I had to admit to myself that much of the IRA's armed struggle boiled down to naked terrorism. Of course, the same went for the Loyalist paramilitary organisations.

I drew a lot from those memories and insights in later years when I had to take a personal position on the armed struggle and violent strategies in South Africa. It helped me to understand that the unnaturally violent nature of the crime wave that is still engulfing South Africa today is largely due to the brutal and excessive violence with which the apartheid system was defended, and to the mindless violence that often characterised the ANC and PAC's armed struggle and some of the internal uprisings. As was the case in Northern Ireland, the main heroes on both sides were often the men of violence.

My fascinating visit to Northern Ireland also ended rather violently, although it was not politically motivated. Towards the end of my trip, I decided to take a few days off at a seaside resort. I went to Portrush and booked into a sweet bed and breakfast.

Some seaside holiday – it rained all the time. Apart from walks in the rain on the beach, I was holed up in my room, writing stories about my visit for a newspaper in Hong Kong, a leftist alternative magazine in the US, a Sunday newspaper in Singapore, and the weekend supplement of the newspapers I worked for.

The establishment belonged to a widower, and he and his daughter managed it. That's where the trouble started.

Her name was Gillian. She had long red hair and she was in her mid-twenties. She was very beautiful in a plumpish, Irish kind of way. Since her mother died, she had known no other life than making breakfast, making beds, doing the books. She was very sharp and very frustrated. She was also the apple of her father's over-protective eye.

We enjoyed talking to each other, and a few times even sneaked a stroll on the beach together. But the attraction was stronger than that.

One thing led to another, and one morning not long after midnight her father kicked open my door. He had a gun in his hands. Gillian covered herself with the blankets, but I was given no such opportunity. I ended up pleading for my life, stark naked, in the entrance hall. The old man gave me forty seconds – he counted down out loud, eagerly stroking his shotgun – to get my stuff and get out.

I was still trying to get my pants on halfway down the block, with half my stuff in my bag in one hand, and a very angry Irish father with a menacing shotgun in pursuit. It was one the most undignified retreats of my life. The price you pay for love.

Gillian and I corresponded for a while, but then she met a proper Irish Catholic, a professional golfer – a much better catch than a raw Protestant Boer hack from the land of apartheid. Mr Golfer made her Da happy, and I sincerely hope her too.

Back in Namibia, my position had become impossible. I was in the employ of a really good company, and I had no doubt that I could have had a bright future with them if I played the game right. But I would be living a lie. Even while I was in Namibia, where apartheid was fast being dismantled, it was becoming increasingly difficult to write for the newspapers I represented; already *Die Burger* and *Die Volksblad* had stopped using much of my copy. I knew it was simply not possible for me to continue as a political reporter for the Afrikaans press back in South Africa.

How could I go on working for an organisation that supported PW Botha, the Group Areas Act, the Immorality Act, the pass laws? I had seen and heard too much, and got to know too many people whom my colleagues in South Africa would brand as 'the enemy'. The doubts that had lingered so long in my mind were now finally confirmed. I knew the time had come for me to make a break.

In 1983 I was offered the position of Senior Editor (Current Affairs) at the *Financial Mail* in Johannesburg. I accepted with some trepidation. I would be working for an English company for the first time, and I would be writing in English. Also, I had my reservations about being in the employ of Anglo American.

But the prospect of working for an organisation that would allow me more freedom and openly criticised apartheid was very attractive, so I accepted. If only I knew.

My then editor, Ton Vosloo, wrote me a letter telling me that I would go far in

Nasionale Pers, asking me to reconsider my resignation. I liked and respected Vosloo, but I knew I could not change my mind, and I went to Johannesburg to tell him so. He was understanding, but not so some of my other colleagues. Willie Kuhn, then an assistant editor, confronted me in the corridor and told me, 'You're making the mistake of your life. You'll come crawling back.'

For years afterwards, journalists at *Beeld* were told that I had been involved in some kind of scandal and was fired. I could never understand why my resignation had prompted such a negative reaction.

I took a long holiday between leaving *Beeld* and joining the *FM*. I had a few things that I had to clear up for myself. I needed to know what communism really was and how socialism actually worked in practice. The easiest place for me to go and see for myself (and to get back to South Africa without getting into trouble) was East Berlin.

I arranged with my friends in SWAPO to ask their contacts in East Berlin to help me. I got a day pass at Checkpoint Charlie, got in touch with the designated contact, and before the day was out, I had permission to stay.

Nothing prepared me for the contrast between the east and west of Berlin. West Berlin, where I had spent time during a previous visit, was bright and loud and busy and energetic, day and night. East Berlin was grey, dull, quiet, sometimes even appearing deserted. No neon signs over shops, no traffic jams, no punks or hobos on the streets. You could not walk for more than five minutes without coming across Russian soldiers or local police.

I needed a scarf to ward off the cold, and was directed to a men's clothing shop in the heart of the main business centre of East Berlin, apparently the smartest in the country. No scarves. It was like *Oom Frikkie se Klerewinkel* in Koppies when I was a child: heavy suits in different shades of brown and grey, heavy soled shoes, white shirts only. There were enough clothes for about five people. I was the only customer.

Next stop a restaurant. The only place I could find in the city centre was a pavement sausage restaurant where you had to stand and eat at the high tables. *Wurst* only, served with cabbage and potatoes. The pleasant surprise was that it cost me the equivalent of about R2.

Okay, I thought, you have to shake off your Western capitalist mindset and open yourself up to a completely different way of life. It worked. I came to appreciate the fact that I could look at everyone I came across in the same way, and only make up my mind about them once we had communicated. In capitalist societies, we notice people's clothes, hairstyles and the cars they drive or the restaurants they frequent, and that influences the way we think about them. The absence of rampant materialism started growing on me.

I settled down in a tiny room in a couple's apartment in a huge block of flats.

The two children moved into their parents' bedroom for the duration of my stay, but Hannah and Karl were very happy to get the extra money. They worked in the same factory, where the wife was the husband's overseer. Karl was very proud of the fact that Hannah was his superior.

My German wasn't great (at the time I had an Austrian girlfriend and I learnt the basics from her), but I could understand it quite well, and with a lot of gesticulation and some English, I could make myself understood.

I met Karl and Hannah's neighbours and friends. Most of them had never met anyone from outside East Germany. East Berlin was an extremely suspicious place, and everybody was constantly on guard against government informers. Right up to the end of my visit, I had the impression that my hosts and their friends were still not entirely sure that I was exactly who I said I was. It was very frustrating, because the main reason for my visit was to get a sense of what it was like for ordinary citizens to live in a socialist state.

But my friends did express their extreme unhappiness with the way they were treated by the police and the Russian soldiers. They treated ordinary people like animals, Hannah said, with no respect and no hesitation to use violence. I could detect a deep resentment towards the Russians.

Karl and Hannah's lives were vastly different from mine, although they both had what were considered fairly good jobs. They never had money for anything but the most basic food, and most days that excluded fresh vegetables or fruit. They did not own a car or a record player, only a radio. Dining out was a concept that did not exist for them, and they never went to the movies or the theatre, only the odd political rally.

I was feeling very sorry for these poor people, when it occurred to me that the vast majority of South Africans were probably worse off, and they lived in a so-called capitalist system.

But Karl and Hannah's children had free education, and they paid virtually nothing for their flat. It struck me that these people had a lot less stress than the average West Berliner or I had. There was almost no crime. There was warmth and caring among ordinary people that I had never seen anywhere else. Neighbours talked to each other and knew each other, a concept alien to me.

The biggest shock to me was the Wall. It was much more sinister than I'd thought it would be. The first time I went to see it from the east, I stood there for an hour, looking at the guards, overwhelmed by it all. I had seen the Wall from the other side, covered in graffiti, but from this side I had the sense of being in the presence of evil.

By the time I left East Berlin, I was somewhat clearer in my mind. A pure socialist system cannot exist in conjunction with the freedom of the individual. By definition, a socialist system has to be authoritarian, and authoritarianism always leads to corruption and abuse. The people I had met in East Berlin were freer of material concerns and competition than their counterparts in the West, but their creativity had been taken away from them. They were prisoners because they were ruled by fear and could not express themselves freely. The human spirit cannot flourish in such a system. The community spirit and warmth I had experienced could have been the result of a less materialistic society, but my guess was that it was more the result of common people connecting with each other because of oppression from the state.

I spent a few days in West Berlin before moving on. It was a shock to my system. The city was too loud, too bright, too hurried. People didn't even notice the beggars or junkies in the streets. The money devil was chasing them.

I concluded then – and my experience in the following twenty years confirmed it – that a certain minimum level of a free-market system had to exist in order for people to be free and creative. When the state is too strong, the citizens suffer.

Yet I also spent six weeks in the United States and saw places like south-central Los Angeles. Unbridled capitalism is as cruel to the unprivileged as hard-core socialism. If a free-market system is not tempered with some state intervention, the freedom it is supposed to provide is a false freedom. There is no freedom in extreme poverty. I saw no extreme poverty in East Germany.

But the Berlin Wall made an indelible impression on my mind. Soviet-style communism was a system I deeply hoped I would never be subjected to.

I wasn't going to become a communist after all. It was a relief, because I was about to join the ranks of the biggest financial publication in Africa.

16

My friend Lubof

IN LATER YEARS, Namibia, like a jealous ex-lover, wouldn't leave me alone. On 11 September 1989, I was in Johannesburg watching the eight o'clock television news bulletin when I saw my old friend Anton Lubowski, by now a senior SWAPO functionary, welcoming SWAPO exiles back to Namibia at Windhoek Airport. I smiled to myself, because he dwarfed everybody around him, almost picking up Andimba Toivo ja Toivo as he bear-hugged him. Anton was in my thoughts the next day, and I thought I should phone him and reconnect.

I didn't phone him the next day. At about ten o'clock that night I got a call from a mutual friend in Windhoek. He simply said: 'They killed Anton.' It was like a cold hand gripping my heart. I knew who 'they' were.

I could not sleep after that. I was deeply sad that a strong life force such as Anton was now no more. I cried for his small children, and for his gentle mother Molly and father Wilfred.

But sadness made way for a boiling anger at the evil men who had shot him in the back outside his house earlier that evening.

I did not need an investigation to know whom to blame. I blamed PW Botha and his ministers of defence and police, Magnus Malan and Adriaan Vlok. They were the political masters of a hate campaign against all who challenged the morality of white oppression and occupation.

Anton was killed in my name: the killers were white Afrikaner males fighting in the name of so-called Christianity for the preservation of a white government dominated by Afrikaner Nationalists.

It made me feel powerless and desperate. If my fellow Afrikaners had sunk to this level of complete disregard for human life, what future did we have but more blood and suffering?

My mind went back to the other people the apartheid state had assassinated because they had voiced their opposition to white oppression. In 1978, there was the Durban academic Rick Turner. His book, *The Eye of the Needle*, had quite an impact on my own thinking when I was in my twenties. They shot him in his own home and he died in the arms of his twelve-year-old daughter Jann, who became my colleague and friend eighteen years later. Rick's killer was never found, but overwhelming evidence indicated that the killer was a member of the security police.

Then they killed Ruth First, a bright academic and thinker, in Mozambique in 1982. Security police captain Dirk Coetzee, himself a killer, told us that the parcel-bomb that killed her was sent by his colleague, Major Craig Williamson.

The same team also tried to kill my dear old friend Marius Schoon by sending him a parcel-bomb in Angola in 1984, but instead it killed his wife Jeanette and daughter Katryn.

In 1981, Dirk Coetzee and his henchmen killed Durban lawyer Griffiths Mxenge and made it look like a robbery.

In December of that same year, a popular medical doctor of Mamelodi, Dr Fabian Ribeiro, and his wife Florence were shot and killed in their home. Pretoria-based security policemen asked for amnesty from the Truth Commission for planning to kill the Ribeiros, but claimed that they were actually killed by two army agents.

In 1982, the security police first poisoned and then murdered a charismatic Eastern Cape youth activist, Siphiwo Mtimkulu.

In April 1988, the same SADF unit that had killed Anton, the CCB, tried to kill academic Albie Sachs with a car bomb in Maputo. He was badly hurt and lost an arm, but survived and is today a judge in the Constitutional Court.

Four months before Anton's assassination, the CCB shot Johannesburg academic David Webster in his driveway. Ferdi Barnard is serving time for this murder.

Not one of the people I have mentioned so far was in any way involved in violence or the armed struggle. And the list of assassinations goes on and on: Robert Smit, Stanza Bopape, the Cradock Four, Zweli Nyanda, Cassius Make, Joseph Mayosi, the Pebco Three – these are among the cases I have personal knowledge of.

Anton was perhaps a flawed man, but he was a man of love and generosity and tolerance. He hated aggression and violence. He was a political opponent of the South African government because he believed in a free, equal and dignified Namibia. His only military connection was the national service he did in the South African army when he was younger.

Anton's killing came as a shock, but we should have seen the signs that he was a prime target. When he announced in March 1984 that he was joining SWAPO, the office of State President PW Botha sent him an insulting letter and withdrew his SADF officer's commission. He was detained several times, the last time in a small corrugated iron hut with only his underpants on. His car was once sprayed with bullets in Katatura.

The day after his death, the *Weekly Mail* asked me to write about Anton. I struggled to write the piece, but this is what I wrote:

On Wednesday there was a front-page picture of policemen putting Anton's corpse into a body bag. My brain just seized up, saying over and over: Lubof doesn't belong in a police body bag. Of all the people I knew, he was the one who adored and loved life the most.

Anton was not your average revolutionary. Unless there is such a thing as a humanitarian revolutionary who can party until the early hours of the morning; who is partial to tailor-made suits, silk shirts and fast cars; who cries openly when he speaks about his children who no longer live with him; who has a sense of humour.

Five years ago Anton and I were drinking beer in the garden of the old Kaiser Krone Hotel when a couple of rough boys at the next table shouted at him: White kaffir!

I remember as if it was yesterday the way his face lit up. It's true, he said, I am a white kaffir.

He was too.

Although his father was of German Namibian stock, I wrote, Anton was actually a *boerseun*, a product of Paul Roos Gymnasium and Stellenbosch University – and a good rugby player.

But as Afrikaans as he was – or perhaps precisely because he was so Afrikaans – he was also inherently a good African. It never ceased to amaze me how easily and spontaneously he fitted into black society, and how warmly and without tokenism the SWAPO community in Katatura welcomed him …

Anton was a gentle and very warm person with a good dollop of charisma and an excess of idealism. Not the kind of person one would expect to provoke the kind of political hatred which ends in death.

But more than this: he had the courage to act out his opposition in a highly polarised community. He made it easier for other white Namibians to leave their fears and inhibitions behind them and to become part of the new Namibian nation.

His death must serve as a warning to all of us on this subcontinent. It is the price we have to pay for decades of the politics of hate, of domination and racial division.

As far as I'm concerned, Anton Lubowski has earned a place in the southern African heroes' acre alongside the Steve Bikos, Victoria Mxenges, Rick Turners and David Websters.

But that is of small comfort to his children, Almo and Nadia, who are going to grow up without a father.

The SADF's propaganda machine was quick off the mark, and early the next morning reporters got an off-the-record briefing that the killing was probably the result of 'power struggles inside SWAPO'.

But later the same day, a Windhoek woman told the police that her tenant had behaved strangely the previous evening, and she saw him carrying something that looked like a rifle in a bag. The man was a shady Irish criminal and hit man called Donald Acheson. He was arrested, and later told the police his handlers were three SADF agents, Calla Botha, Ferdi Barnard and Chappies Maree. They worked for a secret unit cynically called the Civil Cooperation Bureau, the CCB.

My friend Anton was actually killed twice. The second time was four months after his assassination. On 26 February 1990, three weeks before Namibia's independence, the South African Minister of Defence, Magnus Malan, got up in parliament and declared: 'I want to disclose today that Lubowski was a paid agent of Military Intelligence. I am assured that he did good work for the SADF. The Chief of Staff Intelligence, General Rudolph Badenhorst, would therefore never have approved actions against Lubowski.'

It was the most outrageous statement ever made in that parliament. Without even investigating Malan's claim, I knew for certain that he was lying. I would sooner believe that the Pope was a rapist or Desmond Tutu a crack dealer than believe that the man I knew could have sold out his own people.

Anton's family, friends and comrades protested loudly, even the top leadership of SWAPO, including the man who would shortly afterwards become president of Namibia, Sam Nujoma.

But the evil seed of doubt was sown. More than a decade after Anton's death, there are still people who quietly wonder whether he was indeed an agent for the SADF while parading as a freedom fighter.

I realised even then that the suspicions would linger. I knew I owed it to Anton, Almo and Nadia, his former wife Gaby and his parents to make it my business to prove that Magnus Malan was a liar. With my old friend and partner in crime Jacques Pauw and others I investigated every shred of evidence. I have written about this several times in different publications and made two television documentaries about it.

The picture that emerged from confessions, interrogations, interviews and testimony given by some members of the CCB was that the commander of the CCB, Joe Verster, launched a plan in May 1989 to disrupt SWAPO before the November independence elections. Pieter Botes' Region Two, Staal Burger's Region Six (or internal region) and the Namibia Region of the CCB would be involved. Sabotage, assassination and the poisoning of drinking water were among the plans.

The decision to assassinate Anton was taken at a CCB meeting at the Rosebank Hotel in Johannesburg on 1 September 1989. Staal Burger and Chappies Maree appear to have played the central role. Some weeks before that, CCB member Slang van Zyl went to Windhoek to follow Anton and report on his movements and routine. Ferdi Barnard also confessed to having gone to Windhoek to kill Anton, but he 'never got a clear shot' and returned. He did apparently make a videotape of Anton's movements.   ·

On the morning of the assassination, Burger flew to Windhoek under the name Gagiano, and back to Johannesburg the next day. Acheson had flown to Windhoek two days earlier, and the two of them met with Maree, who was already in Windhoek.

Solving the case wasn't actually very hard – for journalists, that is, because the police and the judiciary have still not solved it officially. It is my distinct impression that the judiciary in both South Africa and Namibia went out of their way not to find and punish the killers. It is a most disturbing tale.

In Namibia, murder suspect Donald Acheson was released and left the country for Britian. The police and judiciary bungled their way through two inquests into Anton's death with no clear outcome. During the first inquest, a CCB diary was handed to Judge Harold Levy – but the pages of 31 August and 12 September 1989 were missing: the days David Webster and Anton Lubowski were assassinated.

State President FW de Klerk appointed a commission of inquiry under Judge Louis Harms to investigate the flood of stories of state-sponsored death squads. Some of the information on Anton surfaced before the judge, but the minute evidence got closer to who killed Anton, he would steer it away – because, he said, he had no mandate to investigate what happened outside South Africa's borders.

But when Malan came under pressure to prove his astonishing lies in parliament, the state president broadened Harms' terms of reference to include the question of whether Anton had worked for Military Intelligence – not who killed him, or why, but only whether he was an agent. I hope De Klerk, now a distinguished elder statesman and Nobel Peace Prize laureate, is thoroughly ashamed every time he thinks of the Lubowski case.

Still, a judicial inquiry could at least have cleared Anton's name. No chance. The military told Harms an open inquiry would endanger the security of the state and the lives of other agents, and he ordered the hearing to be held behind closed doors. It was unique in South African legal history; the Lubowski family and their lawyers were barred from the hearing. The SADF presented Harms with their bogus evidence, with only one of Harms' aides also in the room.

It was no surprise when Harms found that Anton had undoubtedly been an SADF agent, because he had seen proof that Military Intelligence had paid R100 000 in three payments into Anton's bank account.

We got hold of copies of the cheques that the SADF had given to Harms. They were from Global Capital Investments. Closer scrutiny revealed that Ernst

Penzhorn, the Pretoria lawyer who acted for Magnus Malan, formed this close corporation. The only director was a woman, but her name and identity number did not appear in the national population register.

I came across Penzhorn quite a few times during the hearings of the Truth Commission, where he represented Malan and several other politicians and soldiers. I once told him that he was the one man who could come out with the truth and clear Anton's name, but he just smiled and walked away. He was clearly a man specialising in shadowy deals involving the military and the arms trade. He also founded a company called Bowett International, an 'import and export' company with PW Botha's son, PW Jr., as MD, and involving senior SADF officers such as Military Intelligence chief Rudolph 'Witkop' Badenhorst.

The SADF initially barred the Lubowski family from investigating Anton's bank accounts, but a Pretoria lawyer working for the Lubowskis, Julian Knight, later showed me his bank statements. The three payments in question were there for anyone to see. It was obvious that the military's suggestion that Anton was desperate for money was untrue; there was more than enough money in his account to cover his debts and pay for his lifestyle.

The *Mail & Guardian* reported in 1999 that Military Intelligence had lured Anton into buying furniture and property for SWAPO (he was their deputy head of finance at the time) through a front company for yet another shady SADF outfit, the Directorate Covert Collection (DCC). The company, Gijima Express, paid him a 5 per cent commission on transactions totalling R2 million. That was the R100 000 paid into his account.

Anton trusted Gijima, because he was advised to use the company by a French businessman and close friend of Winnie Mandela's, Alain Guenon, who was introduced to him by the French embassy.

Julian Knight also got hold of the official forms that the SADF had presented as proof that Anton was a paid agent. In a television documentary, we proved that the forms were bogus.

The third judicial inquest in Namibia into Anton's assassination was more successful. In June 1994, Judge Harold Levy found that Donald Acheson had fired the nine fatal shots with an AK-47 rifle into Anton's body. He had acted under orders of the CCB, Levy found, and named among his accomplices Joe Verster, Staal Burger, Ferdi Barnard, Chappies Maree, Slang van Zyl and Calla Botha.

Namibia never asked South Africa for these men's extradition to be tried for murder in Namibia.

In May 1997, my colleague Jacques Pauw went to interview a senior DCC operative, Rich Verster, in a prison in Dorchester in the UK, where he was awaiting trial on charges of drug smuggling.

Verster told Pauw, and later the investigators of the Truth Commission, that he had been sent by the DCC to Namibia in 1989, among other things to try to recruit Anton Lubowski as an agent or informer – 'because Anton was an Afrikaner'. Anton never showed any sign that he would be disloyal to SWAPO. Verster taped many hours of Anton's telephone conversations, but 'could not find a weakness' he could use, and sent the tapes on to Military Intelligence in Pretoria.

When one of his recruits phoned him on the night of Anton's assassination with the news, he phoned his superior, Geoff Price, at the DCC in Pretoria. Price already knew about it, and told him to return to South Africa immediately. Back in Pretoria, he had access to all the documentation on the Lubowski case, and he says his colleagues at the DCC discussed the case at length. There was never a hint that Anton worked for Military Intelligence.

Verster told Pauw: 'I worked with Lubowski's file, and I would have known if he was a Military Intelligence agent. We were desperate to recruit him, but failed. His signature was faked and documents forged.'

Verster declared himself willing to testify in a court of law that Anton was framed by the military. Verster was never asked.

But Magnus Malan, as was his wont, shamelessly repeated his statement that Anton was a paid agent of the SADF to the Truth Commission. He has never acknowledged the ruling by a Supreme Court judge that Anton was killed by the SADF.

You cannot prosecute someone in South Africa for a murder committed in another country. But to conspire to murder someone is also a grave, punishable offence. I personally put pressure on the office of the Attorney-General to charge Staal Burger, Ferdi Barnard, Slang van Zyl, Calla Botha and Joe Verster with conspiracy to murder. There were more than enough affidavits, statements, testimony and documentation to prove that they conspired on South African soil to have Anton assassinated.

There has been no such prosecution.

PART IV

Playing with fire

17

Diamonds are not forever

IT WAS QUITE a shock to my system: from a free-ranging correspondent in a rough, open country where only bankers and clergymen wore ties, I suddenly found myself wearing suits in Johannesburg's central business district in a very structured newsroom lorded over by capitalists and yuppies. It was 1984, and I was now a political and current affairs reporter for the mighty *Financial Mail* – the fancy title of senior editor merely meant I wasn't a cub reporter any longer.

I disliked the editor, Stephen Mulholland, from the moment we met. That feeling intensified over time and became completely mutual. I thought then that people like him did not belong in my profession, and I still think so today. (Almost twenty years after our first meeting, he wrote in a column in the *Sunday Times* that I was the 'worst unguided missile' he had ever come across. Coming from him, I really took it as a compliment.)

Mulholland's idea was that I was recruited to become the *FM*'s expert on the Afrikaner Broederbond, Afrikaner politics and the National Party. I was a bit of a token Boer. Fortunately my other colleagues didn't see me as such, and some of the more progressive journalists on staff soon became dear friends.

The period between 1983 and 1990 was a tumultuous time in South African politics. In the early 1980s, the government steamed ahead with its policy of black South Africans having to find their political home in one of the 'independent' homelands: Transkei, Ciskei, Venda and Bophuthatswana. This meant that the pass laws were still applied enthusiastically, which meant in turn that hundreds of black people who did not have their *dompasses* on them were criminalised every week. Hundreds of thousands of black people were still being forcibly removed from 'black spots' to townships and bantustans to make the government's plan work.

PW Botha's government was under great pressure to initiate some changes to the rigid apartheid system that was still in place. 'Adapt or die', he declared in a famous speech in Upington – parodied by satirist Pieter-Dirk Uys in a play as *Adapt or Dye*.

In 1983, the National Party published its proposals for a new constitution for South Africa. It was sheer stupidity, but a *verligte* [progressive] Nat's wet dream: co-opt the 'coloureds' and 'Indians' into an uneven system of power sharing, and permanently exclude the black majority from the constitution and citizenship.

In a referendum on 2 November 1983, almost two-thirds of the white electorate voted for the proposals. In August 1984, an election was held for the House of Representatives (coloureds) and the House of Delegates (Indians). Less than 30 per cent of coloureds and 20 per cent of Indians voted, but on 25 January 1985 the new parliament was opened with three houses: the House of Assembly (whites, 178 members); the House of Representatives (85 members, Allan Hendrickse's Labour Party in the majority); and the House of Delegates (45 members, Amichand Rajbansi's National People's Party in the majority). The Representatives and Delegates had jurisdiction over ethnically defined 'own affairs', but the state president always had the final say.

The new dispensation stirred up a deep anger in the majority of South Africans. For more than a year, activists and trade unionists lobbied and organised, and on 20 August 1983 the United Democratic Front (UDF) was launched at a meeting in Mitchell's Plain in Cape Town under the chairmanship of Dr Allan Boesak. It was based on the old Congress Alliance, and its basic policy document was the Freedom Charter of 1956: The people shall govern; the land shall be shared by those who work it; the doors of learning and culture shall be opened to all; there shall be houses, security and comfort; there shall be work and security; the work shall be shared among all people.

The resistance generated by the UDF turned out to be the final stretch in the long journey for democracy and human rights in South Africa. Only six years later, the NP government started secret talks with leaders of the banned ANC leadership. But those were six long, bloody years.

The original UDF leadership reflected names that would be prominent in national politics twenty years later. Among the patrons were Robben Islanders Nelson Mandela, Govan Mbeki and Walter Sisulu, as well as internal activists such as Helen Joseph, Smangaliso Mkhatshwa and Beyers Naudé. Prominent in the executive were people such as Trevor Manuel, Mohammed Valli Moosa, Azhar Cachalia, Frank Chikane, Mosiuoa Lekota, Popo Molefe, Abrey Mokoena, Andrew Boraine, Cheryl Carolus, Steve Tshwete, Murphy Morobe, Dan Montsisi, Ebrahim Rasool and Jeremy Cronin.

The UDF was more non-racial that any African liberation group ever before. This fact, and the role of progressive whites still in parliament at that time, such as Van Zyl Slabbert and Helen Suzman, as well as white leaders inside the exiled ANC such as Joe Slovo and Ronnie Kasrils, contributed in large measure that the struggle for liberation never had a strong racial element.

The resistance was taken to the streets, and from 1984 onwards the country was gripped in a cycle of revolt and repression. In late 1984, the first state of emergency was declared. There was a Total Onslaught on South Africa, Botha said, and it needed a Total Strategy to counter it.

These were insecure times, and insecurity makes capitalists nervous. The current affairs pages of the *Financial Mail* were dominated by news and analysis of strikes, boycotts, detentions, protests, negotiations, the birth (in 1985) and first campaigns of the Congress of South African Trade Unions (COSATU), and mass mobilisation campaigns.

Mulholland and other big business types who liked to call themselves liberals were in a tight spot. Up to this point they were very comfortable in proclaiming to the world that they were against apartheid. But now their bluff was called. Distancing oneself from the crudities of apartheid imposed by thick-wristed Boers didn't work any more. It was time to stand up and declare oneself in favour of a full democracy in a unitary state, like the UDF did, or quietly support the white-dominated government. That's the way the capitalists decided to go in the mid-1980s, although after 1994 they denied it vehemently.

The upshot was that we were under increasing pressure at the *FM*. At one point, Mulholland even imposed a quota on us: no more than two 'black stories' per edition, he declared, because the readers were squealing.

I had deeply annoyed Mulholland when I put hostile questions to business leaders at a press conference after one of their chummy summit meetings with PW Botha. But our worst confrontation was not to be about South Africa, but about my old stomping ground.

While I was working in Namibia, I had heard rumours that CDM, a Namibian subsidiary of the South African diamond giant De Beers, had been 'raping' the diamond deposits at Oranjemund. It was one of the richest diamond deposits in the world, and the mine was the backbone of the Namibian economy. But I couldn't get a proper grip on the issue, and I knew that this was the kind of story where you had to be 100 per cent certain of your facts. Anglo American was the one company you didn't mess with without consequences.

I should admit that I harboured a deep resentment towards Anglo American. I had long believed that one of the most destructive aspects of South Africa's racial policies was the migrant labour system.

Black workers, mostly miners, were brought in from all over the country to mainly the Witwatersrand. Their families were not allowed to accompany them, and they were housed in huge, single-sex labour 'compounds', or 'hostels'. Once in six months or once a year they were allowed to go home.

No other facet of apartheid damaged the social fabric of black society as much as this system. Families were destroyed and social structures disturbed. Children grew up without fathers. The hostels became festering sores.

The main culprits were the mining companies, the biggest of which was Anglo. Yet Anglo had the public image of being an opponent of apartheid. That's what irked me. When Harry Oppenheimer died in 2002, all honoured him, including the ANC and the Mbeki government. I wrote an angry column reminding people of the other side of his legacy. It was not well received.

Early in 1984, the issue of CDM's 'overmining' of the Oranjemund mine was again mentioned at hearings into government corruption in Namibia. This time I got hold of a solid source: Gordon Brown, a senior man at CDM who had serious moral qualms about what they were doing to the mine. He started briefing me on the technical issues and gave me a number of documents with explosive content.

An understanding of CDM's unique position in Namibia is important in order to grasp the overmining story. CDM mined the world's richest diamond field in terms of an agreement with the South African administration in Namibia, who was bound to act in compliance with a League of Nations mandate to protect the interests of the people of the territory.

The agreement was known as the Halbscheid Agreement, and was signed in 1923. CDM was given exclusive rights to prospect and mine all minerals in an area the size of a small country (2.8 million hectares) along the Namibian coast called the *Sperrgebiet* [forbidden territory], where no one is allowed without the permission of CDM. They paid the grand sum of R812,40 for these rights.

But there was a price to pay for this generous offer. The Halbscheid Agreement stated: 'CDM, when working an area pegged under this, shall conduct operations as thoroughly and economically as it does on its other mining fields and shall carry on mining satisfactorily to the administrator and not with a view to exhausting the superficial and more valuable deposits to the detriment of the low-grade deposits.'

This last part is the crucial part: *Not with a view to exhausting the superficial and more valuable deposits to the detriment of the low-grade deposits.* The idea was that the diamond field should provide Namibia with a source of revenue and employment for as long as possible.

CDM, I wrote in my first piece in the *FM*, was in breach of the Halbscheid Agreement because it was, in mining-speak, 'picking the eyes out of the mine': preferentially mining the richer deposits at the expense of the mine's future profits.

I had CDM's own documents to back this up. The official 'Life of Mine Forecast' of 1977 stated: 'The objectives of this forecast are to specify the production policies and requirements that will maximise profit each year within the constraints of plant headfeeds and overall carat call.' And, 'from 1980 onwards the carat call was determined by overmining by 20 per cent on the average remaining grade at the beginning of each year'. It reported that overmining on grade in 1976 was 70 per cent, and it estimated 69 per cent for 1977, 60 per cent for 1978 and 63 per cent for 1979.

The smoking gun was a document called 'A Life of Mine Review', drawn up by the then manager at Oranjemund, Jack Forster, in September 1981. 'Treatment throughput has increased from 5 million cubic metres per year in 1968 to the current 9.3 million cubic metres of ore per year. Throughput, excluding any which might come from expansion in capital projects, will start declining rapidly from 1990 with first the closure of the screening plants and then of No. 1 plant in 1991.'

And then Forster used these words, devastating any fancy explanation CDM could come up with: 'To me this is best described as a power dive and unless we have a conscious change in strategy, effective some time in the future, *we will power the mine into the ground* and we will be unable to conduct the reclamation and cleaning operation which could extend the life of the mine by three or four years.' (My italics.)

I published CDM's response on the same page. Predictably, they denied any wrongdoing: 'CDM has consistently followed a sound long-run mining policy in accordance with the Halbscheid Agreement. At no stage has CDM's mining policy ever resulted in payable ground being rendered unpayable.'

Then CDM came out with the smokescreen they would keep up for the months and years this controversy continued: 'overmining' doesn't actually mean 'overmining'. They stated: 'The term "overmining" describes the grade actually mined in relation to the average grade of the whole area containing diamonds whether all of such areas are payable or not.'

The statement added: 'CDM's mining policy has nothing to do with CDM's attitude towards independence for Namibia. The company's policy towards the political evolution of the country has been frequently stated in speeches by its chairman and directors, and the company's actions speak for themselves.'

The morning of the publication of my story, Mulholland walked to my desk, slammed the magazine down and asked: 'What the hell do you think you're doing?' He said I knew nothing about mining: 'It is clearly news to you that mining companies are in the business for a profit.' I tried to explain about the 1923 agreement, but he didn't want to discuss the merits. He warned me to drop the story.

I checked with Gordon, who said my story was spot-on. He also explained why CDM's statement wasn't truthful. I vowed not to leave it there. A few weeks later, when Mulholland was out of town, I wrote a follow-up story, sticking to my line.

Mulholland was livid. He accused me of damaging the reputation of the *FM*. He dismissed my explanations by saying I was 'clearly ignorant'. But the story hurt enough for CDM to take out full-page advertisements in the Johannesburg and Windhoek press to defend their mining practices. I told Mulholland that I thought it was my ethical duty to follow through with the story.

CDM's – or was it Mulholland's? – next move was to invite me to a briefing where they would explain everything. Mulholland informed me of the invitation and said he would join me. On the day, he told me that he would meet me at 44 Main Street, the Anglo head office in Johannesburg.

We met at the entrance to the famous building and were taken to a huge and impressive boardroom. Mulholland introduced me. As I heard the names and titles, it dawned on me that this was the entire upper hierarchy of the De Beers empire, including the chairman, the Oranjemund mine manager and the top man of the Central Selling Organisation in London. I also realised, to my surprise, that I did not feel intimidated at all.

Mulholland told the assembled gathering that I was a good journalist who genuinely believed that they were doing something wrong in Namibia. He thanked them for taking the time to brief us.

The De Beers men proceeded to explain their definition of overmining. They explained that all diamond mines had to adjust their mining policies according to the needs of the market, because the diamond industry would collapse if there were violent instability.

I understood and accepted their explanations, but I wanted them to explain the documents I had in my possession. Clearly annoyed, they explained some of the technical stuff, and I had the impression that they were deliberately using technical terms that they thought I would not understand. In fact, at more than one point they said that the details would be difficult for a layperson to comprehend. But Gordon had briefed me well, and I did follow all their arguments.

I started putting more documents on the table to counter what they were saying, especially the mine manager's statement that CDM was 'powering the mine into the ground', and Mulholland lost patience. He silenced me, thanked the De Beers bosses profusely, and apologised for my stubbornness, more or less saying that *he* was satisfied with their explanations, which was all that counted. I was ushered out.

This showdown meant the end of my career at the *FM*, and I accepted an offer from Tertius Myburgh, editor of the *FM*'s sister paper, the *Sunday Times*, to become their political correspondent.

But it wasn't the end of the CDM story; it was the beginning, although the *FM* would no longer take part in the exposé. The *FM*'s opposition magazine, *Finance Week*, had by now taken up the story, as had the Namibian press. Mr Justice Pieter Thirion soon expanded his inquiry into maladministration in Namibia to include an investigation into the diamond industry and the workings of the Diamond Board.

Gordon Brown came out of the shadows and gave devastating evidence before Thirion.

The Thirion Report, published in March 1986, vindicated every word I had written, and more. The documents Brown had given me were extensively quoted in the report – and they were given Brown's interpretation, which I in turn had used in my reports and in the sham briefing with CDM.

Judge Thirion found that CDM had breached the Halbscheid Agreement by excessively depleting the Oranjemund diamonds for at least twenty years. 'The excessive depletion of the deposit was a preferential depletion of the more valuable deposits to the detriment of the low-grade deposits. The probabilities are that the effect of the excessive depletion of the deposit will be to shorten the life of the mine and to detrimentally affect its profitability towards the end of its life.'

The next year, Brown was the star of a powerful Granada documentary made by producer Laurie Flynn and shown on ITV, titled *The Case of the Disappearing Diamonds*. It found that De Beers had secretly stripped Namibia of R3 billion's worth of diamonds through overmining. Brown went on to appear in the BBC documentary *The Diamond Empire*, and became a central figure in an authoritative book on violations by southern African mining companies, called *Studded with Diamonds and Paved with Gold*.

But Brown was to pay a heavy price for blowing the whistle on De Beers, first with the reports he gave me, then by giving evidence to Thirion and finally by appearing in the documentaries.

An elaborate trap was set for him. He was asked by an acquaintance, a dealer in rough diamonds who turned out to be a police informer, to evaluate a parcel of diamonds on his next business trip to Namibia. Brown was given assurance that these were legal diamonds from Angola, and that the necessary permits had been issued and the legal requirements complied with.

The Diamond and Gold Branch of the Namibian police then pounced and arrested him on an illicit diamond buying charge. He was found guilty in court and sent to jail.

Brown claims he was denied the fundamental right to a fair trial. He says his conviction was based on the perjured testimony of a single state witness, a De Beers employee. This witness subsequently confessed in an affidavit made to Namibian justice department officials.

Shortly after his incarceration, Brown was released on bail pending an appeal hearing. He tried his best to get the police and justice department to investigate prosecutorial irregularities and misconduct, but nobody would do anything.

Brown says he then lost faith in the justice system in Namibia and decided to skip bail. He actually had to swim across the Orange River to his freedom in South Africa. He continues to work in the diamond industry in South Africa.

'As long as De Beers appointees sit on government regulatory bodies and their security people hold top positions in the Gold and Diamond Branch of the Namibian police,' Brown told me, 'no serious critic of De Beers can survive criminal charges from the police or De Beers themselves, and you certainly cannot expect a fair trial on such charges.'

That's what happens to you when you mess with Anglo American.

18

The struggle heats up

THE POSITION OF political correspondent at the *Sunday Times*, the biggest newspaper in South Africa, was considered a plum job in the 1980s. I also thought it was a pleasant job, but for the wrong reasons.

I was by now thoroughly disillusioned with South African journalism. The few progressive editors of English-language newspapers were nervous. Their owners didn't want to annoy the government too much, and they were more worried about losing white readers, and thus profits, than serving the truth. Apart from the odd critical remark in an editorial every now and then, the Afrikaans newspapers were solidly behind PW Botha's government.

There were two courageous newspapers: the *Rand Daily Mail*, which was closed down by its owners in 1985 for the reasons mentioned above, and *The World*, which was closed down by government decree. I remember the day *The World* was banned because of the news posters on the lampposts: 'Government closes down *The World*'. They would too, if they could, I thought.

My editor at the *Sunday Times*, Tertius Myburgh, was a charming, intelligent man who could switch from speaking Afrikaans like a Boer to a posh Queen's English. He liked the company of the captains of industry, cabinet ministers and diplomats, and they liked him. He revelled in his position as the most influential editor in the country, and laughed at offers from the government and the opposition of a top position in politics.

Colleagues gossiped about Tertius, even after his death, that he was 'a closet Nat', or even that he was in cahoots with the security police or Bureau of State Security. I didn't think he was much of an ideologue. He was more of a Machiavellian. His editorials, opinion pieces and political reports were all carefully considered to influence those in positions of power.

Tertius never ordered me not to pursue a certain line or stopped me from writing something. But he was very clear about the kind of political reporting that would fit into his scheme of making the *Sunday Times* the most influential voice. Instead of slashing my reports when he didn't like them, he would phone me and discuss the report in terms of political strategy. And then he would gently sculpt it into what he wanted it to be.

When it came down to the basics, he would support the National Party in a roundabout way, or praise them with faint condemnation. That way he remained, to the end, an insider with the *verligtes* in PW Botha's government. He even had the reluctant respect of Botha himself, because Tertius was always strong on 'national security'. But he never really alienated the white opposition either.

I never had a serious showdown with Tertius, but I hated what I was doing. My brief was mainly to cover the tricameral parliament, while South Africa's political future was being determined outside it. The fact that I had a proper salary, a generous parliamentary allowance and an equally generous expense account seduced me into staying. I lived a rather hedonistic life, spent mostly in style at my cottage on Bakoven beach, with Fridays and Saturdays at my parliamentary office.

The real political drama was unfolding in the townships and streets of South Africa, and to a lesser extent in Lusaka. The United Democratic Front had become a formidable, non-racial, mass-based force the like of which Africa had not seen before. The movement mobilised the ordinary people, urban and rural, like the ANC had never done. It was an alliance of 640 political, religious, sports, student, youth, community and civic organisations, and, of course, the mighty trade union organisation, COSATU.

The UDF launched a Call to Whites campaign in 1987 to welcome more whites into their ranks. Several organisations with mostly white members were affiliated to the UDF: the National Union of South African Students, the Black Sash, the Johannesburg Democratic Action Committee and Women for Peace. In 1989, the UDF affiliate Afrikaanse Demokrate was formed in my lounge. (I was a co-founder, but lost interest after a few months when members couldn't agree on a constitution.)

A certain amount of local autonomy developed within the UDF. A civic body or an area committee or even a youth club could interpret the movement's policies according to their own circumstances. Classlessness and a devolved power structure made for active participation by communities and individuals unknown to the struggle before or after. It was People's Power at its best.

Tertius Myburgh, like most white political commentators, and indeed the government at the time, viewed the UDF as the internal wing of the ANC – a sly move by the leadership in Lusaka to have a legal presence inside the country. It was a gross oversimplification, and one the ANC itself did nothing to dispel.

The two organisations had in common the Freedom Charter as their blueprint for a democratic South Africa, and the UDF did honour ANC stalwarts such as Nelson Mandela and Walter Sisulu as their patrons. But the UDF was not the initiative of the ANC leadership, nor was it at any stage its puppet. The UDF had much stronger participation from the religious communities than the ANC, and a much less powerful communist lobby. Church leaders such as Alan Boesak, Beyers Naudé and Desmond Tutu were among the most prominent figures in the UDF.

The most important difference was that the majority of the ANC's exiled leadership were completely out of touch with conditions and the mood of the people inside South Africa. Most of them had been in exile for a decade or more by then. Their experience was of Angola, Zambia, Tanzania, Mozambique and Uganda. Intellectually, the Cubans, Russians and East Europeans, who trained them, influenced them. Their armed wing, Umkhonto we Sizwe, played a very important role in their thinking and in their strategies. The ANC was also a far more secretive and authoritarian movement than the UDF.

Not that one should romanticise the UDF era too much. These were rough and bloody times, especially between 1985 and 1987. Many townships were indeed, as the slogan went, made ungovernable. Quite a number of black local councillors were murdered by the UDF's shock troops. Boycotts and strikes were enforced by sometimes very cruel means. 'People's Courts' meted out rough justice.

'No education before liberation' was a campaign that inflicted severe long-term damage on the youth. The youngsters who perpetrated the violence were called the 'comrades'. Later, when most communities were sick of their violent behaviour, they were often referred to as 'comtsotsis' – comrade *tsotsis*.

The necklace method of killing – a car tyre doused with petrol, hung around someone's neck and then set alight – was initiated during this time and used frequently. I witnessed the aftermath of one such killing, and saw two others on video footage, shot clandestinely. One never forgets it.

According to a white South African theory, necklacing became popular because of a primitive belief among blacks that if a person's spirit is not killed as well, the person can come back – only fire can kill the human spirit. I made a television documentary about necklacing years later, and established that no such motivation existed.

The poet and journalist Sandile Dikeni, himself a militant UDF youth leader during the 1980s, gave the only explanation that I thought made any sense. No one knows who came up with the idea of necklacing, but by the time the second one occurred, it was big news on television and on the front pages of newspapers. Dikeni says that's precisely why it became popular: through this terrible deed, the black youth felt that they were at last being noticed; their anger was finally acknowledged by society. And so necklacing happened again and again.

Of course, it did not help matters that the UDF leadership at the time did not immediately get up and loudly and repeatedly condemn the practice – Winnie Mandela once even appeared to encourage it, when she said that with 'boxes of matches' the country would be liberated.

The UDF leaders did in the end put a stop to it, and leaders such as Murphy

Morobe and Azhar Cachalia even risked the wrath of the ANC in order to condemn the all-powerful Winnie Mandela for her and her so-called Mandela United Football Club's outrageous behaviour.

Ten years later, Cachalia did not skirt this issue when he declared to the Truth Commission: 'Having looked at this question long and hard among us, we conceded that the language used by some of us from time to time could have provided the reasonable basis for some of our members to infer that violence or even killing was acceptable.'

Morobe added in his submission that 'we accept political and moral responsibility. We cannot say these people have nothing to do with us. We organised them, we led them.'

I have little doubt in my mind that this culture of violence in the 1980s is at least partly to blame for the overwhelming crime wave that hit South Africa in the period after 1990.

What I did know for certain at that point from my cosy front seat in parliament was that neither parliament nor the cabinet was running the country any longer. PW Botha's State Security Council, a body of generals, securocrats and selected cabinet ministers, did. They had unleashed an unprecedented repression on the population with a succession of states of emergency. Many thousands of people were detained, many activists were tortured, and some were murdered. But it took me a few years to get my own hands dirty and help expose how terrible it really was.

In 1989, I got hold of a weighty document with proposals on how to deal with the UDF, which was read by all the State Security Council officials. It was based on the 500-page PhD thesis of police general Stan Schutte, and titled 'A police analysis of the UDF'. He proposed that the different local structures of the Security Management System be used to improve social conditions in townships, and that SABC radio and television be used to communicate this to the population. Schools used by the black youth to 'create a climate of unrest' should be closed and the leaders detained.

The state should under no circumstances negotiate with the UDF or its affiliates or give it any recognition, said Schutte. 'It must be made clear to the community that the UDF as extra-parliamentary organisation does not have any right to political status or negotiating status.' And: 'No political compromises should be made with the UDF or its affiliates.' The document even urged that 'candidates who have expressed positive sentiments towards the UDF by way of negotiations with the ANC outside the country, should not be allowed to have parliamentary status'.

Almost to the end of the 1980s, the State Security Council followed General Schutte's line of thinking. Give the blacks better houses, water and electricity, and tar their roads to make them happy. And if they're not, beat the hell out of them.

The obvious solution, a political solution, was only considered towards the end of the crisis.

By the time white opposition politicians and concerned business leaders, and even the government and its security forces, realised that South Africa's internal turmoil would not disappear through more repression, it is ironic that they did not first turn to the UDF leadership for negotiations. Instead, they went outside the country to seek out the ANC's exiled leadership.

This was partly because of ignorance, partly because the UDF also claimed Nelson Mandela and other Robben Islanders as their leaders, who were all mainstream ANC, and partly because of the romantic myths surrounding exile and the armed struggle.

When the ANC was eventually unbanned in 1990 and the exiles returned to South Africa, the UDF was simply swallowed up. At the time of the twentieth anniversary of the UDF's formation, Alan Boesak said in an interview: 'Allowing the UDF to disband was one of my darkest moments.' He claimed it was disbanded under orders of the ANC leadership.

The exiles were too arrogant to even consider properly integrating the UDF into the ANC, or using the movement to introduce themselves to the people. The mass participation and devolution gave way to apathy and the centralisation of party power.

The demise of the UDF also meant the slow demise of non-racialism in the resistance to apartheid. Good comrades from the Cape Flats who had risked their lives for the UDF or sat in jail started feeling so alienated that they joined the party they had fought so bravely against, the National Party. I can tell dozens of stories of Indian and white South Africans who were active in the UDF who are today supporting the Democratic Alliance, or have simply become politically apathetic.

Today the ANC has very little support among the minority groups in the country. Non-racialism is all but dead. And far too many highly talented UDF leaders have been sidelined instead of being in top positions in the cabinet and civil service.

I had a strong sense during those days that we were seeing the final stages of the 'revolution', and that things wouldn't just quieten down before there was a major shift. But I thought it would take at least a decade or more, because from where I sat in the parliamentary press gallery, the Bothas and Malans looked intent on seeing the country go up in flames rather than compromise.

I was frustrated that I could not really get my teeth into these developments when I was with the *Sunday Times*, or even when I transferred to *Business Day* as their political correspondent in 1987. But I made the same mistake of thinking that the exiled ANC leadership was the only key, and every year in January I would make the trip to Lusaka for the ANC's annual press conference. My contacts with the leaders in Lusaka were better than my contacts inside the UDF leadership, even though my sentiments were with the UDF.

I got to know the ANC's media man in Lusaka, Tom Sebina, quite well, and had regular telephone contact with him. But from 1985 I started to get to know the rising star in the ANC better, and interviewed him several times: Thabo Mbeki. He was charming, sophisticated, well informed, and very friendly and cooperative. After every contact I had with him, I would return to South Africa and tell everybody who would listen: *Thabo Mbeki is going to play a major part in our future, and a better man you can't get.*

Mbeki knew how important the *Sunday Times* constituency was, and in an interview late in 1985 he used me to send out one of the very first, strong signals that the ANC wanted a negotiated solution rather than a protracted struggle. He said there would be no preconditions for the first meeting on talks about talks. Mbeki was flying a kite, and it worked – but that I only found out much later.

There were two influential and powerful men, in parliament, who felt the frustrations of spending their time and energy in that institution: PFP leader Frederik van Zyl Slabbert, and party chairperson Alex Boraine.

Slabbert was an icon to progressive young Afrikaners like me. A Polokwane boy from a broken home who shone as a brilliant student (and rugby player), and then as lecturer successively at Stellenbosch, Rhodes and Wits universities, he was blessed with a powerful personality, good looks and the sharpest analytical mind I have ever come across in politics. He was drafted into the PFP as a kind of Moses who had to lead the white opposition out of obscurity. In a way he did. (An Afrikaans magazine actually called Slabbert the 'Afrikaners' Mandela' recently.)

Boraine was the president of the Methodist Church of Southern Africa before entering politics. I got to know him personally when I had a relationship with his daughter.

Boraine had much in common with Slabbert: tall, handsome, strong-willed, highly intelligent and charismatic. The two of them made a good team. But for some, he didn't have the added attraction that Slabbert had: he wasn't an Afrikaner.

In fact, Boraine, the 'turbulent priest', was branded by the Afrikaans press as a *Boerehater*, someone who hated Afrikaners. My personal experience of Boraine over many years was quite the opposite: he had a real soft spot for Afrikaners. He came from a working-class background and spoke Afrikaans fluently. Probably because he knew and understood Afrikaners so well, he was able to put his finger on their selfishness and paranoia, which irritated the Afrikaner establishment no end.

Along with Boraine, two other prominent white English-speaking figures were branded as *Boerehaters*: former *Rand Daily Mail* editor Allister Sparks, and former *Business Day* and *Sunday Times* editor Ken Owen. I have well-developed antennae with which to pick up anti-Afrikaner prejudice, but I never detected it in these men, whom I knew well. The explanation is the same as for Boraine: they both spoke Afrikaans fluently and understood Afrikaners well. They therefore didn't hesitate, as others sometimes did, to sharply criticise Afrikaners when they deemed it necessary.

Slabbert and Boraine's frustrations with the white parliament came to a head in 1985. They were continually lied to about the military's exploits in neighbouring states, and generally felt that they had little impact on government's decision-making, while at the same time their presence afforded parliament some legitimacy.

In December 1985, Slabbert drew up a position paper that he shared with his fellow PFP MPs. It said that he was going to resign from parliament if the government did not give a clear indication 'that it intends restoring freedom of choice on a non-racial, non-ethnic basis for the purposes of participating in the constitutional, social and economic spheres of South Africa'.

Slabbert concluded: 'I am not prepared to carry on as before. According to my own light and wisdom I have done whatever can be done with the available opportunities and to continue as before I would be bluffing myself and others.'

Slabbert's idea was, I thought at the time, brilliant, and could have drastically changed the face of politics in 1986. He wanted his caucus to resign, and thus force by-elections in their constituencies. They would then ask their voters for a mandate not to return to parliament until the National Party committed itself to the ending of apartheid. 'I prefer to go out with a bang rather than to whimper along in the slipstream of the government's repression and incompetence,' Slabbert told his MPs.

Slabbert had no takers other than his friend Boraine, and the caucus believed that the planned resignation was therefore off. But Slabbert and Boraine had made up their minds.

It became the most difficult secret I ever had to keep. I was told they were going to resign at the end of the no-confidence debate a week after the start of the 1986 session of parliament, but their own caucus did not know. It was dynamite, but I could not tell a soul.

Half an hour before Slabbert's reply to the debate, he told his caucus he was going to announce his resignation. They were stunned.

That Friday I was the first journalist to take my place in the press gallery above the Speaker's chair. This was high drama.

The show opened with PW Botha's response to the debate. He was in top form, hissing and threatening and finger-wagging. His prime victim that day was his foreign minister, Pik Botha, who had recently publicly suggested that South Africa might one day have a black president. Pik was cowering in his bench.

Everybody was sitting up to hear Slabbert's take on the issue. He did not even mention it. He delivered a most devastating condemnation of the National Party and of the way in which they used the white parliament.

It was political theatre such as I had never seen before. It was a brilliant speech delivered with great conviction. The 170 or so MPs of all sides sat spellbound, as did the public and press galleries. 'In the course of the week I have tried to gauge my predominant feeling about the debate as it has developed,' Slabbert said. 'It was an overwhelming feeling of absurdity. Last year, in 1985, our country was torn apart. Things happened to our people which may never be mended … Parliament's reaction to 1985 in its first week of the 1986 session was, as far as I am concerned, a grotesque ritual in irrelevance. We carried on as if nothing happened.'

When Slabbert ended by saying he was resigning from parliament, I could see the shock registering in the eyes of Botha and his colleagues.

Slabbert had asked Boraine to delay his resignation in order to stabilise the PFP after the shock. But he had no choice but to resign himself a week after Slabbert.

The PFP caucus was livid, especially veteran MP Helen Suzman. She accused Slabbert of betrayal and of being unreliable. She said he was selfish and had simply become bored with parliament. 'The manner in which he quit was unforgivable,' she said. 'I don't think the captain of the bloody team walks off the field when the game is just starting.'

A member of the PFP caucus told me then – and I checked again before writing this book and he confirmed it – that Suzman said of Slabbert: 'What do you expect of a bloody Afrikaner?'

I love and admire Helen Suzman, and I think all South Africans should thank her for the way she stuck to her guns as an opposition politician through several lonely decades. But this time she was dead wrong. The 'game' she was referring to wasn't just starting, it was fast fizzling out. The real game was about to start, and the white parliament had very little to do with it.

I think even Slabbert and Boraine underestimated the medium-term effect of their dramatic departure. For many activists in the UDF and ANC, their resignations presented a ray of hope for an alternative to violent conflict between the white power bloc and the black majority. It seriously undermined the rigid distinction between 'parliamentary politics', meaning the orderly, constitutional place where all decisions were made, and 'extra-parliamentary politics', meaning crazed revolutionaries trying to overthrow the government by force.

The president of the ANC, Oliver Tambo, was asked by a British reporter at a press conference in Addis Ababa whether a man like Van Zyl Slabbert was really an alternative to the apartheid system – a man who had walked out of his own party, the PFP, not long ago.

Tambo's response was, 'Precisely. We trust him precisely because he did that.

He left the South African parliament because he came to the conclusion that no change can come through that institution, that apartheid racist parliament.

'To get out of the party,' Tambo said, 'and join extra-parliamentary forces of change, that is the only sort of change, a very correct move, and we have called on the rest of the members of the PFP to leave that body and join us to work for real change.'

Tambo referred quite respectfully to Helen Suzman and her three decades of hard work in parliament, then added: 'It is just that she is working through an institution that is not going to bring about changes.'

To the white electorate, Slabbert and Boraine's departure was advance warning that a new political drama would soon unfold. To those who still thought that the tricameral parliament was a solution, it was a signal that ethnic politics and the exclusion of the majority were dangerous.

For me it meant that I was stuck in a place that was even more irrelevant than before. I was becoming a very lacklustre political correspondent because my heart wasn't in my job. I had to get out.

The decision was made for me the next year.

Slabbert and Boraine had formed the Institute for a Democratic Alternative for South Africa (Idasa) after they left parliament. Idasa was holding workshops and conferences to build bridges between black and white and prepare for a democratic future.

Early in 1987, Slabbert called me aside at a conference we were both attending. He explained that he was planning a meeting between white, mainly Afrikaans-speaking opinion formers and academics from inside the country and the exiled leadership of the ANC at a venue in West Africa. He wanted me to come along, but asked me to keep it quiet because he feared that if the government heard about it, they might want to stop the initiative.

I had no hesitation in accepting. I was excited, because I sensed that this might be an event that could make a difference at a crucial time. Still, I knew that I could not participate in a potentially controversial gathering while I was the political correspondent of a newspaper. I would have to quit, and after the event find another job as a journalist. Or perhaps leave journalism altogether and become a full-time activist in one of the UDF structures.

Slabbert and poet Breyten Breytenbach were behind the initiative. Slabbert had negotiated Breytenbach's early release from prison when he was still Leader of the Opposition, and the two became close friends. Breyten was living in Paris and had developed contacts in West Africa, as well as with Danielle Mitterand, wife of the French president, who headed an institute called France Liberté.

In 1986, France Liberté organised a conference in Dakar, capital of Senegal, which included a music concert on Gorée, the former slave island. After the concert,

Slabbert and Breytenbach talked about taking a group of Afrikaners to Senegal for a meeting with the ANC. In Slabbert's words, he thought that 'the situation at home was screwed down so tightly that something like that could be a loosening-up event'.

Slabbert soon got the green light from Thabo Mbeki, whom he knew quite well by then, and the rest of the ANC leadership. Alex Boraine and Slabbert then had to finance the event, and were eventually given money by the international financier George Soros, the Scandinavian countries and the German Naumann Foundation.

On 6 July, the sixty invited participants went through passport control and customs at Jan Smuts Airport as individuals, stating that they were on their way to London. They came together for the first time in the lounge of the departures hall.

It was a real mixed bag of people: academics, economists, writers, artists, business people and theologians – politically ranging from middle-of-the-road *verligtes* to progressive, with a few on the left; quite a few heavyweights, but not quite representative of Afrikanerdom. Several prominent Afrikaners had declined Slabbert's invitation.

News of the venture had leaked out in the last few days before our departure. If the delegates had any doubts, the leaks confirmed that the government was incensed by the initiative.

Most of the group were very nervous: not only had they never been to Africa outside of South Africa's neighbouring states, they had never been remotely involved in anything clandestine.

But the nerves made way for excitement as we headed for London to catch a connecting flight to Dakar. The Dakar Safari, as it soon became known, was on its way.

The first glitch came when our Air Afrique aeroplane from London to Dakar could not be refuelled at Charles de Gaulle Airport outside Paris: the West African airline hadn't paid their bills. But after a while a solution was found, and we were on our way back to Africa.

Nothing could have prepared us for our arrival at Dakar Airport.

19

The New Voortrekkers

THERE WERE SOME very nervous Afrikaners sitting in the Air Afrique aircraft as it turned low over the lights of Dakar and approached the runway. Only a handful of them had had any contact with the ANC before, and they were struggling to contain their subconscious prejudices before the first contact.

The ANC was, after all, officially a Marxist socialist movement engaged in a violent armed struggle against the South African government. In 1960, the government declared the ANC an illegal organisation, and one could go to jail for a long time merely for being a member. White South Africans were brought up to believe that the ANC was 'the enemy': a dangerous group of communist terrorists.

When the doors of the aircraft opened, the hot, sweet West African air gushed inside. As we walked down the steps, I recognised some of the faces in our welcoming party: a grinning Thabo Mbeki, pipe in hand; the mysterious Mac Maharaj with his greying goatee; the big frame of Steve Tshwete, senior UDF figure until he skipped the country the year before; the tall, handsome frame of Essop Pahad.

We were nervous; they were excited. Mbeki rushed forward and hugged Slabbert, Breytenbach and Boraine. There was a lot of hugging, smiling and backslapping going on. Most of our party was in a daze – so this is the enemy?

Dakar Airport was the most chaotic airport I have ever been through, but the exhilaration of the moment made the heat, ineptitude and chaos tolerable. We got into a bus and followed the smart police motorcycles with their flashing lights into town and to the Dakar Novotel.

After breakfast the next morning, we were ushered to a square outside the hotel, where we walked into an amazing spectacle of colour and music. There were bands, drums, dancers, gymnasts, and people in costumes and masks; lots of energy and very loud. The ANC delegation was there, but also the two-metre tall figure of the president of Senegal, Abdou Diouf. A more spectacular welcome was hard to imagine – it was a reception fit for a visiting head of state.

Diouf formally opened the meeting in the hotel's conference hall. He was warm and strong in his praise for the 'New Voortrekkers' who risked their own government's wrath to make this bold trip. His message was one we were to hear over and over in the next few days: Africa sees Afrikaners as white Africans, and are prepared to welcome them into the bosom of the continent as soon as they got rid of apartheid, which Diouf stressed was a crime against humanity.

Slabbert's speech, appropriately, was much more low-key, and he emphasised the symbolism of the meeting. He echoed Diouf's sentiments by saying he hoped that the event would 'seize the minds of white South Africans by making them realise they are part of Africa'.

Then it was time for introductions. Each person had to walk on stage, say his or her name into the microphone, where he or she was born and what his or her position was. It took quite some time. In our group, among others, were political scientists André du Toit, Hermann Giliomee, Lawrence Schlemmer, Jannie Gagiano and André du Pisani; authors André P Brink and Ampie Coetzee; theologians Beyers Naudé and Theuns Eloff; famous rugby Springbok Tommy Bedford; PFP members of parliament Peter Gastrow, Errol Moorcroft and Pierre Cronjé; business consultant Christo Nel; filmmaker Manie van Rensburg; painter Hardy Botha; economist Johan van Zyl; labour expert Blackie Swart; free-market lobbyist Leon Louw; educationists Jakes Gerwel and Franklin Sonn; law professor Gerhard Erasmus; jurisprudence professor Louwrens du Plessis; professor of medicine Jacques Kriel; and veteran journalist Hennie Serfontein.

Then it was the ANC's turn: Kader Asmal, law professor at Trinity College in Dublin; historian Pallo Jordan, member of the ANC national executive; Lindiwe Mabuza, poet and ANC representative in Scandinavia; jurist Penuel Maduna; ANC Secretary for Arts and Culture Barbara Masekela; the editor of *Sechaba*, an ANC publication, and member of the NEC Francis Meli; philosophy lecturer, former Stellenbosch student and political prisoner Tony Trew; the Pahad brothers Aziz and Essop (born in Schweizer-Reneke); Harold Wolpe, ANC lawyer who escaped from a South African prison; Steve Tshwete and Mac Maharaj.

The last man on stage was the head of the ANC delegation and the ANC's Director of Information. He walked onto the stage, smiled broadly and said: 'My name is Thabo Mbeki. I'm an Afrikaner.' He brought the house down. His words certainly melted away some of the nervousness.

We settled down for three days of talks. There were some learned papers delivered on the political situation and the economy back home, but mostly the two groups just wanted to talk to each other.

One theme dominated from the start: the ANC's armed struggle. Actually, most, if not all, the delegates from inside accepted the armed struggle as a historical reality and as a response to the intransigence of the South African government. André du Toit, who emerged as the group's unofficial spokesperson, made it clear that there was great appreciation for the ANC's reluctance to engage in an armed struggle until 1960, and after that restricting their campaign to hard targets and sabotage.

But he voiced the opinion of most of his colleagues when he stated his opposition to the killing of civilians, the attacks on soft targets and the apparent lack of control over some guerrillas. 'Not only does it tend to frighten the more conservative groupings and the majority of whites politically into the National Party's *laager*, it also creates the kind of conditions in which the state can unleash its massive powers of repression with greater impunity and turn loose vigilante groups and reactionary forces to wreak havoc in local communities.'

Du Toit argued, with support from his group, that it was the ANC's responsibility to generate meaningful political initiatives to break the deadlock in South Africa, instead of providing 'a reactionary and destructive coercive showdown'.

The ANC leaders who dominated the discussion were Mbeki, Pallo Jordan, Mac Maharaj, Kader Asmal and Essop Pahad. They made it clear that they viewed the ANC's armed resistance as inevitable and morally sound. Jordan reminded the Afrikaners in the room that their ancestors, too, had used violence, in their case against British colonialism. I could see that remark hit the spot.

Just to remind us that we were actually talking about a very real situation, a powerful bomb destroyed part of the Witwatersrand Command offices in Johannesburg during our Dakar stay. The government responded that it was the ANC's way of thanking the whites for trekking to Dakar. The Minister of Police, Adriaan Vlok, immediately blamed the only known white Afrikaans operative in MK, Hein Grösskopf, son of a former editor of *Beeld*. Vlok had no proof and did not produce any. The temptation to blame a 'white terrorist' at a time when a group of 'white fellow travellers' was talking to the ANC was just too great.

The bomb was not the only reminder. During the same week, we received news from home that South African police agents had assassinated a rising star in the ANC and member of the MK High Command, Cassius Make, in Swaziland. Make had been a personal friend of some of the ANC delegates in Dakar.

The ANC said that they shared the concern about indiscriminate violence. It would be strategically stupid to kill white civilians while they were trying to win over white South Africans to the dream of non-racialism. They called attacks such as the bomb in an Amanzimtoti shopping centre, which killed five civilians in 1985, 'mistakes', and explained that it was sometimes very hard to control units of Umkhonto we Sizwe operating inside South Africa. They had little influence over acts of violence not perpetrated by MK. And, of course, they repeated the standard excuse that 'in a war, civilian casualties are regrettable but sometimes unavoidable'.

The discussions became quite intense. One ANC speaker suggested that the white delegation ought to support the armed struggle in principle. A white delegate said across the table: 'How can you expect me to support you if my wife or child could be killed by one of your bombs tomorrow?'

The Idasa delegation was also unhappy with the ANC's position on necklacing.

ANC delegates said that they had never called for it and did not encourage it. But they refused to publicly condemn those who carried out necklacings.

André du Toit summarised the Idasa delegation's position in a briefing afterwards:

I don't think they have answered this to our satisfaction. This concerns not only the proliferation of uncontrolled violence. It concerns the actions of all those people who claim to act on behalf of the ANC, whether or not they are part of an organised and disciplined hierarchy of political control.

What is happening more and more in the emerging civil war in South Africa are all the ambiguous cases, all these cases where it is not clear who should accept responsibility for, for instance, the bombing which took place earlier this week in Johannesburg. In that context I think what we are seeking from the ANC is a clearer statement: if they are in general, as they say, committed to an armed struggle not aimed at civilians, then, in these dubious cases, they must be prepared to take a clearer stand on repudiating and renouncing where civilians do become the victims.

The ANC leadership also made it clear that they would declare a ceasefire the moment they were convinced that the South African government was serious about finding a negotiated solution. But, they said, a unilateral cessation of armed operations would not be considered. It remained, along with internal resistance and international pressure, their strongest weapon to persuade the Botha government to negotiate.

By the second day of talks, it was clear that there were as many differences of opinion among members of the Idasa delegation as there were between them and the ANC. We had intense debates, and differed in view on sanctions, cultural and sports boycotts, the role of the Communist Party in the ANC, a free-market system versus strong state intervention in the economy, possible nationalisation of industries, and a future bill of rights.

The Senegalese government laid on another big reception for the two delegations with the country's best musicians and food fit for kings, and treated us to a guided tour of a giant flea market and a cloth factory. Wherever we went, you could hear the debates raging on.

By the third day, the favourite social activity of many of the delegates was both drinking a lot and making a lot of noise. A few bottles of ten-year-old KWV brandy that I had smuggled through customs as a peace offering proved very popular. There were many early morning moments of tears, nostalgia, singing, burning patriotism and eternal brotherhood. Alcohol, as was proved over and over in the next few years in South Africa, was an excellent political lubricant.

I was fascinated by what I saw happening in the room. I had met and even socialised with senior ANC leaders several times before in Lusaka, but this was very different. I wasn't wearing a neutral journalistic hat and I wasn't looking for a story. I was here as a South African and an Afrikaner who was deeply concerned about the future of my country and its people.

At the start, I suspected that the ANC leaders were a bit cynical and opportunist and didn't like the Boere much, but had to be sweet to them because the show was clearly good for the ANC's cause and image. There was indeed a measure of opportunism on the side of the ANC, but I watched tough, hard-nosed men such as Mac Maharaj, Steve Tshwete and Pallo Jordan melt before the sincerity and commitment of the white delegates and getting swept along with the significance of the moment.

(The one bit of 'opportunism' came from Maharaj. He walked with the aid of a walking stick, and the story doing the rounds was that he suffered from kidney damage after being tortured, and was on his way to Moscow for treatment. But it was a ploy to make the South African security police believe that he was sick, while he was actually planning a dangerous trip to South Africa as part of Operation Vula.)

I also carefully studied my own delegation as they sat around the table. A few of them – especially the writer and artist types – appeared eager to be accepted as comrades by the ANC. Some were bowled over by the warmth and openness of the other side, but at the same time they could not forget that they were talking to communists who were fighting a war. A few were a bit overwhelmed and slightly out of their depth. There were also the professional cynics who would not allow themselves to be moved by any emotion as vulgar as some of the stuff going on. And a number of the academics were intent on showcasing some of their learned models and superior wisdom.

But mostly the Idasa delegation struck me as deeply sincere, curious and eager to learn, and serious about making this exchange of views and ideas worthwhile. Theuns Eloff was an example. A minister in the conservative Gereformeerde Kerk, he probably had more to lose from his presence in Dakar than anyone else. He spoke and argued with great conviction and clarity, often taking on ANC speakers very directly. He was undoubtedly one of the big stars of the whole exercise. After Thabo Mbeki, that is.

The main event of the discussions was the 'coming out' of Hermann Giliomee. During the late 1970s and early 1980s, Giliomee had gained a reputation as an Afrikaner dissident, and moved from Stellenbosch to Cape Town University. But here he was, delivering a strong plea for a race-based solution in a post-apartheid democratic South Africa.

Giliomee called his concept 'bi-communalism'. He used the conflict between the Israelis and the Palestinians in the Middle East and the Catholics and Protestants in Northern Ireland as examples of how competing nationalisms should be allowed to coexist, rather than try to suppress each other.

Dirk Mudge, one of the leaders of the
Democratic Turnhalle Alliance

Foreign affairs minister Pik Botha and
Martti Ahtisaari, the UN Special Representative
in Namibia, January 1979

Anton Lubowski and Andimba Toivo ja Toivo on 11 September 1989,
the day before Lubowski was assassinated

Max du Preez, editor of *Vrye Weekblad*, December 1989

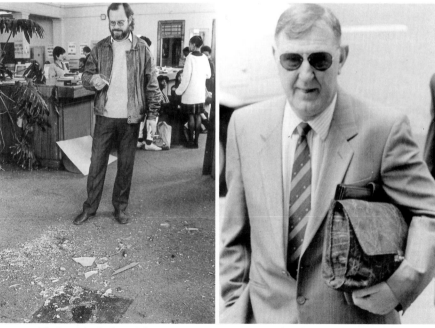

The bomb in the foyer, July 1990

General Lothar Neethling during the
Neethling vs *Vrye Weekblad* case

Max and Leslie Lesia, a paid agent of the CCB,
outside the Supreme Court, November 1990

Max and journalist Jacques Pauw

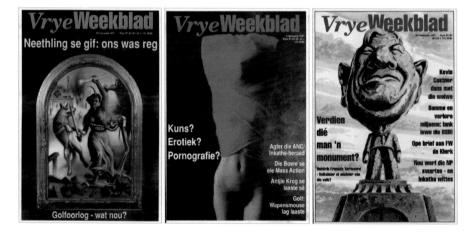

Covers from *Vrye Weekblad*'s inception in
November 1988 to its final issue in February 1994

Thabo Mbeki and Van Zyl Slabbert, circa 1991

Anton Lubowski's mother Molly holds up a
bullet-ridden picture of her son at the TRC hearings

Alex Boraine and Archbishop Desmond Tutu during the TRC hearings

The *Special Report* team: Back left to right: Jann Turner, Hanné Koster, Lienkie Biermann, Gail Reagon, Nantie Steyn, Max du Preez. Front: Anneliese Burgess

Max receives the Foreign Correspondents' Association of South Africa's
Award for Outstanding Journalism from Nelson Mandela

Cartoonist Zapiro's take on the two recent Max du Preez controversies

Whites, Giliomee said, would never accept an ANC government in a winner-takes-all system. Holding out for a victory for the revolution and armed struggle, or for sustained repression, would destroy South Africa. Instead of Afrikaner nationalism and black nationalism competing against each other, a system should be found wherein the two could coexist. Only that would assure a permanent peace, he said.

I was astounded. After three centuries of colonialism and forty years of apartheid, here was a progressive academic with an anti-apartheid reputation trying to sell a solution to the liberation movement that would not be a proper democracy; that would again keep black and white South Africans apart; that would again limit the rights of black South African citizens. It smacked of the 'own affairs' doctrine of the National Party's tricameral system.

I must confess that I never understood how Giliomee thought 'bi-communalism' would work in practice. Separate parliaments for white and black? A parliament with chambers for whites, blacks, coloureds and Indians? He didn't spell it out in Dakar. Months later, at a meeting at the Rand Afrikaans University, when I asked him how his system would differ from apartheid, he angrily refused to answer.

I don't know when and why (or if) Giliomee abandoned his idea of 'bi-communalism', but, after the 1994 settlement, he frequently accused the National Party of having sold out the whites and Afrikaners to the ANC by accepting a 'simple' democracy without guaranteed minority rights.

Giliomee's proposition wasn't well received – not by most of us from inside the country, and definitely not by the ANC. Some Idasa delegates criticised him sharply for comparing Afrikaners to the Jews, in effect equating Afrikaner nationalism with Zionism. Several delegates distanced themselves from his premise that a black majority would oppress minority groups.

But Giliomee's contribution proved extremely valuable. His position and his fears were much closer to how the majority of whites and Afrikaners felt than many of the rest of us in Dakar. Quite a few members of our delegation shared some of his views, but didn't feel brave enough to express them directly to the ANC. But fear of controversy was never one of Giliomee's weaknesses.

Giliomee's bombshell loosened up a lot of discussion around the possibilities of minority rights, protection of minority cultures and languages – especially Afrikaans – and a Lancaster House-type interim constitution.

But the ANC stood firm: a future democratic South Africa could not be based on race or ethnicity. Instead, they proposed a new constitution that would guarantee the rights of the individual, from which cultural and language protection would stem. They gave abundant assurances (with Pallo Jordan and Essop Pahad stressing the point by speaking in Afrikaans) that a future ANC government would not allow the Afrikaans language and culture ever to come under pressure. The debate between Giliomee and Jordan, both historians, was highly entertaining.

I found it interesting now, sixteen years after the event, to look back at the pieces I wrote on that Saturday 11 July 1987, which appeared on the front page of the *Sunday Star*, forerunner to the *Sunday Independent*. They were virtually the only positive stories to appear in the South African media about the initiative. (I was actually bending the rules a bit, because the talks were not open to the media. But I was careful not to mention names or be too specific.)

The historic workshop between a delegation of mainly Afrikaners and an ANC team ended here last night with both sides astounded at the extent of common ground reached in three days. They were enthusiastic about the impact it could have on the future of South African politics.

There was a strong feeling among delegates that the contact should go on and that more workshops be organised in future. Despite strong fears among the Afrikaner delegation of victimisation back home, they have openly come out in support of a non-racial democracy; they accepted the historical realities of the ANC's commitment to the armed struggle; and they see the ANC as a crucial element in any future solution in South Africa.

The man behind the talks, Idasa executive director Frederik van Zyl Slabbert, said last night that the workshop was definitely a worthwhile project in the quest for a democratic alternative for South Africa. It was certainly not, in the words of Dr Slabbert, just a 'gentle chat', but a real and tough debate on crucial issues such as political violence, the role of communists and the leadership role of the ANC in the struggle against apartheid.

The ANC had never so fully and comprehensively explained its stand on all relevant matters before.

One of the few ANC members who can still be quoted in South Africa, Dr Pallo Jordan, said last night the initiative was a resounding success and gave African nationalists new hope that the South African conflict could possibly resolved with relatively little bloodshed.

Earlier sharp divisions on the issue of violence emerged during the talks. Vital issues, such as the shape of the economy and how the ANC would govern after apartheid, were left in the air despite gruelling talks. Despite wide agreement on the desirability of a non-racial, one-man-one-vote democracy, the means to that end caused much disagreement.

The ANC officially rejected the government's invitation to blacks to elect members of the proposed National Advisory Council and demanded to lead the forces of opposition to apartheid.

Some Afrikaner delegates said an escalation of the armed struggle and bombings would make it all but impossible to get a significant number of whites to accept ANC leadership.

In a bid to protect the white delegates from possible reprisals, the ANC appealed to Western allies of South Africa, the US and West Germany in particular, to exert pressure on Pretoria to ensure that delegates are not victimised on their return home.

News from down south confirmed a campaign of vilification was being waged against the whites who trod the road to Dakar. President Botha denounced them for associating with the ANC, the SABC described them as 'political terrorists' and extremist Afrikaner organisations such as the Blanke Bevrydingsbeweging and the Afrikaner Weerstandsbeweging made threats of personal reprisals when they returned and urged the government to charge them with high treason.

One delegate received news from home that his young daughter had to be removed from her Pretoria school after being victimised by other pupils 'because her dad was talking to terrorists'.

In another piece I wrote:

More myths and prejudices have been exploded during the last three days in this West African capital than in many years, possibly even decades, of the South African conflict.

When the some four dozen Afrikaners and a few other South Africans arrived here earlier this week, they were greeted by 16 members of the ANC. But the smiles were rather plastic and the handshakes cold.

Yesterday morning the 65 South Africans were slowly emerging from their rooms for breakfast. They met in the hotel foyer. The cold handshakes had turned into warm African hugs. The smiles were now also in their eyes.

What happened between Wednesday and Saturday? Three mind-blowing, extraordinary days that will certainly have an influence on the course of South African history.

Three days which fundamentally changed the views and approach of most of those present at the conference.

It started with the overwhelming welcome by the people and government of Senegal. It could not have had a higher profile. It was treated as a full state visit, a happening such as Dakar had never seen. The Senegalese went overboard. An opening ceremony by the president, preceded by a wild welcome from tribal dancers and people in traditional dress; eight pages of news and pictures in the local paper, a state banquet in the presidential palace, a traditional sheep braai hosted by top government officials; white South Africans being stopped and welcomed in the streets of Dakar.

The message was clear to the white South Africans: we see you as Africans and we want to help resolve your problem, the isolation of white

South Africa has nothing to do with skin colour or ethnicity – only with the ideology of apartheid.

On Thursday the first discussions started on strategies toward a democracy. Some ANC delegates confessed afterwards that they had been stunned by the overwhelming acceptance of non-racialism. One by one the Afrikaners stood up and talked about strategy on how to get there – a dominee, academics, businessmen, writers.

The ice was melting fast, but as the two sides got more familiar, the questions became more honest, the statements more forthright and the tension was beginning to increase.

One by one the internal delegation started pushing on two issues that had the potential to blow up the whole exercise: the armed struggle and the role of the SA Communist Party. Mac Maharaj spoke with an astounding honesty and eloquence. By the end of the day he said that the questions were so fundamental and important that he wanted to consult with his leadership.

Friday morning. ANC crown prince Thabo Mbeki took the floor. The atmosphere was intense and for an hour Mbeki spoke – probably the most honest, direct and comprehensive explanation of the ANC's positions ever given to people outside the organisation.

Several Afrikaner delegates remarked later that if a transcript of his statements could be released inside South Africa, it would fundamentally change the understanding most whites have of the ANC.

Mbeki did not shy away from anything. He spoke freely about the ANC's concern with uncontrolled violence; the difficulties of controlling guerrillas inside South Africa; the role of the Communist Party; a negotiated settlement versus a transfer of power; the possibilities of a suspension of violence; the unhappiness of radical youth in the townships; attitudes towards other groups such as Inkatha.

The Afrikaners were stunned by his performance. Said one: 'Mbeki will make PW and Pik look like amateurs – and then he's honest on top of it.'

A prominent Afrikaner remarked over a beer: 'If I were God I would hand over government in South Africa to Theuns Eloff and Thabo Mbeki. They will sort us out.'

The friendlier the atmosphere, the more direct the remarks became. Several times arguments broke out about comparisons between Afrikaner and black nationalism. But in the end there was a reminder of the Afrikaner struggle for power as a model for the struggle against apartheid. Those who complained about the extreme rhetoric in publications of the ANC and over Radio Freedom were reminded of the revolutionary and fiercely nationalistic songs, poems and statements in Afrikaner history.

It was tough and it was tense. But not once was there any aggression.

The Afrikaners had stressed their appreciation of the sacrifices of the ANC members, and ANC delegates spoke often of their understanding of Afrikaner fears and the problems facing delegates when they go back home.

Thabo Mbeki bowled everyone over with his sincerity, sense of humour, intellect, clear thinking and straight talk, his charm and charisma. I had experienced his charm and diplomatic skills before, but this was a spectacular performance.

There were some clever commentators who later said that the ANC did not send their A-team to meet with us. But I did not think it would have been appropriate for ANC president Oliver Tambo to be there personally. It would also probably not have been a good idea to have Joe Slovo, a senior white MK and Communist Party leader, at this meeting. I did find it a pity that Chris Hani, senior military leader, wasn't present. It would have been good for him and us.

But, as for the rest, it was a senior team, seven of them from the ANC's national executive. Eight of the delegates became cabinet ministers after 1994, one became president, two became ambassadors and two became senior civil servants.

Before we went home, and after lots of consultation and a few arguments, the Idasa delegation issued a concluding public statement. Looking back, it sounds almost prophetic:

> We met with representatives of the ANC in Dakar because of our deep concern at the escalating violence and a drift towards authoritarianism in South Africa.
>
> The conference in Dakar was planned by Idasa, but the group consists of people from many walks of life, including academics, teachers, politicians, churchmen, farmers, architects, lawyers, writers, artists, journalists, students and businessmen. Most, but not all, are Afrikaners. What unites us is our total rejection of apartheid and minority domination and our commitment to a multiparty, non-racial democracy.
>
> We never imagined that we could negotiate with the ANC. We do not have the power, nor do we have a mandate to do so. We did not try to speak on anyone's behalf excepting our own. Indeed, we differed among ourselves on many key issues. What we do share, however, is a common belief that serious discussions with the ANC must form part of the search for the resolution of conflict and the transition towards a peaceful and just future.
>
> We believe that as a result of our conference in Dakar, we have demonstrated that such discussions can take place and that they can be constructive. We hope that what began in Dakar will continue inside and outside of South Africa and will eventually involve the South African government itself.
>
> In our discussions, we found that it was possible for South Africans,

who are in many ways far apart, to have frank and cordial exchanges on crucial issues facing our country. We agreed that we are all South Africans, that we share one country with a common history and a common destiny and that our commitment was to work towards a non-racial democracy which offers hope and opportunity for all.

In fact, there were many differences between ourselves and the ANC, particularly in terms of strategies towards change. Amongst the issues addressed and explored were the following: the ANC's historical commitment to the armed struggle as a response to state repression; the dangers posed by the proliferation of uncontrolled political violence from whatever source; the problem of white fears and Afrikaner cultural and language concerns; the serious obstacles to national unity as a consequence of entrenched ethnic, racial, economic and ideological cleavages; the importance of a bill of rights, an independent judiciary and a multiple party system to safeguard human and civil rights and to ensure a future political democracy; the need for distributive justice, the redistribution of wealth and concretely righting the historical injustices which have scarred our nation; the importance of economic growth as a determinant in planning a truly liberated economy.

We did not expect to find consensus on all these issues, nor did we. But the importance of these discussions cannot be underestimated.

We realised from the beginning that this initiative would be misunderstood by many. Also that the government would be highly critical and that our objectives would be misrepresented by some of the South African media. However our concern for our country, facing as it does a grave political crisis, outweighs the risks involved. We firmly believe that it is our duty and that of every concerned South African to explore every possibility to find a way out of the ever-deepening conflict in our country.

Finally we were greatly encouraged by the enthusiastic and warm reception we received from the President and government of Senegal. President Diouf's welcome and encouragement illustrate the readiness of black Africa to assist black and white South Africans in their common search for a non-racial democratic alternative to the system of apartheid.

The fact that the ANC was prepared to meet with a group of predominantly white Afrikaners is also cause for hope. The prevailing myth is that the ANC and Afrikaners are sworn enemies and can never meet except in conflict and on the battlefield.

We have experienced an openness and a readiness to talk and this will redouble our efforts towards a negotiated settlement rather than the inevitability of inconclusive and escalating violence.

Even more caucusing and consulting took place during the writing of a joint communiqué by the two delegations. Every word was weighed, because every word would later be scrutinised in Pretoria and Lusaka. It read in part:

> Although the group represented no organized formation within South Africa, their place within particularly the Afrikaans-speaking communities and the fact that they were meeting with the ANC, invested the conference with an overwhelming atmosphere that this was part of the process of the South African people making history. In similar manner, the international community focused its attention on the conference. Participants could not but be aware that some of the adherents of apartheid regarded the participation of the group as an act of betrayal, not only to the apartheid state, but also to the community of Afrikanerdom.

The communiqué further stated:

> The group listened to and closely questioned the perspectives, goals, strategy and tactics of the ANC. The main areas of concern arose over the ANC's resolve to maintain and intensify the armed struggle. While the group accepted the historical reality of the armed struggle, although not all could support it, they were deeply concerned over the proliferation of uncontrolled violence. However, all participants recognised that the source of violence in South Africa derives from the fact that the use of force is fundamental to the existence and practice of racial domination. The group developed an understanding of the conditions which have generated a widespread revolt of the black people and the deep resolve of the ANC.
>
> Conference unanimously expressed preference for a negotiated resolution of the South African question. Participants recognised that the attitude of those in power in South Africa is the principal obstacle to progress in this regard. It was further accepted that the unconditional release of all political prisoners and the unbanning of organisations is a fundamental prerequisite for such negotiations to take place.

20

The Dakar legacy

THE DAKAR TALKS made a great impact on the white delegates, and undoubtedly had an effect on the political climate back home. But an unexpected and equally significant development was the emotional discovery by the Afrikaner delegates that they were real Africans – and welcomed as such by Africa.

President Abdou Diouf of Senegal had made the point when he welcomed the delegation at the beginning of the visit; Thabo Mbeki and his colleagues repeated it; and ordinary Senegalese proved it through their interaction with the South Africans on the streets of Dakar. But the real African experience was still to come.

After the four-day workshop in Dakar, the two delegations became one South African group and boarded a ferry for the twenty-minute trip to the island of Gorée.

It is a small island, one can walk around it in half an hour or so. The first Europeans set foot on Gorée in 1444, and at different stages the Portuguese, the Dutch and the French occupied the island. They left an interesting collection of colonial architecture, now quite rundown.

From the little harbour we walked to the Maison des Esclaves, the House of Slaves. Built in 1770 by the Dutch, it is today one of the best-known international symbols of the slave era. For more than three centuries, Africans were hunted down, and hundreds of thousands of them were brought to this island and put on slave ships to the Americas.

The curator of the museum, Boubacar Joseph Ndiaye, first took us to the cells where the men were held: fifteen to twenty in a cell measuring 2.6 m × 2.6 m with a low roof. They were chained around their necks and arms, chains that Ndiaye showed us.

When the group moved on, I stayed behind in one of the cells. I sat down against the wall as the slaves once had. I closed my eyes. It was a feeling as intense as I had seldom felt before.

We went to the cells where the 'temporary unfit' men were kept – if a slave weighed less than sixty kilograms, he was fattened on beans like a goose, then shipped out. We visited the women and children's cells, where they were kept like sardines in a tin. Families were split up according to market demand; the father could be sent off to Louisiana, the mother to Cuba and the daughter to Brazil.

The sweeping double staircase in the centre of the slave house became imprinted in our minds, because it was something so aesthetically elegant and beautiful in such a place of horror. Hardy Botha subsequently used the staircase in many of his paintings and etches – it features on the side of the ox wagon on the cover of this book, for example.

The South Africans stood there in stunned silence. After an intense four days, this was almost too much. Apartheid cannot be equated to slavery, but man's inhumanity to man was in the back of all our minds. Here was where human beings' relationships started going wrong; the dehumanisation of black people that had started with slavery was still continuing in our country in the form of apartheid.

Then we walked down a narrow, dark corridor with a bright light at the end. The light was coming through a hole in the wall, probably a metre-and-a-half high and a metre wide. On the other side, the Atlantic Ocean was quietly lapping the rocks.

This was the Gate of No Return. This was the last the African slaves ever saw of their continent. They were pushed through this hole onto a loading dock and then onto boats that would take them to the slave ships. Escape wasn't an option; the waters were infested with sharks that fed daily on the bodies of the dead and dying thrown into the sea.

The vision of that hole in the wall will never leave my consciousness. To most of us there that day, seeing the Gate of No Return also meant that there was No Return for us, no going home and continuing as before. Witnessing this together, Afrikaners from inside South Africa and ANC leaders in exile, was an intensely moving experience.

I have been back to Gorée since. Only a sociopath or fundamental racist will not be deeply moved by the House of Slaves, but that first time was different.

The next day we boarded an Air Afrique Boeing and flew to a place few of us had heard of and nobody, at first, could spell or pronounce: Ouagadougou, the capital of Burkina Faso, the Land of the Upright People, formerly known as Upper Volta.

The welcome we'd received in Dakar had been quite outrageous, but this was completely unreal, totally over the top. Thousands and thousands of cheering Burkinabe lined the streets for kilometre after kilometre as our bus drove behind half a dozen outriders from the airport to the hotel. I have never seen anything like it before or since.

It was almost embarrassing, and we felt like telling them that they'd misunderstood: we were just ordinary citizens. But for days before our arrival, the good people of Ouagadougou had been told that a Boer delegation was going to visit with a group of comrades, and that this was an important blow to apartheid. Few of them knew anything else about South Africa and hadn't even seen anything about it on television, but it was remarkable that they felt that apartheid was also an assault on them personally.

Ouagadougou is a flat, brown city, and in its streets are thousands of bicycles and mopeds. It is a desperately poor place, but somehow it manages to portray dignity.

Our first stop was to attend a public tribunal in a huge enclosed stadium, where a dozen or so civil servants were on trial for corruption. There was a prosecutor and an advocate for the defence, but the public in the stand also participated. I remember that one poor soul's crime was that he had stolen the equivalent of twelve dollars. This, our guide explained to us, was how President Thomas Sankara dealt with the scourge of Africa. The next morning, we saw a large group of people doing physical exercises in front of public buildings. We were told that they were civil servants – the president had declared that too many of them were fat and lazy, and ordered them to do physical training every morning before work.

Our next appointment was to attend the laying of the first stone of an anti-apartheid monument in the city. Thabo Mbeki and Beyers Naudé did the honours. It was a simple stone structure, but the idea was that it would only be completed once apartheid had been eradicated.

A noisy crowd attended the ceremony. They were chanting in French, and all we could hear were the words 'apartheid' and 'Botha'. Someone explained that they were chanting 'Down with apartheid' and 'Put Botha on the stake'. This sounded a bit bloodthirsty to some of our delegation, and several expressed their unhappiness at being made to participate in such a scene. They also felt that Sankara, who'd assumed power through a military coup, was using our trip to further his own causes.

But the flamboyant president himself soon dispelled these fears. At a function in his humble official residence, he mixed freely with the South Africans. Late evening he invited us to join him and several members of his cabinet, including his deputy, Blaise Compoare, for a conversation on his verandah.

Sankara said that Burkina Faso would from this day on, by presidential decree, be the South African visitors' alternative homeland. The meeting between the two delegations in West Africa had been 'the most important act since Moses crossed the Red Sea with his people' the president said.

Sankara and his cabinet, all dressed in the beautiful traditional striped cotton attire, then sang some of their country's folk songs. It was beautiful, moving and very odd to be serenaded by a president and his cabinet. But what was even stranger still was that we then replied with a song of our own. Forty-odd Afrikaners singing the generations-old and traditional 'Sarie Marais' to the president and cabinet of Burkina Faso on the presidential verandah must rank among my most bizarre memories. It was quite a sight, and brought even the most pompous and self-important among our delegation down to earth.

But it wasn't even a proud rendition of 'Sarie Marais'. None of us could actually risk singing too loudly. We all had diarrhoea from either the food or water in Ouagadougou.

Next stop Accra, Ghana, where they had to change the law before we could be allowed in with our South African passports. What a contrast. Here the post-colonial decay had little dignity. Ghana was a lot wealthier and more modern than Burkina Faso, but the people, or at least the elite with whom we made contact, had not progressed nearly as far as the Burkinabe in decolonising their minds.

On our arrival we were met by a group of hostile, aggressive journalists who attacked the ANC delegation for associating with and trusting whites. If this was a test, Thabo Mbeki passed it with flying colours. Equally aggressively, he responded that the colour of one's skin did not determine one's political attitudes, and that his white guests were as African as the Ghanaians and he himself. In fact, he said, there were white people serving in the ANC's army.

We met with President Jerry Rawlings, but I was far more impressed with his wife. He acted like a testosterone-charged bantam rooster; she was warm and engaging, and knew more about South Africa than her husband.

Slabbert and Mbeki were at their best at an 'open forum' held in the state convention centre the next day. About a hundred intellectuals, officials and journalists fired questions at them, mostly in the same vein as the earlier press conference with its strong anti-white undercurrent.

And then it was time to go home – for us, not for our ANC compatriots. It was a sad farewell, with more than one ANC member asking us to kiss the South African soil for them, or to drive through Johannesburg and wave to the people on their behalf.

It was an exhausting trip, and we were keen to be home again and to share our experiences with family and friends. We craned our necks to look at Johannesburg as we came in to land, just as if we had been away for years.

But the homesickness quickly turned into bitterness and disillusionment. Security officials came on board and asked us all to get into a bus instead of going through the arrivals hall like the other passengers. It was for our own safety: AWB thugs in khaki and camouflage had virtually taken over the airport and were baying for our blood. Their posters and slogans accused us of being traitors, communists and terrorists, and called on the government to charge us with high treason.

We were taken to police offices on the perimeter of the airport, and only later were allowed to leave in small groups. We were angry, but it did prepare us for the hostile reaction we were to get from much of white South Africa.

We did see some of the press reports that were appearing in South Africa while we were in West Africa, but we didn't appreciate the extent and fierceness of the hostility and condemnation. The SABC led the vilification campaign, but a strong second was the newspaper group I had worked for until four years earlier: *Die Burger, Volksblad* and *Beeld.* They had their own correspondent in Dakar, Chris Koole, who dug deep to find negative stories to write and was quite bitter because most of us had shunned him. (He later became a press spokesperson for the National Party.) But even the English-language newspapers were critical, at most lukewarm.

We were crudely charged with being unpatriotic and disloyal to South Africa, and of aiding and abetting terrorists. The stories suggesting that the ANC had used us simply to promote their own image, increase their legitimacy and weaken the resolve of law-abiding South Africans to resist the revolutionary onslaught were subtler. We were the 'useful idiots' of the manipulative communists; they had sweet-talked us into believing they were peace-loving democrats.

I discussed this allegation with Professor Blackie Swart of the Stellenbosch Business School on the flight home. 'I have done enough hard labour mediation to know when I get taken for a ride,' he said. 'They felt about this like we did: it was a historic breakthrough and it bodes well for our future.' Tommy Bedford chipped in: 'This was like a tough rugby tour. There's no way these guys could have fooled me.'

It was an insult to people of the calibre of Van Zyl Slabbert, Alex Boraine, André du Toit and other heavyweights to suggest that the ANC had pulled the wool over their eyes. I had sat around the same table, witnessed the interactions and took part in the debate myself. Of course the ANC politicians put a positive spin on issues whenever they could and bent over backwards to be accommodating. But after the first day, I could see that they were also moved by the experience. I was convinced that what we had heard from them was pretty close to what they really felt and thought.

But we don't have to argue about it. I write this book nine years after the ANC took over the government of a democratic South Africa. The negotiation process and the way in which they have governed so far are completely in line with what they told us.

There's just one big unanswered question: What on earth happened to the charming, smiling, generous, warm, straightforward Thabo Mbeki we got to know in Dakar? The man who is today the president of South Africa does not possess one of the above attributes.

So what do I believe was the legacy of the Dakar Safari? I am surprised that the more respected books on South Africa's transition, such as those by Patti Waldmeir and Allister Sparks, hardly take note of Dakar. Perhaps that is due more to ignorance than bad judgement. Graham Leach, a BBC journalist who wrote a book on South Africa titled *The Afrikaners – Their Last Trek*, asked for my help when he wrote about Dakar. I gave him the full transcripts of the speeches and debates, and he interviewed several of the Idasa delegates.

He wrote in 1989: 'There was no major breakthrough towards peace; that had not been the object of the talks. But it was nevertheless a landmark. If one day the South African government does decide to negotiate with the ANC, it may only be possible because the Slabbert delegation, and others following, have paved the way. The mission to Dakar was the beginning of a process which will slowly make it acceptable and respectable for Afrikaners to talk to the ANC.'

Slabbert himself has always been very careful not to overstate the effects of Dakar, always emphasising the symbolism of the meeting and the fact that it countered the demonisation of the ANC in Afrikaner eyes and of Afrikaners in the ANC's eyes. 'The ANC discovered that Afrikaners have minds also,' he was quoted as saying at the time.

Several times after the Dakar meeting, Thabo Mbeki said that both groups had arrived in Dakar expecting the other side to have horns.

According to Breyten Breytenbach, Dakar was 'the beginning of the *ontdooiings-proses* [thawing process] that brought the road to negotiated settlement in sight'.

Slabbert remarked in his book *Afrikaner/Afrikaan*: 'The fact that the meeting played a significant role to launch the politics of negotiations and to legitimise negotiations with the ANC internally, only dawned on them and on us much later.' It 'secularised' the ANC of most of the stereotypes the government had created. 'It equally undermined the prejudices the ANC had about Afrikaners, especially the monolithic-brainless-pap-en-wors-bully-from-the-Bushveld variety.'

Fourteen years after Dakar, Kader Asmal, now Minister of Education, spoke at the farewell for Theuns Eloff, who was no longer a *dominee*, but the director of the powerful National Business Initiative. It was August 2003, and Eloff had just been appointed rector of Potchefstroom University. Asmal said:

I first met Theuns fourteen years ago when a group of Afrikaners travelled to Dakar to meet the ANC in exile. We have lived a lifetime in the intervening period, so much has happened.

A lot has been contributed by people like Theuns and his fellow comrades, if I may use the term more generally, who travelled to Dakar. If we look around at the Dakar class of 1987 we will see people from both sides of that delegation, from the President down, playing leading roles in public life in South Africa. That meeting, like a number of other events in our history, was a lever for change in South Africa.

I must confess that before then I do not think that I had met an Afrikaner who wasn't a special branch policeman or immigration official. It was a learning experience for all of us. Many of the Afrikaners who took part in that trip had considerable adversity to deal with on their return to South Africa. They had to deal with hell; they and their families were threatened and they were often ostracised by their friends in the community, but they stood their ground.

We have quickly forgotten the South Africa we left behind, or at least we have quickly moved on to a strong, non-racial democracy. This is due in no small part to that group of white, often Afrikaans, South Africans whose latent goodness flourished in the face of adversity.

In fact, Theuns Eloff's story is an example of the spin-off effects of the Dakar initiative. A former chairman of the student's representative council at Potchefstroom University, he was a Dopper [Reformed Church] minister little known outside his own circle when he went to Dakar.

After Dakar, his own church and some of his congregants, as well as PW Botha, who attacked him by name in parliament, singled Theuns out as a target. His life as a minister became so unbearable that he eventually quit and took over the leadership of the influential National Business Initiative (an association of progressive business leaders) from a fellow Dakarite, Christo Nel.

When the real talks between the National Party and the ANC started at the World Trade Centre in Kempton Park after 1991, Theuns became the head of administration and an active facilitator at the multiparty talks that resulted in a new constitution for South Africa. He is one of very few South Africans respected by all sides of the political spectrum. His current job is not his easiest: to transform the Potchefstroom University for Christian Higher Education into a progressive, non-racial institution serving all South Africans.

The Dakar initiative led to several similar meetings between internal delegations and the ANC. Business leaders had more than one meeting; progressive Stellenbosch students had a gathering in Maputo; and Idasa itself organised further meetings in Zimbabwe, Zambia, Germany, France and the US. Not one of these meetings provoked the hysteria of Dakar; in fact, it became quite a common part of the political landscape. And when the National Party itself started negotiating publicly with the ANC, the same people and newspapers that had called us 'useful idiots' welcomed it.

And that, in my opinion, was the value of the Dakar Safari and the reason why I think it should be regarded as an important moment in our recent history: within a few months after Dakar, only the right wing believed that the ANC should not be part of a future solution. Dakar triggered a new consciousness inside South Africa; a realisation that we have to find a different type of solution than the ones the government had come up with.

The Dakar initiative also sparked off a new progressive movement in Afrikanerdom, in music, theatre, art and the media. The full emotional realisation we'd had in Senegal and Burkina Faso, that we were full-blooded Africans, was spreading to young Afrikaners who refused to bow and scrape before the fathers of the *volk*.

A footnote: All of us in Dakar wondered who the spy among us was – operating under the suspicion that there always was one. I know that one of our prominent delegates gave a full written assessment of the talks to the National Intelligence Service. But we were not doing anything subversive, and as it was a good thing that the NIS were properly informed about the discussions, I'm not sure whether he actually was a 'spy'.

NIS chief Niel Barnard later told Nelson Mandela's official biographer, Anthony Sampson, that he had 'discreetly' supported the Dakar trip. He was either lying or he meant that by not preventing it from happening, which I suppose was in his power, he was 'supporting' it. Slabbert and Boraine, who organised the finances for the trip and the meeting itself, deny vehemently that Barnard or any of his officials ever did anything to help or even encourage the trip to Dakar.

Two years after Dakar, the same Barnard stood in the witness box of a Johannesburg court giving evidence *in camera* against me, describing the ANC as the enemy of the South African state and a threat to our civilisation. More about that later.

But in the end, the real spy did not come from the Afrikaner delegation – he came from the National Executive Committee of the ANC. Francis Meli, editor of *Sechaba*, was later unmasked as a long-time agent of the South African security forces.

PART V

The
Vrye Weekblad
Years

21

Going alternative

OUAGADOUGOU, 15 JULY 1987. A few of us were sitting at the poolside of the Intercontinental Hotel. It was hot and humid, and we were weak from two days of diarrhoea. We were also mildly depressed, because some of the news reports that had appeared in South Africa had been faxed to us. They reminded us of our diarrhoea.

I was loudly lamenting the state of the South African media, especially the Afrikaans newspapers. How would Afrikaners ever know what was really being done in their name by the National Party government if the newspapers did not start telling them?

'Well, what are you going to do about it?' asked Beyers Naudé, *dominee* in the NG Kerk who had broken with apartheid years ago and was ostracised, banned and demonised for it. Van Zyl Slabbert fixed me with a stare. 'Yes, you can't just moan about it. If you're that unhappy, do something about it.' The others nodded in agreement.

Do what about it? There was only one thing one *could* do: launch a newspaper that would have the idea of an open, non-racial democracy as its credo. In Afrikaans. But that would mean taking on the National Party government and the Afrikaner establishment, and probably getting into trouble with the security forces. It wasn't really feasible. In fact, it was madness.

Back home, after the hue and din of Dakar had died down, the Ouagadougou challenge came back to haunt me. Do I go back to journalism as if nothing had happened, or do I join one of the UDF structures as an activist, or do I actually take on *Oom* Bey's challenge?

I went to talk to Slabbert and a few like-minded people. Slabbert encouraged me, but he didn't think anybody would give me money for the project and warned me that I was saddling a tiger.

So I decided to go about it the 'proper' way: get a committee together to advise on the project, consult stakeholders, get mandates – all that boring struggle crap. There was great enthusiasm for an alternative Afrikaans newspaper among the assembled committee, but little enthusiasm for my participation. We had meeting after meeting, which I mostly had to finance out of my own pocket. They talked in circles, and mostly behind my back. (I decided not to embarrass the members of this committee by naming them.)

After several months of talking and bickering, I forced the issue. At last I was told what the problem was. They didn't think I was the ideal candidate to be the editor. They said they wanted someone more acceptable to the Afrikaner establishment, and I came from English newspapers. Also, I was too young. (I was thirty-five at the time.) Later I found out that some of them had thought I was too radical; one said I was too abrasive; another – a prominent academic – expressed the opinion that I was most likely a spy for the security police.

'Who then?' I asked them. Finding a job for me wasn't the priority; launching an alternative Afrikaans voice was the issue. But they didn't know, although one did come up with the name of Jan Spies, editor of the DTA newspaper in Namibia, *Die Republikein*. I had to laugh. Not only was Jan, a dear man and a friend of mine, not a South African, he would also be considered a *verligte* Nat in South Africa. He had spent the last ten years fighting a propaganda war against SWAPO.

I realised my committee's vision of what was needed radically differed from mine. We did not need a gentle, *verligte* mouthpiece for the Progressive Federal Party. We wanted a kick-ass publication that would show apartheid and all its practices for what they really were; that would investigate without fear or prejudice; that would let all the muzzled voices be heard; that would stimulate a new progressive Afrikaans culture. Afrikaners had had enough sugar coating.

I understood enough about media politics in South Africa to know that it would be stupid to go for a mass circulation paper – for that, we would have to compromise too much on our politics in order to be acceptable to the market, and the message would be lost. We didn't have the money for a big staff or massive print runs; we would never be able to afford big marketing budgets; we would probably not attract much advertising with the kind of message I was hoping we would bring; and the big guys in the business would crush us if we became serious opposition. We didn't need to be big capitalists; we needed to be media guerrillas. We needed something that would be very different – a catalyst rather than a mass circulation paper.

My friends in the committee didn't understand this. They thought we should publish *Huisgenoot* magazine with a column on democracy tucked in somewhere.

So I gave them an ultimatum: they could continue as a founding committee and find someone to drive and finance the project, but if they hadn't done anything in a month's time, I would do it myself. I never heard from them again.

I was on my own, it was several months later and I'd spent a few thousand rand on aeroplane tickets. I also needed to make a living. Two people supported the project through these times: Van Zyl Slabbert and Abraham Viljoen, farmer, theologian, part-time Idasa official and twin brother of the head of the South

African Defence Force, Constand. In the later stages of preparation, I worked from Braam's Idasa offices in Pretoria while staying with my sister.

By now I had no doubt that this newspaper should happen. Braam Viljoen came up with the obvious name for the new newspaper: *Vrye Weekblad*. When he said the name, I knew it was right. *Vrye* means free and independent, and *weekblad* simply means weekly journal.

I then did what I should have done from the start: I got journalists involved. Elsabé Wessels was the first, and became a formidable force in making the newspaper a reality. Like me, she had worked for *Die Burger* and later the *Sunday Times*, and, like me, she was frustrated and dreamt of being a journalist who could once again write in her own language without having to support the government's apartheid policies.

A young state prosecutor from Cape Town whose sister I dated at the time, Karien Norval, was so excited about the concept that she moved to Johannesburg to be the manager and coordinator, and do whatever else needed to be done. (Karien later became our lawyer.)

Elsabé and I started assembling a small team of journalists. We could not offer them competitive salaries, long-term employment, a pension fund or health benefits. We could only offer them a rough, exciting ride and the opportunity to be pioneers – and to serve the cause of a non-racial democracy.

We couldn't have found better people even if we had offered great career prospects. Chris du Plessis was an unorthodox, creative, gifted writer on music and the arts. Koos Coetzee was a somewhat antisocial genius and a brilliant sub-editor who had been at university with me. Victor Munnik was a talented writer and thinker, and a gentle soul with a great passion for the environment.

I think that Van Zyl Slabbert, by this time, had grave doubts about the project. But – may God bless his soul – he hung in there right to the end, even when we acutely embarrassed him with some of our antics. He and I went to see rugby boss and fertiliser/beer millionaire Louis Luyt, who had just had a falling out with the National Party. He was polite, but he knew what was good for business and never reached for his cheque book. Van Zyl eventually did get some seed money from a foreign source; I can't even remember who it was.

We went around Johannesburg looking for very cheap office space. Then we discovered, almost as if by divine intervention, that the beautiful old Standard Bank building in rundown Newtown on the edge of Johannesburg's central business district had been standing empty. We rented it straightaway, I think for R1 500 per month. (The building is now the head office of the National Union of Mineworkers.)

It was a good place to be: around the corner from the blossoming Market Theatre precinct in an area where apartheid didn't really apply. As importantly, across from the Market Theatre was the Yard of Ale, a restaurant and watering hole run by an old acquaintance. It was to become our second office.

I was sitting in the Yard when a clean-cut young Afrikaner came up to us and introduced himself. He said he was working for *Huisgenoot* magazine, but wanted to be a real news reporter again and do investigations. His name was Jacques Pauw. Elsabé, Jacques and I became the core of the news team, with Chris in charge of the arts pages and Koos the chief sub.

We found some desks and chairs in the building we were renting, broke down the partition that used to separate the bank tellers from the customers, and used the wood to make a huge table for editorial meetings.

Now we only needed computers. It was the beginning of the era of desktop publishing, and the only reason why starting up a publication such as this one was possible in the first place. At a fraction of the prices at the time, we got someone to build seven PCs from assorted parts, mostly made by a nameless factory in Taiwan.

But we still could not afford a more powerful, sophisticated computer with which to do the desktop publishing. Then we had a breakthrough: the Canadian embassy, which remained sympathetic right to the end, gave us R75 000 for computers. I cashed in my insurance policies and pension and sold my paintings, and with the Canadian money we were ready to go. Much later we also received money from the Dutch anti-apartheid NGO Komitee Zuidelijk Afrika (KZA) and the Scandinavian governments for the training of new journalists, but they knew we used a lot of it to pay distribution and the printers. Elsabé's contacts in the diplomatic world saved us from giving up before we'd even started. After our second year, the European Union became our biggest financial benefactor.

I formed a company called Wending Publikasies Ltd, which would act as the publisher. I approached a small Afrikaans venture capital group in the hope that we could publish a prospectus and entice shareholders, but it was soon clear that this was never going to be a substantial source of finance.

To limit the potential risks to others, I remained the nominal owner of Wending Publikasies Ltd, and thus *Vrye Weekblad*. But, in practice, it was understood that the paper was jointly owned by all who worked there, and that our editorial board would in effect be the board of directors. Our board consisted of Van Zyl Slabbert, rebel Stellenbosch economist Sampie Terreblanche, business consultant and fellow Dakarite Christo Nel, progressive Johannesburg entrepreneur Chris Otto and myself.

We were planning to publish the first edition in July or August 1988, but it wasn't possible. So we aimed for the first Friday in November.

Our timing wasn't very good. Black and English-speaking journalists who shared our dreams and frustrations had established three other 'alternative' newspapers in South Africa by mid-1988. Journalists from the defunct *Rand Daily Mail* pioneered the *Weekly Mail*; jailed ANC leader Walter Sisulu's son Zwelakhe was the editor of the *New Nation*, a paper close to the ANC; and *South* was published in Cape Town.

South was closed down by the government between May and June that year, *New Nation* from March to June, and the *Weekly Mail* for the month of November.

We could go the same way, we thought, but we bargained on two things: that the National Party would hesitate to close down an Afrikaans-language newspaper, perhaps simply out of fear that it would make us appear more important; and the fact that there was massive external pressure on the government to stop banning newspapers after the closure of the *Weekly Mail*.

We were right, but we didn't bargain on another, far more effective strategy the government would use against us.

The weeks before the launch were utterly chaotic. Starting a publication from scratch was much more complicated than we'd thought – we were mere journalists, after all. Elsabé and I abandoned our efforts to find advertising for the first edition, because it was clear that nobody was even going to contemplate touching this strange new animal with a bargepole before it showed its true colours. (Of course, once they saw what we were all about, they *definitely* didn't want to be associated with us.)

There were only seven of us to do all the preparatory work (and get stories to run in the first edition), and we literally worked twenty hours a day. We had to organise printing, distribution, telephones, fax machines (it was the time before the Internet), bank accounts, freelance contributors, etc.

It was nerve-wracking and tempers flared quite often, but at the same time we sensed that we were doing something really worthwhile – in a small way, making history.

Vrye Weekblad wasn't going to be the first 'alternative' Afrikaans publication: before us there were *Veg, Ster, Die Afrikaner* and *Patriot*. But they were all published by the extreme right wing and were started by politicians, not journalists. Only *Die Afrikaner*, mouthpiece of the Herstigte Nasionale Party, and *Patriot*, mouthpiece of the Conservative Party, existed for any length of time.

Vrye Weekblad would be the first anti-apartheid newspaper in the history of the Afrikaans language. The magazine *Die Suid-Afrikaan*, founded by Hermann Giliomee and later run by André du Toit and Antjie Krog, was also critical of apartheid, but it was a quarterly journal of opinion and analysis with a rather academic approach. As I said in an interview at the time: '*Die Suid-Afrikaan* has good manners, *Vrye Weekblad* doesn't. *Hulle sê* pardon, *ons sê vlieg in jou moer*' [They say pardon, we say go to hell].

Three weeks before the launch date, we remembered that we were legally obliged to register the newspaper. A nominal deposit of R10 was required in those days. The reason for the registration was merely to have the owners of the new publication on record with their address and telephone numbers. We duly filed the necessary papers, and thought nothing of it when we didn't get a response before 4 November.

The evening of 3 November 1988 is forever etched in my mind. After all the pain and blood and guts, our small team was at the printers. The deep, low thunder of the printing press, the vibrations you feel under your feet and the smell of fresh printer's ink would become a part of my life for the next few years, but it never lost its magic.

The winding snake of freshly printed newspapers rolled towards us, and we grabbed the first few. Through the tears in my eyes I could see the tears in my colleagues' eyes. Our dream had become a reality.

With our primitive equipment and mad rush to meet the first deadline, it wasn't exactly a good-looking front page. To me, at that moment, it was the most beautiful thing that had ever appeared in print.

Below the red masthead we proclaimed '*Die Nuwe Stem vir die Nuwe Suid-Afrika*' – 'The New Voice for the New South Africa'. (When FW de Klerk stole the 'New South Africa' bit just over a year later, we changed it to '*Onafhanklik, Onverbonde, Onverskrokke*' – 'Independent, Non-Aligned, Fearless'.)

Our front-page lead headline read: '*Mandela: 'n Nuwe Era*', written by and Jacques and myself. The story didn't contain much new information, but we wanted to tell our constituency that South Africa stood on the brink of a dramatically different time. The time of white rule and repression was almost over, and they'd better get used to a man called Nelson Mandela and the politics of negotiation. (Mandela was only released fourteen months later.)

We also speculated about the debates in the cabinet and State Security Council, about whether and how Mandela should be released, and made the point that releasing him without unbanning the ANC and SACP at the same time would be a dangerous farce. And we quoted a wide range of community and political leaders, including the Conservative Party and the AWB on the role Mandela could and would play after his release. Only Beyers Naudé seemed to grasp the real potential of a free Mandela: 'He will be the most important bridge builder between black and white in South Africa.'

I wrote in the editorial:

People close to the state president say it is important for him in this last part of his public life to do something that would make history remember him as a statesman. We can understand that. We cannot think of any better step the state president can take than to release Nelson Mandela.

But then it has to be now, and it has to be unconditional. And his Rivonia friends such as Kathy Kathrada and Walter Sisulu should also be released unconditionally. To ban them after their release like the government had done with Govan Mbeki will be a huge mistake. In Mandela's case it could actually lead to dangerous levels of bitterness.

With Mandela a free man, South Africa will be able to start walking the road to normality and democracy. Mandela's role as a potential force for reconciliation should not be underestimated.

He looks like the one man who could take the black population – including the radicals – with him on the road to reconciliation and national unity, while at the same time allaying white fears.

It will probably be a rocky, uphill road, but the reward is great: peace and prosperity.

But then PW Botha and the State Security Council will have to talk to him when he walks free. South Africa might never get a chance like that again.

Elsabé, who had just attended another meeting organised by Idasa between white opinion leaders and the ANC leadership in Leverkusen, Germany, took the front-page picture. It showed two Afrikaner leaders who had just left the National Party for the new Democratic Party, Sampie Terreblanche and Wynand Malan, sitting next to a smiling Joe Slovo, leader of the Communist Party and top MK commander. Elsabé also wrote about the conference on the middle-page spread.

(A few months later, the National Party used the photograph on their election posters and in newspaper advertisements to discredit the Democratic Party. It gave us great joy to get a late-night urgent interdict against the party on the grounds that we had copyright on the picture and they never asked permission to use it. The NP had to take down all their posters, and in the full-page ads in the newspapers the day after, they had to leave the space where the picture was blank, with an explanation that it was *Vrye Weekblad*'s picture. We could never have afforded that kind of advertising.)

We also published our credo in the first edition, in which I stressed our independence: we didn't have any ties or special loyalties to any political grouping, nor did we belong to a big company. Our only loyalty was to the people of South Africa. That was why we could supply citizens with information they could trust, and for Afrikaans-speakers that had become a rare commodity.

'We say: to hell with the Total Onslaught that is being manipulated to keep South Africans in the dark. Afrikaans speakers are not children and they are not stupid. We have a right to know what happens in our country and what our rulers and fellow citizens do and think.'

We promised to reflect the views of everybody 'from Eugene Terre'Blanche to Oliver Tambo', but we did also have a basic philosophy: 'We believe in an open, non-racial democracy; the rule of law; basic human rights like freedom of speech and association; the rejection of all forms of violence; free enterprise without exploitation; negotiations, reconciliation and national unity; and responsible, effective and clean government on all levels.'

We did not believe in losing:

> We don't believe it's in the interest of the Afrikaans-speakers to define themselves out of the majority like Ian Smith in Rhodesia was doing. Too many of Smith's 'white minority' are today in South Africa, and they are hardened, embittered racists. It is not in our or anybody else's interest that we be classified as a minority, with special privileges that would only last a few years anyway and would only perpetuate other South Africans' suspicions.
>
> Afrikaans-speakers have exactly as much right to Africa and South Africa as black Africans and South Africans.
>
> It must be clear by now that we are unashamedly Afrikaans. We probably read the history very differently than Eugene Terre'Blanche, but we are equally proud of it. We love Afrikaans as the youngest African language very much and will do our best to forward its cause – also to free it of the stigma which decades of white rule had given it as the language of the oppressor.
>
> For us there is no conflict between being completely Afrikaans and being against white domination. We believe with others that Afrikaner nationalism was the first form of organised anti-colonialism in Africa and that we are Africans in our blood and in our hearts. In fact, we want to see the proud Afrikaner tradition of an uncompromising struggle for freedom and justice live on.
>
> At the same time we believe racism is a greater danger to peaceful co-existence in South Africa than communism, or any sort of 'ism' or onslaught or threat.
>
> Although we strongly believe in classic liberal values such as freedom of the individual, we are not a bunch of liberals. We are South African nationalists.
>
> As we prepared for our first edition, we saw signs that certain English-speaking elements view us as 'cute' and 'liberated' Boere, and that certain black elements are waiting for us to undermine the 'Afrikaners'. We have a surprise for them.

I ended the credo by explaining why we had chosen the name *Vrye Weekblad*:

> Because we are free of ideologies; free of propaganda and slogans; free of narrow inhibitions; free of manipulation by state presidents, cabinet ministers, Broeders, generals and big capitalists – free to say to the modern

Afrikaans-speaker: read and decide for yourself. As our motto says: 'We conceal nothing.'

We had a launch party that Friday. The guests were mostly diplomats and UDF politicians, including a few friends and almost the entire Afrikaner left of Johannesburg (it was a small party). A few minibus taxis stopped outside, and out popped a Soweto women's choir. I still don't know whose idea it was or who invited them (they claimed they came of their own accord), but it was just perfect. We partied well into Saturday morning. On Sunday morning, it was back to work.

In our second edition, we reported on the back-stabbing in the National Party cabinet. 'At the heart of the problem was frustration with PW Botha's poor leadership. His bombastic and dictatorial style is breaking his cabinet apart,' we wrote.

Jacques interviewed a young Conservative Party leader, Pieter Mulder, who said his party believed the homeland system should be expanded to also include a homeland for coloured people.

I wrote a piece under the headline 'The Grammar of Racism' about the official *Dictionary of the Afrikaans Language*, a massive work of several volumes, printed by the State Printer. For decades, I wrote, Afrikaners said that apartheid was actually a fair policy of separate development and wasn't based on racism. It is generally accepted that a language reflects the soul of a people, I said, and then pointed out that twelve pages of the dictionary, 303 words in all, were devoted to the word *kaffer*, the derogatory name for black people.

The dictionary notes twenty-two other meanings for the word 'kaffir', such as '*stinkasem*' [stinkbreath], '*houtkop*' [woodhead], '*swartgoed*' [black thing], '*kroeskop*' [peppercorn head] and '*Gamsgeslag*' [Ham's people].

When you call someone a 'kaffir', the dictionary states, you mean that he is 'an uncivilised, uneducated, ill-mannered, rough person'. But, it could also be 'a fictional person used to scare children'. 'Kaffir' can also be used as a prefix to depict something inferior: a 'kaffir dog' is a mongrel, 'kaffir sweets' are cheap sweets of inferior quality 'like those manufactured for the Kaffirs'. An example of an old edition of *Die Burger* is used to explain the use of the word: 'You get three types of students: the good ones, the bad ones and the kaffir-bad ones.'

It borders on the bizarre. 'Kaffircourtship' means 'lovemaking in the kaffir way, in which the lover hurts/bullies the girlfriend in a playful manner, for example by pinching her or beating her with a light cane'. 'Kaffirwork' means work regarded as beneath the dignity of whites. But a 'Boerkaffir' was 'a kaffir of good character'.

In the second edition, Jacques wrote that PW Botha and his foreign minister, Pik Botha, had had lunch with the notorious Mafia boss Vito Palazzolo. He based his story on an affidavit that an accountant, Clifford Bentley, had made to the Harms Commission of Inquiry, but which was kept secret.

Mark Swilling, a young Wits University academic who attended the Leverkusen meeting, wrote an opinion piece on the debate around the 'national question' at the conference. He reported that Hermann Giliomee had repeated his 'bi-communalism' theory, and wrote: 'Joe Slovo rejected the two-nation thesis, arguing that South Africa should be understood as a special kind of colonialism. He said that colonialism had created a ruling settler class in South Africa that uses a series of racial and ethnically based mechanisms to divide and rule the black majority.'

And then the shit hit the fan.

I was charged under the Internal Security Act that prohibited quoting a banned person – in this case Slovo.

PW Botha sued *Vrye Weekblad* for defamation for reporting that he had had lunch with a Mafia boss. He demanded R100 000.

The Minister of Justice, Kobie Coetsee, warned me in an official letter that he was of the judgement that *Vrye Weekblad* was going to be used to 'disseminate the opinions of illegal organisations' and so stir up a revolutionary climate in the country. He informed me that he was considering banning the newspaper under the provisions of the Internal Security Act of 1982. The Act excluded recourse to the courts.

Years later, I saw the report by two senior policemen, General Basie Smit and Major W van der Westhuyzen, who were tasked to investigate us and report to Coetsee, and on which the minister based his opinion. The report, marked 'secret', advised: 'The influential awareness-raising role which the *Vrye Weekblad* plays and may play among the targeted Afrikaans-speaking market should not be underestimated. The degree of publicity, particularly of discussions with the ANC, in the first two editions indicates the future political approach.'

In another 'secret' document on 'the legal options open to punish *Vrye Weekblad*', Colonel AZB Gouws reported to the minister: 'Declaring the newspaper an illegal publication in terms of the Internal Security Act or seizing it in terms of the state of emergency regulations, could possibly be challenged successfully in court.' But, the colonel wrote, the editor could be sent to jail for six months for publishing the newspaper before the minister had granted registration, and he could also be charged with publishing a picture of Mandela and publishing the words of a banned person. The colonel added that he would discuss the possibilities with the local Attorney-General, Advocate Klaus von Lieres und Wilkau.

I took our lawyer, David Dison, with me to see Coetsee in his office. We sat down around a table and, like good Afrikaners, first exchanged niceties about the weather and our families (Coetsee knew my father). I treated him like an uncle, and even said that I was sure he and I had the same dreams for our country and our people – our methods were just different. I asked him to reconsider his threat to close the newspaper down, assuring him that we had no intention of undermining the security of the state.

The meeting was pleasant enough, but Coetsee didn't say much. Two days later, his office informed me that the minister was prepared to provisionally register the newspaper – if we paid a deposit of R30 000 instead of the usual R10. It was the highest deposit ever demanded of a newspaper by the government.

We issued a public statement, which we sent to Coetsee and published in the 2 December 1988 edition:

> We believe the Minister of Justice's decision was unreasonable and out-rageous. *Vrye Weekblad* has shown since its first edition on 4 November that it was a balanced, responsible newspaper with the interests of all South Africans at heart.
>
> It is clear to us that the government is very sensitive that an Afrikaans newspaper for a change writes straightforwardly on issues such as mal-administration, ineffective government, the crippling divisions in the cabinet and the consequences of the government's racial policies.
>
> The government's attitude is further proof of their arrogance. If the minister had considered our oral and written submissions reasonably, we believe he would have asked for the standard R10 deposit. The amount of money the minister wants is a blow to our company. The government knows that we are a new and small company with no support from big capital.
>
> We cannot be blamed if we called the government's attitude a low-intensity war against *Vrye Weekblad*.
>
> We believe in what we are doing. We believe Afrikaans-speakers have a right to know what is going on in the country and the government.
>
> We are not going to break the law, we will not be a mouthpiece for any-body, and we are not going to stir up a 'revolutionary climate' in South Africa.
>
> But we shall not shy away from our duty as professional journalists and responsible South Africans.

In the same edition we published a cartoon depicting 'PW Botha's New Cabinet'. It was a drawing of a wolf with the caption 'Minister of Chickens', a cat was 'Minister of Mice', a crocodile was 'Minister of Goats', and then there was a drawing of Kobie Coetsee, 'Minister of Justice'.

On the same day, two police officers from John Vorster Square arrived at my office. They were there to officially inform me that I was being charged with publishing an unregistered newspaper; publishing a picture of Nelson Mandela; and for putting the box with the name of the newspaper's publisher and address on the wrong page of the newspaper.

I laughed in their faces, asking them whether they were not ashamed of doing the government's petty dirty work for them instead of fighting crime. They did not respond.

It was actually quite funny. The government holds back on registering the newspaper in order to figure out that they want a bigger deposit, and then they charge us with publishing a newspaper without that registration! The photograph of Mandela that we used was the size of a postage stamp and, as we indicated in the caption, was copied from a publication issued by the Department of Information.

Not long after that, I was charged under the Internal Security Act: we had contravened the regulations of the national state of emergency by writing about police actions in the townships, the state claimed.

This was to be the pattern for the next four years: endless harassment by the police and the Attorney-General. Due to increasing international pressure, the Botha government did not want to close us down by decree, so they tried to do it by involving us in endless criminal and civil court cases – they knew very well how small our financial resources were.

A few months later, my trial on charges of quoting a banned person took place in the Johannesburg Regional Court. It was the first such prosecution in years.

My only witness was the head of the Department of Communications at the Rand Afrikaans University, Professor Nina Overton. She said that the paragraphs referring to Slovo did not quote him, but merely referred to his position and should be seen as 'academic and critical'.

My legal counsel, Eberhard Bertelsmann, SC, told the court that the charge was outrageous. 'It certainly could not have been the aim of the legislator that the ordinary South African shouldn't even know about Joe Slovo. How can a South African develop his own political thinking if he does not even know what his enemy is thinking or where the danger comes from?'

Bertelsmann pointed out to the court that Slovo's words were quoted verbatim in fifteen other newspapers at the time, including *Beeld, Die Suid-Afrikaan, Rapport*, the *Sunday Times* and the *Financial Mail. Vrye Weekblad*, which only referred to his arguments and never quoted him, was the only one charged.

Bertelsmann further said that the Act prohibited giving a voice to banned people and disseminating inflammatory messages, but the piece in *Vrye Weekblad* was a neutral summary of Slovo's position.

Magistrate Pieter Bredenkamp either did not agree, or he had his orders. He said he did not care that while most newspapers had quoted Slovo directly, *Vrye Weekblad* was the only one brought before court. He sentenced me to six months' imprisonment, suspended for five years, and fined Wending Publikasies, as publisher, R1 000, suspended for five years.

It was the beginning of a rather long criminal record I assembled as editor. Because, as we declared on our front page in June 1989, the government and the

Johannesburg Attorney-General, Klaus von Lieres und Wilkau, were clearly abusing the judiciary in their vendetta against *Vrye Weekblad*.

Von Lieres und Wilkau sued me for defamation for writing that, as well as for constantly calling him by his full names, Klaus Peter Constantin Otto von Lieres und Wilkau, SC, or sometimes 'Herr Klaus Dinges' in our satirical column, *Brolloks en Bittergal*. It hurt him in his personal and professional capacities, and damaged his international reputation, he claimed.

By this time we had also been sued for defamation by three police generals and the state president himself. (One, General Leon Mellet, sued us for reminding our readers that in his younger days he had been the hero in a smutty picture book, *Kaptein Duiwel* or *Captain Devil*.)

In all these cases, also Herr Dinges's case, the state or the taxpayer was footing their legal bills, which meant that they could drag the case out for as long as possible, and use the most expensive counsel.

The case by Herr Klaus Dinges was not about a principle. He was just a silly, self-important civil servant who had been given the green light from somewhere higher up to make our lives hell. At the time his case was about to go to trial, we were engaged in a serious and extremely expensive long-term court case against one of the generals, and we felt we could not afford another trial.

So we offered Herr Klaus Dinges an apology, R15 000 for the first claim and R5 000 for the second. He accepted the R15 000, but not the R5 000 for the second claim. So we went to court. The offer of R5 000 was a secret tender the judge didn't know about.

Mr Justice AP van Coller agreed with Herr Klaus Dinges that we had indeed defamed this important man by saying he was guilty of selective prosecutions. He ordered me to pay a further R5 000 on the second claim.

But this was exactly what we had offered, which meant that the days in court were wasted. According to the rules of the Supreme Court, that meant Herr Klaus Peter Constantin Otto von Lieres und Wilkau had to pay all our legal costs plus his own. We calculated he had to pay in the region of R100 000.

Never was a victory sweeter. But, of course, it wasn't the end of the prosecutions. There were months where I spent more time in the courtroom than in the newsroom.

When we heard nothing from PW Botha's lawyers about his defamation suit, we taunted him and challenged him to serve the papers. We knew we could not lose the case, because the information was based on an affidavit before a judicial commission, and we merely reported on it. But then PW had a stroke, and soon after disappeared from public life.

22

Golden years

PAYING *VRYE WEEKBLAD*'s bills was the biggest nightmare of my life. As the driving force behind the whole enterprise, the financial responsibility rested heavily on me. I could handle the risks, the court cases and other high drama. But the finances gave me sleepless nights and tore at my guts.

Twice we had to skip an edition because the printers refused to print before hadn't paid our bills. We changed printers four times in the process. Twice the sheriff of the court arrived to confiscate our computer equipment because we hadn't paid our bills. (And twice we succeeded in hiding the computers used for design and layout.)

But the worst was when there wasn't enough money to pay salaries. In the end we always paid, but sometimes it was up to three weeks late. If ever there were journalists who deserved every penny of their salaries, it was the *Vrye Weekblad* team. Some of them had families and bonds to pay. It broke my heart.

Once, in 1990, I faced a month-end without enough money to pay salaries. A friend of mine cooked up an excuse to introduce me to a woman whose husband had died a few months earlier. She was lonely and frustrated, he said, but she had more money than she knew how to spend. Now if I could …

I hate to admit it, but I did. I spent a weekend with her. If I remember correctly, I returned with R50 000.

My colleague Jacques Pauw, whom I'd stupidly told about the plan, spread the story. Only, he added a little tail: I was supposed to get R100 000, he claims, but I was deemed only worth half of that.

But I did pay salaries that month.

I was often accused of being reckless and inviting prosecution while we had no money. But that's not the way it worked. NGOs and Western governments could not give us money for operating costs. But it was easy to lobby for money around freedom of expression issues. I had no qualms whatsoever using foreign money to ward off the government's vendetta through the courts.

Thanks to the good people of Canada, Sweden and Holland, and NGOs and press lobby groups all over the world, we could pay the phalanx of lawyers and expensive advocates who kept us from being closed down and me as editor from going to jail. Almost half the money ever spent on *Vrye Weekblad* went towards legal expenses.

I had to swallow my principles and accept the petroleum giant Shell and the South African multinational Anglo American as our first – and for quite a few months, only – advertisers. The white, English-speaking, 'coke-sniffing, yuppie scum' – as I used to call advertising agencies' employees – didn't even acknowledge *Vrye Weekblad*'s existence. All they cared about when one of our advertising salespeople or I met with them was our circulation. We never sold more than 25 000 copies – and at the beginning quite a lot less – and therefore they were never interested.

In fact, *Vrye Weekblad*'s readers should have been an advertiser's dream. They were by definition innovators, mostly aged between twenty and forty-five, and our surveys showed that nine out of ten held a university degree or were studying towards a degree, and almost four out of ten held more than one degree.

But while the non-Afrikaans-speaking business world didn't advertise out of ignorance, the Afrikaans business sector avoided us because they were scared that they would alienate the National Party and the Broederbond. One fairly big Afrikaans corporation advertised a few times, with a lovely full-colour full-page ad, but their MD was quickly summoned and told that there was an 'agreement' among Afrikaans businesses never to advertise in *Vrye Weekblad*.

We also had huge distribution problems. Nasionale Pers's distribution company, National News Distributors, would have been our natural choice, because they went to exactly the areas where we wanted to sell. But they refused us. So the Argus Group's distribution company distributed *Vrye Weekblad*, and it was a nightmare. On top of that, many outlets, like the shop in Stellenbosch University's student union, refused to sell our newspapers and simply hid them below the counter when they were delivered.

So we tried to concentrate on subscriptions. But, for the first eighteen months or so, the numbers weren't high enough for a distribution company to handle. So, on Thursday nights when the paper came off the press, readers and supporters joined us in our offices to hand-fold and stamp the newspapers to be delivered to the post office. We had many enemies, but we also had warm and loyal friends.

In late November 1989, just weeks after one of *Vrye Weekblad*'s sensational exposés on state-sponsored political violence, I attended an Idasa conference with the ANC leadership outside Paris. At a meeting in the French parliament, two of South Africa's most famous authors, André P Brink and Breyten Breytenbach, referred to the role we played in South Africa, and appealed to the French to support *Vrye Weekblad* financially. Back in South Africa, *The Citizen* reported on the meeting and launched a vicious attack on us for trying to obtain foreign aid. (After all the hullabaloo and gossip, we did not receive one cent from the French government or any of their NGOs.)

I responded in *Vrye Weekblad* under the headline 'Here's the whole story'. I wrote:

> *Vrye Weekblad* is the property of the journalists working for it. It was founded with much idealism and the minimum of capital, and still is anything but financially strong … We treat donors in the same way as advertisers: no matter how big their assistance is, there can never be any question of influence on the editorial policy of the newspaper. Our policy and political principles were spelled out in the first edition. No political party, pressure group, donor or advertiser will make us deviate from that.
>
> We regard *The Citizen*'s commentary about the matter as absurd and presumptuous. And on top of that, it comes from a newspaper that was started in a devious way with taxpayers' money!

But being dependent on foreign donations remained a sensitive issue to me right to the end. I wish we could have done without it, because it opened us up to accusations – especially among xenophobic conservative Afrikaners – that we were doing the dirty work of 'South Africa's external enemies'.

Of course, the situation was impossible. I cannot think of one South African newspaper that was profitable at the time; all of them had to be subsidised by the owner company from other commercial activities. Add to that the conspiracy among Afrikaans businesses not to advertise with us and the fact that we could never grow a mass circulation because of the nature of what we were trying to do, and it was no wonder that we needed assistance – as did the *Weekly Mail, New Nation, South* and *Die Suid-Afrikaan.* If any of our sources of funding had ever even hinted at trying to influence what we were writing, I would have sent their money straight back.

It wasn't cheap to practise our kind of journalism. From the first edition, we put a large chunk of our resources into hard investigative journalism.

In our second edition, our regular contributor and veteran investigative journalist, Martin Welz, exposed one of Bloemfontein's most prominent Afrikaner citizens and National Party supporters for swindling poor whites through his speculation in state-owned houses. The next morning, the man and his friend were found gassed in his Rolls-Royce outside the city with a copy of *Vrye Weekblad.*

I was shocked. But Welz's reply? 'That's how a journalist fucks up a crook.'

Two months later, Welz wrote a front-page lead with the headline: 'Botha's Era of Corruption'. It was the first in a series of exposés on corruption in high places. We carried a cartoon of cabinet ministers sitting in church, one minister trying to steal from the collection plate, and PW Botha hissing, 'Put it back, minister!'

On 18 January 1989, PW Botha had a stroke. A month later he resigned as leader of the National Party but, surprisingly, not as state president. Most people in politics and journalism knew he wasn't fit to be president, but nobody said it publicly. *Vrye Weekblad* did. We pointed out that his signature was very different after the stroke compared to before, and asked: 'Is this the Soviet Union or is this South Africa? Is it not our right to know exactly how mentally and physically capable our president is?'

In February 1989, Anton Steenkamp, a young lawyer who had joined our staff, wrote that a controversial right-wing judge, Jan Strydom, actually had six criminal convictions before he was appointed as judge. Someone with a criminal record could not become a member of the Bar, and therefore a judge, in South Africa. One of Strydom's convictions was for car theft. All the crimes were committed when he was a member of the ultra-nationalist Ossewa Brandwag paramilitary in the 1940s.

Shortly before this exposé, Strydom gave a white farmer who had beaten a black worker to death a suspended sentence. We were not endearing ourselves to the judiciary.

On 17 February, we were among the very first to write about Winnie Mandela's so-called football club of thugs. We linked them to the deaths of the child activist Stompie Seipei and Dr Abu-Baker Asvat. We also reported that the football team was suspected of killing one of their members, Maxwell Madonde, that week. In March we carried two pages of new information on the controversy.

In the same edition, we launched a competition for readers: 'Draw a picture of FW de Klerk and win your own homeland!' We received dozens of very entertaining cartoons over the next few weeks.

On 7 June, Elsabé wrote about her exclusive interview, the first, with the controversial 'Afrikaner terrorist', MK member Hein Grösskopf, in Lusaka. At the time, his face was plastered all over police stations and magistrate's courts as a wanted criminal. 'I am a political soldier,' he told Elsabé. 'If I killed you because of who and what you are as a person, it is murder. But if I killed you because you were standing in the way of peace, it isn't murder.'

A week later, I was criminally charged with 'undermining national conscription'. The charges stemmed from verbatim quotes during a court case in which a conscientious objector, Charles Bester, testified that he believed it was God's will that he refused to serve in the army, because God was against apartheid. A few months later, I was again charged under Regulation 5(b) of Proclamation R99, because we had published a paid advertisement of the Mandela Reception Committee advertising a legal meeting – an advertisement that had also appeared in other publications.

A few months later, Jacques Pauw and I publicly signed a register of 780 white South African men who refused to do military service.

Our first birthday party was a much bigger affair than the launch party – and more unruly. We were going up in the world – we even had a few ambassadors as guests.

But a fortnight later, on 17 November 1989, *Vrye Weekblad* published the most important story in its existence. There was a big picture of security police Captain Dirk Coetzee on the cover, with the headline 'Bloedspoor van die SAP' ['The SAP's trail of blood']. And then the words: 'Meet Captain Dirk Johannes Coetzee, commander of the SA Police's death squad. He tells the full gruesome story of political assassinations, poisoned cocktails, bomb attacks and letter bombs.'

It was the biggest story to break in South African journalism in many years, if not decades. It was followed up in the following months by revelation after revelation of death squads, assassinations and torture by the South African Police and Defence Force. (See Chapter 24.) It also sowed the seed of our eventual destruction.

Nobody could ignore *Vrye Weekblad* any longer, although the mainstream media tried very hard to ignore our weekly scoops. Our sales slowly climbed, as did our meagre advertising revenue. Our cover price paid for printing and distribution, but advertising revenue didn't actually cover our salary costs – to augment it, we had to pinch off some of the money we received from the European Union for training young journalists.

While I made many enemies, I didn't really hate anyone. Well, in the case of National Intelligence chief Niel Barnard, I came close. In 1990, I wrote a piece on FW de Klerk's advisers, singling Barnard out as the 'superhawk' who gave the new president the wrong advice. He was deeply annoyed.

Then I wrote a story exposing a prominent Stellenbosch academic who also worked for the NIS. He actually used his cover as a Sovietologist to spy on the South African Communist Party. It annoyed Barnard even more.

Shortly afterwards, Jacques Pauw and I were invited to lunch by two very senior National Intelligence (NI) men. We were curious, and met them in the Yard of Ale. We completely misunderstood Barnard and NI, was the men's message; they had been strongly supportive of negotiations with the ANC long before De Klerk's speech. In fact, they said, they had the same end goal as we did, so why didn't we work together?

We were probably a little paranoid, but I knew that spooks such as these often used this kind of method to blackmail journalists. They could have had a microphone or a camera hidden somewhere to record the conversation and use snippets to compromise our position. Jacques turned to the people at the tables around us and said something like: 'These guys are from National Intelligence, and they just tried to recruit us.' It was hilarious.

In 2003, a man who had worked for NI during my time at *Vrye Weekblad* contacted me to volunteer the information that he had been tasked with listening to my phone conversations. I didn't have a problem with that; in fact, I appreciated him telling me. I asked him if he knew anything about that meeting in the Yard of Ale, and he assured me that the two men who had lunched with us were actually the nice guys in NI, and would definitely not have tried to trap us. Maybe he's right.

But they probably reported to Barnard that we weren't going to be their spies after all, as the next thing we heard was that Barnard had ordered that I be prosecuted under the Protection of Information Act. The case was ordered *in camera*, because information could be revealed that would 'threaten the security of the state'.

No such information was revealed. The crux of the state's case was that I had revealed the name of a secret agent of the state, and thus endangered his life.

I argued in court that although that may technically be true, I wrote the piece on the same day, 2 February 1990, that the state president announced the unbanning of the ANC and SACP, and the release of Nelson Mandela and others. By the time of the trial late in 1990, the government had already started negotiating with the ANC. Perhaps my story might have done some damage had it not been for all these developments. Now, however, it was completely harmless and, in fact, in the public interest.

Then Barnard took the witness stand. The only people allowed in court were the magistrate, the prosecutor, a policeman, my lawyer and myself. Barnard proceeded to inform the poor intimidated magistrate how nothing had really changed; the ANC was still the enemy of the state – a communist, subversive movement. He spoke for several hours.

I sat there in disbelief. I seriously contemplated breaking the *in camera* rule by telling the rest of the country what this powerful man had said in court while he was pretending to negotiate with the ANC in good faith. But my lawyer warned me that such an act would be seen as extreme contempt of court, and I would go straight to jail.

Back in open court, the magistrate sentenced me to a fine of R7 000 and two years in jail, suspended for five years. I hadn't bargained on being found guilty, and if I had, I certainly wouldn't have dreamt that I'd get such a stiff fine. I therefore didn't have the money on me. I was led down to the cells, while my lawyer went to my office to find the money for my release.

As I walked down the steps to the cells, my thirteen-year-old daughter Annéne leaned over the railing with shock in her eyes. She thought I was going to go to jail for a long time. I didn't even know that she was in court and not at school.

It broke my heart. There I was, in the basement cell with rapists and hijackers, and I was crying. They must have thought I was crying because I had just been sentenced. But I was crying because, in that instant, I realised what I was doing to my children.

My ex-wife was working for the United Nations and was stationed in Sarajevo. Annéne and my son John were living with me. Down in that basement, it struck me for the first time what price my children were paying for my obsession with *Vrye Weekblad*.

A Supreme Court judge later threw out the magistrate's judgment, harshly commenting on his bias and lack of competency. And we got the R7 000 back.

While I couldn't tell the world what Barnard had said in court, I could take my revenge on him in other ways. In November, we published a letter Barnard had sent to the right-wing leader of the Namibian National Party, Kosie Pretorius, in the days when they were still fighting Dirk Mudge's DTA. He was reacting to a DTA proposal for schools in Namibia to be made multiracial, and he thanked Pretorius for opposing it. 'We [in South Africa] are also fighting a fierce fight against the Philistines,' he wrote. 'Therefore we are all the more thankful to the men who take firm positions under difficult circumstances such as in South West. In the long run it will also be what matters in the affairs of state.' He then waxed on about the Total Onslaught on South Africa, and lamented the DTA constitution's provisions that meant all races 'had to bend the knee to the same laws'.

I found Barnard a devious and despicable man, and was shocked when he was retained in a senior position in the National Party-controlled Western Cape provincial government after 1994.

My experiences with the courts didn't exactly engender a feeling of trust in me. Of all the judges and magistrates I saw from the dock, only one was straight and didn't have political orders. (A joke in our office at the time was: What do you call Max du Preez in a suit? Accused Number One.)

A Pretoria judge's strange ruling when I appeared before him makes for an interesting story. But in order to tell it, I first I have to tell another story.

In June 1992, I published an article over seven pages on security policeman Colonel John Horak, who had confessed all his sins to me. It was sensational stuff. He told how he had manipulated the news while he was the security police's operative at the SABC, and how he became the spy on the *Natal Mercury*, the *Sunday Express* and the *Rand Daily Mail*. At the time he moved freely in left-wing circles, and became a close friend and confidante of Winnie Mandela and Veronica Sobukwe, wife of PAC leader Robert Sobukwe.

Horak gave details of incidents where the security police planted bombs and attacked people, and then blamed it on anti-apartheid activists; where the police had stolen cheques from trade unions to sow dissension; and other dirty tricks. He also told me that the security police had a thick file on a progressive KwaZulu-Natal judge, John Didcott, and continued to tap his phone.

Horak also told me that a close friend of his, a brigadier who then became a lecturer in criminology, had asked him to relay another story to me for publication.

In January 1987, the leader of the Labour Party in the House of Representatives and a minister in PW Botha's cabinet, the Rev. Allan Hendrickse, illustrated his opposition to the apartheid laws by going for a public swim at a whites-only beach in Port Elizabeth. The pictures were all over the media, locally and internationally.

PW Botha and his Minister of Constitutional Development, Chris Heunis, were deeply annoyed about this. So our brigadier received the order to 'scare Hendrickse off' and 'teach him a lesson'. The brigadier then ordered a security police captain to 'do the job'.

The Pretoria-based captain flew to Port Elizabeth, drove to Hendrickse's private home and threw a hand grenade at his front door. Nobody was injured. The captain flew back to Johannesburg early the next morning.

The next day, the police issued a statement saying that they suspected 'ANC terrorists' of the attack.

I wanted to publish the story, because I knew that the SAP often used this kind of 'false flag' operation, and it had to stop. But, like a good journalist, I thought I should give the police a chance to respond before I went to print. So I phoned the Commissioner of Police, General Johan van der Merwe, who asked me to fax him my story so that he could make inquiries before commenting.

The next morning my lawyer phoned me, and said that he had just been informed that the police were applying for an urgent interdict against me in the Pretoria Supreme Court. We rushed over and arrived minutes before the case started. Of course, it was again held *in camera*.

I could not believe my eyes. One of the applicants for the interdict, with the Commissioner of Police, was our brigadier, the source of the story. The commissioner and the police captain who threw the hand grenade were the other applicants.

They argued that the story was completely false and, if published, would irreparably damage the image of the police. They could prove that the captain did not travel to Port Elizabeth on that day, they said.

I could not tell the court that the source of the story was one of the applicants, because a journalist should always protect his sources.

I tried to tell Mr Justice de Villiers that I had a very senior and reliable source, and explained to him that it would be normal practice for me to publish the story, with the police denial, and if they felt aggrieved they could bring a defamation suit against me. The story was clearly in the public interest, I argued.

The judge didn't even pretend to listen. He slapped an interdict on me forbidding me to publish the story, and added the unusual rider that I wasn't allowed to tell anybody about it – ever. Nor was I allowed to state that such a case was brought against me, and that the police had obtained an interdict against me. My lawyers said that they had never before heard of such a ruling in South African law.

Of course the story was true. I later received information that the police had dispatched someone to the offices of South African Airways to destroy the documentation of the captain's flights to and from Port Elizabeth on that day.

For years, senior political journalists have debated whether we should report on the private scandals of cabinet ministers. Most of us were witnesses at some point or another to the excessive drinking, extramarital capers, and decadent and depraved parties of some of the ministers in the cabinets of PW Botha and FW de Klerk.

I'm still not sure. On the one hand, I'm against journalists who tell stories in private instead of publishing them; their readers also need to be informed. On the other hand, even politicians have a right to privacy, and if there is no direct proof that their private behaviour negatively affects the execution of their duties, we shouldn't report it. (This question became very real in my life when I called the president of South Africa a womaniser on national radio. More about that later.)

In the past, *Vrye Weekblad* reported that one of the reasons why the negotiations between South Africa and Cuba – which centred around Namibia and Angola – on the island of Sal in the mid-1980s had been so successful, was because the Cuban officials and their South African counterparts had all drunk themselves into a stupor and behaved like teenagers.

But mostly we dealt with these stories in our satirical column *Brolloks*, and without revealing names. Like the visit made by several cabinet ministers and young boys and girls to Bird Island off the Eastern Cape coast. Like the minister flying back to South Africa after an overseas trip who collected all the available liquor in a huge vase, then drank it all and passed out in the aisle.

But we couldn't resist publishing John Horak's story of a cabinet minister well known for his sexual antics who nearly got caught with his pants down. Again, we preferred not to divulge the minister's identity.

This was what Horak told me: 'The minister in question went, as he had done several times in the past, to visit a certain prostitute in the centre of Johannesburg. But his timing was terrible: that same evening a huge bomb exploded at the nearby Johannesburg City Hall. And the minister was, of course, without his bodyguards.

'Newspapers reported the next morning that the minister was on the scene shortly after the explosion.

'General Jaap Joubert, one of the best policemen we have ever had, was called in by the Minister of Police, Adriaan Vlok, the next morning. Vlok demanded to know why the minister did not have his security guards with him, and Joubert replied that Vlok should ask his cabinet colleague himself.

'Vlok wanted to know whether Joubert knew where the minister was that night. Joubert said yes he did, but when Vlok asked him to say where, Joubert refused to tell.

'That was the beginning of the end of Joubert's career. The next day he was transferred, and that morning, in front of several officers, General Johan van der Merwe apologised to Joubert because they had to transfer him – meaning it was Vlok's decision, not his.

'Senior security policemen were very worried about this particular minister because he had become a serious security risk,' Horak continued.

'One day, as he was about to board a plane at Jan Smuts Airport, a police officer dressed in the uniform of a South African Airways pilot quickly handed the minister a letter. In it were the full details of the woman he was having a relationship with and his visits to her.

'The police thought it would scare him and make him more careful, but the minister gave the letter to Niel Barnard of National Intelligence and said there was a security leak Barnard should investigate – because how could someone get so close to him to hand him the letter without being checked by security officials?

'The sexual antics of this minister have become famous among his bodyguards and senior security policemen – they just love to tell the stories,' Horak said.

And then there was the story of the cabinet minister holed up with a sex worker in a Durban hotel when the Vice Squad raided the place for prostitutes, not knowing that the politician was there. The minister's private secretary told the police that the prostitute was his guest, while the minister hid in a cupboard. The private secretary later got a very senior and cushy job as reward for his help – and his silence. But I didn't write that story either.

A regular visitor to *Vrye Weekblad*'s offices, senior UDF leader Terror Lekota (now known as Mosiua Lekota, Minister of Defence), once rebuked me for our complete lack of security. I told him the idea of locked doors, bodyguards and regulated access would be completely against the spirit of what we were trying to do.

The truth was that we had no idea whether we were in any danger, and what kind of danger that could be. If the agencies of the state wanted us dead, we could not stop them with security measures. We worked under the assumption that they were tapping our phones, bugging our offices, monitoring our bank accounts (we never did get any money from Moscow) and opened our mail, so we kept our noses clean and conducted secret dealings secretly.

The security police sent us a few messages informing us that we were vulnerable. In the first few months after November 1988, my trusted old Lancia had its wheel nuts loosened three times overnight. In the first instance, the one wheel came loose before I was driving at speed, and on the other two occasions I spotted it and tightened the nuts before I drove off. A few months later there was a mock attack on my house – people viciously hammering on the doors and windows in the early hours of the morning. I phoned the police, but they never came. I phoned some friends, and when they arrived they saw the attackers speed off in a police van.

But, in 1991, matters turned serious. Just after midnight, and not long after the last staff members had left the building, a bomb ripped apart the front door and foyer of our offices. No one was hurt.

A Sandton-based security police officer later informed us that a man called Leonard Veenendaal had confessed (after being just slightly tortured, we were told) to planting the bomb. He was a known right-wing militant, and was wanted for serious crimes in Namibia. But he was also an operative of the shady SADF outfit, the Civil Cooperation Bureau (CCB), which we had recently exposed. Veenendaal was never charged with the bombing.

Five years later, Veenendaal reported to the Truth and Reconciliation Commission as a victim of gross human rights abuses. He had the audience in stitches when he described how the security police had tortured him: they squeezed his 'gentiles', he said in English. Veenendaal was in the newspapers again just the other day, living a happy family life in rural England, where he is the local school's rugby coach.

Then there was the night we had a frantic phone call from an academic we knew in Potchefstroom. Two men from the extremist right-wing group the Church of the Creator were on their way to kill Jacques and me, he said. We were the only ones left in the office that evening, and before we could flee, two men started banging on the doors and windows. Jacques and I, scared to death, tried to hide under desks and in cupboards. But the men kept shouting that they knew we were there, and we'd better let them in. We reckoned that by opening the doors for them, there was at least the chance of talking them out of it, so we let them in.

They each had an attaché case, which they plonked down on the desk. Each one contained a Bible and a pistol. But they hadn't actually come to kill us, they said, they'd come to warn us that they *would* kill us if we kept on doing what we were doing.

I only found out long after *Vrye Weekblad* had closed down that the military had more serious plans for me than blowing up our offices. A senior military intelligence officer confessed to Jacques that he had recruited my farm neighbour to report when I would be arriving from Johannesburg. One day, the officer was informed that I was going to be on my farm on a Friday, and he went on ahead of me. He waited in the mountains near my house, his rifle trained on my front door. That's where I was supposed to die.

For some reason I changed my mind and never arrived that weekend. And for some reason he never tried to assassinate me again.

Jacques introduced me to the guy one day over lunch in Pretoria. I found it odd that I didn't resent, or even dislike, him.

There was another night when I thought I was going to die – twice. For months after the existence of the CCB had been exposed, little was known about the inner workings of the unit. Then Jacques met Pieter Botes, a senior CCB man who wanted to spill the beans – the same man who had blown up Albie Sachs with a car bomb in Maputo and claimed he had assassinated six activists.

But a day or two before we were going to blast his confessions all over the front page, Botes told Jacques he wanted to see us both in Pretoria. He was having second thoughts. We desperately wanted to print the story, because it exposed the entire workings of this evil unit. I sat listening to his macho blood and guts stories all night, matching his brandy and Coke one after the other. Botes was enjoying this. Every now and then he would look at me and say: 'Yes, Mr Editor, and what's your story?'

Then he took us to his home and introduced us to his very potent pear *mampoer*. But by now I had imbibed more alcohol than I normally drink in six months, and we still had to drive back to Johannesburg. We said thank you, but we couldn't drink any more.

Botes got up and fetched a brown sack, from which he pulled a Russian RPG, a rocket-propelled grenade. He fixed the grenade onto the launcher, primed it, pointed it at us and ordered us to drink his *mampoer*.

I had no choice but to drink the vile stuff. I could see Jacques dumping every second or third glass into a potted plant next to him, but there was nothing near me; I had to swallow.

We finished the bottle, then got in the car and drove back to Johannesburg. I was driving, but halfway to Johannesburg I went completely blind. Blind, as in I could not see a thing. I opened and closed my eyes, but it stayed dark. I knew it was probably not safe for me to continue driving, so I stopped right in the middle of the highway and Jacques took the wheel. Somehow we made it all the way to Johannesburg.

I collapsed on Jacques' couch, and only regained my eyesight late the next morning. For a week, I felt like a corpse. So that's one for medical science, if they don't already know it: alcohol poisoning can cause temporary blindness.

But it was all worthwhile. Our cover story was very dramatic.

Vrye Weekblad spent a lot of time and column inches on the horrific violence that plagued KwaZulu-Natal and the East Rand between 1990 and 1994. There were mass killings virtually every week, but nobody was ever caught and nobody claimed responsibility. It was threatening to consume the country's hopes for peace.

In 1991, the *Weekly Mail* exposed the dealings between the SADF and the Inkatha Freedom Party (IFP), a scandal that became known as Inkathagate. The government gave the assurance that the R250 000 they had given to Mangosotho Buthelezi's organisation was the first and last money donated in such a way. In August, *Vrye Weekblad* published the confessions of one Larry Barnett, a security police agent, to Jacques that they had only shortly before delivered huge bundles of cash to Inkatha. He also gave information on the delivery of new guns to Inkatha.

Barnett decided to talk to us after his handler ordered him to steal documents and notebooks from the newsrooms of *Vrye Weekblad* and the *Sunday Star*.

Vrye Weekblad, the *Weekly Mail* and *New Nation* were the first to allege that there was a Third Force, meaning a shadowy group other than the two protagonists, Inkatha and the UDF/ANC, fomenting the violence. We suspected that it was the

South African security forces, but could not prove it. Of course, the government denied it stringently.

Then, in September 1992, we found the smoking gun.

The owner of a nightclub and restaurant in Yeoville, the Black Sun, arrived in our offices one morning with a black man in tow. He introduced him as João Alberto Cuna, one of his employees. He told us a remarkable story.

Cuna had deserted from the Mozambique army and was working illegally in Johannesburg. He found accommodation with the family of a Narcotics Bureau policeman, Joseph 'Boy' Schultz. When Schultz discovered that Cuna was a former soldier, he took him to a meeting with six white men in a room in the Johannesburg Sun Hotel. One introduced himself as a farmer from Natal. They asked Cuna whether he would be prepared to shoot ANC members and plant bombs. Cuna said yes, but ran away the next day because he didn't want to get involved in murder.

But Schultz found Cuna, and towards the end of March 1992 took him to Pietermaritzburg, where they booked into a smart hotel. They bought him new clothes and treated him royally, he said.

One evening, Schultz and the man who said he was a farmer took him to a big face-brick building in Durban, which was guarded by soldiers. There, another black man joined them, and they all got into a light-brown Kombi with tinted windows. They were each given an AK-47 assault rifle with a spare magazine, and were then driven to one of the black townships, where the white men pointed out a specific house. Cuna didn't know KwaZulu-Natal and couldn't tell us which township it was, but he could describe it.

'Me, the other black man and the white man who was picked up at the brick building which looked like a police station then put balaclavas over our faces,' Cuna said. 'The white also had dark glasses on.

'We drove past the house four times and then the farmer dropped us off. We got out and ran up to the windows. The white man went to a back window. I saw between seven and nine people inside the house. They were standing there talking. Most of the people were men but there were women also.

'Then we started firing. I saw people falling and they were screaming as well. One man ran away. I only saw him when he was already far away. I don't know how he got outside the house.

'We then stopped firing. I do not know whether anybody inside the house was dead. We did not go inside. We stopped firing and ran back to the Kombi. We got inside and went back to the taxi rank. There the three of us, except for the driver, shot through the windows at people who were still at the rank. I shot three people, but I'm not certain about this because the farmer was driving very fast.'

Back in Johannesburg, the white men gave Cuna R4 000 and a passport in the name of Malefetsane Johannes Mokoena. Cuna said the men now wanted to force him into doing the same thing again, and that's why he went to his employer and asked him for help.

Pearlie Joubert, a journalist with *Vrye Weekblad* who interviewed and looked after Cuna during the weeks we investigated the story, could not pinpoint the exact date and place of the attack. Cuna was a bit bewildered, couldn't speak English very well, and had never before or since been to Durban or Pietermaritzburg. Selvan Chetty of the church organisation Practical Ministries, which monitored the violence in the Port Shepstone area, listened to Cuna's story. He said it could have been any one of five attacks at the time in the KwaGcaba and Murchison areas. In all these attacks, unidentified men with balaclavas had fired into houses with AK-47s, and in some of the cases a light-brown Kombi was used.

We published the story on 30 October under the front-page banner headline: 'At last proof of the Third Force', with a picture of Cuna.

In my editorial that day, I wrote: 'Now we know: there is a Third Force.' I listed the large number of exposés in *Vrye Weekblad* about misconduct, dirty tricks and murders by the security forces, and pointed out that the government had done nothing to curtail this culture. This time, I said, the De Klerk government dared not fail to act, because the violence fomented by the Third Force was threatening a negotiated settlement. 'Imaginative, firm action by the state president is the only thing that can save us.'

During that same week, the Commission of Inquiry Regarding the Prevention of Public Violence and Intimidation under Mr Justice Richard Goldstone had its first meeting in Pretoria. We persuaded João Cuna to offer his testimony to Goldstone.

Cuna was very nervous when he sat down before the commission. My lawyer and I were sitting right behind him. Moments before Judge Goldstone entered the room, we saw a white man staring at Cuna, pulling his finger across his throat – the universal sign for: 'I'm going to kill you.' Cuna became very upset and refused to testify. Goldstone decided to hear his evidence *in camera*, and refused me permission to attend.

The commission later declared that they couldn't make any findings on Cuna's testimony. I was outraged and began to doubt Goldstone's bona fides.

But I was wrong. They were just playing a cat and mouse game. Cuna proved to be the key to uncovering one of the SADF's dirtiest little secrets.

Goldstone asked one of the few straight policemen at the time, Colonel Henk Heslinga, to investigate. He took Cuna back to Pietermaritzburg and showed him hotel after hotel, until he recognised the one where he had stayed before the attack on the house.

Heslinga looked through the hotel's credit card slips for the time Cuna said they were staying there, and found a Diners Club slip for three rooms in the name of Africa Risk Analysis Consultants (ARAC).

Diners Club informed the Goldstone Commission that ARAC was their biggest customer. More than forty cards were listed in the names of ARAC employees, and they spent many millions each year on hotel and travel expenses.

Heslinga and Torie Pretorius, the Deputy Attorney-General in Pretoria and Goldstone Commission official, went to ARAC's offices in Pretoria. Just by looking at the place, they knew that this would be a big operation, and asked for a contingent of uniformed policemen to accompany them.

Pretorius, surrounded by policemen, produced his search warrant to the stunned employees of ARAC. He demanded all their files relating to Ferdi Barnard, the only man they could identify from Cuna's experiences.

Pretorius and Heslinga were astonished. They had stumbled upon a highly secret front for military intelligence called the Directorate Covert Collection (DCC).

One of the files seized by Pretorius covered Operation Baboon, aimed at gathering information with which to blackmail senior ANC leaders and anti-apartheid activists. Another file exposed a brothel, used to photograph important people.

In my opinion, the Goldstone Commission made a grave mistake that day. Judge Goldstone was over-cautious, and ordered Pretorius to take no other files than the ones that related to Barnard. He later explained that he had feared that a general search would have led to an urgent court application against his investigation. But, in the days after Pretorius and Heslinga's raid, the Directorate Covert Collection removed or destroyed a large number of even more sensitive files, the contents of which we will never know.

Richard Goldstone called a press conference for the following Monday to make the sensational information public. It just so happened that State President FW de Klerk was that very morning returning from a rugby test match he had attended with British prime minister John Major. At Heathrow Airport, a journalist asked De Klerk about the Third Force allegations, and De Klerk confidently gave his standard response: the South African security forces were not involved in political violence and the Third Force theory was false.

But at more or less the same time, Goldstone disclosed to an international press conference that he had proof that the South African military were engaged in clandestine operations, including murder, against opponents of the National Party government. They were the Third Force.

De Klerk was livid.

23

Anarchists at work

WHAT DO YOU get when you throw a bunch of foul-mouthed, ill-mannered individualists and anarchists together? *Vrye Weekblad*'s newsroom.

Vrye Weekblad's offices were always in a mess, and always highly charged with energy and, often, conflict. At any given time you could walk in and find two people (the one was frequently the editor) engaged in a heated argument about something that was supposed to or not supposed to go into the next edition.

There was far too much drinking – some staff members kept sleeping bags for the two hours between the end of the party and the start of the new working day.

It was the most wonderful, creative, exciting space I had ever been in or heard of. It was close to my dream of the ideal newsroom: no rules, no formalities – just a free flow of ideas.

To everyone who worked there, it was so much more than a job. There were no fixed working hours, dress codes or prescribed style. You know you had do dig deeper, get more, write better. Press statements and news conferences were not sources of news, but tip-offs that there might be a story. We had to reflect the events of the country, but we also had to tell our readers who or what was behind it. We had to reflect the whole of society to itself, and especially to Afrikaners who had been shielded for so long. And we constantly had to smoke out crooks, killers, torturers and racists.

Vrye Weekblad drew creative people like a magnet, and our staff levels grew steadily. The iconoclastic Ryk Hattingh, a well-known Afrikaans playwright, became our chief sub-editor, and brought a whole new anarchistic dimension to the paper. He was also rather eccentric and a bit of a philosopher.

Koos Coetzee specialised in dredging up the worst insults imaginable to describe the reporters' copy he had to sub or rewrite. It often resulted in stand-up screaming matches across the floor. But everybody loved Koos and learnt a lot from him, even though he sometimes slept in the office and didn't go home for a week. He also wrote a sometimes-strange column on food.

A favourite form of entertainment was looking out for the weird scumbags, murderers or torturers whom Jacques Pauw brought to the office. He had a remarkable talent for getting these people to confess their evil deeds to him for publication. More policemen and soldiers spilled the beans to Jacques than to the Truth Commission years later.

Pearlie Joubert came to do her practical with us at the end of her postgraduate year in journalism at Stellenbosch, and never left. She was wild, loud (she had an affinity for calling people, including me, the Afrikaans word for female genitalia), stubborn, and had no respect for anybody or anything. But never before had I seen such natural journalistic talent in a person. Within months she was writing cover stories, and soon she had her own loyal following among our readers.

Pearlie undertook an epic train trip through the country in 1992, and wrote about the people she came across and the places she visited. It was some of the most beautiful writing I have ever seen in an Afrikaans newspaper.

Martie Meiring, a veteran journalist who joined us in 1993, wrote in our last edition: '*Vrye Weekblad* gave you something of Mickey Spillane, something of Damon Runyon, something of Tom Wolfe – and all in Afrikaans!'

Andrea Vinassa was a magnet who attracted the cream of South Africa's *avant* artists, performers and writers to the office and onto our arts pages. There have been other cultural writers who were as opinionated and outrageous as Andrea, but none were ever taken so seriously.

Our parties became notorious, and I was often really ashamed of my colleagues and myself. At one such party, the 'respected investigative journalist' Jacques Pauw ran around with a box of red wine, squirting it on the shirt fronts of esteemed diplomats, prominent political leaders and media colleagues. At another, I crashed into the Dutch ambassador while driving my old Vespa scooter around the office with Pearlie on my back.

Okay, there were some ordinary, decent-looking, well-behaved people too, but never one with a boring mind. People such as Esma Anderson, Christelle Terreblanche, Ina van der Linde, Louis Kirstein, Martie Meiring, and the only journalist in the history of the world who could not type or use a computer, Hennie Serfontein. (Van Zyl Slabbert once referred to Hennie as the 'best Afrikaner' he had ever met. That's quite something for Hennie, a man who had been fighting the Broederbond and the Afrikaner establishment since the 1960s.)

In our second year, *Vrye Weekblad* underwent a metamorphosis. The reason? A man called Anton Sassenberg. He turned every rule in the newspaper design handbook on its head and made every page a work of modern art. And the next week he would do it completely differently. He even changed the masthead while I was away for a week.

After 1992/93, one could see Anton's revolutionary ideas creeping into most magazine designs in South Africa. He was the original design guerrilla. Anton designed and made his own clothes – my favourite was a Kentucky Fried Chicken-red double-breasted suit he wore without a shirt. The only human being he respected was David Bowie. And he shaved his head ten years before it became fashionable.

Virginia Keppler was the last trainee reporter we appointed. She arrived as an innocent, decent girl from Eersterust, Pretoria. She left a journalist. This is how she remembers *Vrye Weekblad*:

> One Monday morning I pitched all dressed up for an interview at *Vrye Weekblad*. The place was a mess and made no impression on me, because to a brown-skinned Afrikaans girl like me it wasn't actually proper ...
>
> I learnt that Afrikaans was a sweet language and that I could be proud that it was my mother tongue. And the Boere who say Afrikaans is their language, well, I have news for them. It is my language too, because I am a real Afrikaner!
>
> These people were a different kind of Boere who really didn't take any shit from Boere with guns.
>
> And then there was the swearing. Sis, I said in the beginning, because I was one of those well-mannered, religious girls who even taught Sunday school at one point. But I soon discovered that swearing was a part of *Vrye Weekblad* just as I later became a part of it. If you really wanted to hear swearing, then you should have been at one of our editorial meetings. Pearlie always said: 'There's nothing wrong with swearing, it's just a different language.'
>
> Then there was the drinking. The designer breezed into the office early in the morning with a bottle of Beefeater gin under the arm. The editor sometimes came back from lunch with a nip of brandy, and the rest of the lot bought liquor on credit at the liquor store across the road. And so I learned to drink – not a lot, just enough to make my acquaintance with the toilet floor of the Yard of Ale. It was all Max's fault, Nanna!
>
> And it wasn't a place where you held your tongue. Oh, no. We were so democratic. If you didn't speak out, you didn't belong there.

Thinus Horn, sports editor and cartoonist, looked back in our last edition:

> During *Vrye Weekblad*'s rougher days, the sports editor was a bit like *Sports Illustrated*'s political correspondent. You're there, but a little removed from the action. But it was fun. What are your chances at *The Star* or *Beeld* to meet a real, genuine member of a death squad? At *Vrye Weekblad* there was a new one every week. Or at least a bomb on the front stoep.
>
> The fact that your phone was tapped made you feel important in an odd way, even though you were only listening to Fulton Allem telling you what a brilliant golf player he actually was.

But, best of all, one could write what one wanted to write. I have a message for the little grey men who have been predicting *Vrye Weekblad*'s demise for a long time and are probably smirking now: oh, fuck you.

Pearlie Joubert said *Vrye Weekblad* was 'like low-budget parties on the wrong side of the tracks that were suddenly discovered by the clients of the trendy uptown spots'. Andrea Vinassa remembers:

I could wax pompous about working for a publication with a mandate to bring about justice in our evil society … but it was more like jolling in a cheap spy novel. Max tries to present to the outside world a united front of busy *Vrye Weekblad* bees buzzing in harmony, but half the fun of working there was the conflict between the different personalities.

All of us more or less agreed that Something Had to be Done About the Government, but that's where the agreement ended. Within that broad directive, we were eager to express a multiplicity of viewpoints that generated unbelievable conflict in the newsroom. Blood flowed often. Only the most ruthless survived.

At most newspapers, editors surrounded themselves with sycophants in white shirts, assistant editors promoted to deputy editors because they agree with each other. Not so with *Vrye Weekblad*. The paper seemed to attract the outsiders, the space cadets, the egomaniacs, the geniuses and the loudmouths.

The newsroom was teeming with testosterone-charged Boere with beards, but under those beards beat hearts of individualists with agendas of their own. And the only difference between the men and the women was that we had no beards. We learnt very quickly that to survive we had to stake out our territory.

Editorial meetings were battlefields … no polite euphemisms here. We were granted freedom of expression, and, boy, did we use it. Criticism was often acrimonious and new recruits were dumbfounded (or maybe just bored?) at the viciousness of the arguments which were often esoteric and fought on matters of principle.

Readers would often complain of inconsistency and chaos evident on the pages, but *Vrye Weekblad* derived its character from obstinate individuals who refused to compromise – a luxury no other publication can afford. If a shrink got hold of our psychographic profile he would have locked us away in a loony bin.

Much of the inconsistency had to do with the absolutely crippling workload. We produced more copy in a week than most magazines in two months. The stress was unbearable because we were breaking barriers, pushing out the frontiers, defying the legal system, pissing off the *dominees*, winding up the politicians and behaving like adolescents who had stolen dad's car.

Vrye Weekblad often looked like a cross between a master's thesis and a fanzine because we were eager to give our readers in-depth analytical stories without crushing them to death with turgid facts and theories …

We functioned on adrenaline, nervous energy, irrational rage and humour – the best and the blackest kind. We veered between exhaustion and ecstasy. *Vrye Weekblad* was obsession-inducing and all-consuming.

Vrye Weekblad's uncompromising political reporting and dramatic exposés of apartheid evils and police and military dirty tricks attracted the most attention. But there was a substantial group of loyal readers who bought the paper for its arts and culture pages and creative writing.

With writers such as Andrea, Chris du Plessis and Ivor Powell, our coverage of film, theatre and visual arts was on the international cutting edge, and certainly the sharpest and most incisive ever seen in Africa. In hindsight, perhaps our cultural impact was greater than that of our exposés on apartheid's death squads and other evils.

But our 'cultural wing' tended to run away with us, and sometimes I had to fight hard to keep them from becoming so *avant-garde* that they would lose most of our readers.

Andrea saw it differently. 'Max spent all his time trying to reign in the artists and madmen and (god forbid) writers of fiction trying to hijack his paper. If it were up to Ryk Hattingh, Anton Sassenberg and I, we would have changed the masthead every week.

'In journalism, cultural writers and news journalists are natural enemies. Editors of newspapers are not very bright when it comes to things intellectual. Max was more enlightened than most, but we [the cultural wing of *Vrye Weekblad*] still had to wage a fierce battle against the forces of anti-intellectualism. I wanted to keep my arts pages experimental, spontaneous and anarchic. I wanted to undermine and question the larger project of the newspaper and journalism in general, i.e. that so-called objective reality should take precedence over the emotive and subjective.'

It was an accusation I often heard – sometimes overheard being said behind my back: I was a tyrant, a despot. I had consciously appointed individualists, mavericks and anarchists, because that was where the raw creativity lay. I also introduced a unique culture to the newsroom of joint decision-making – a Boere version of an editorial collective. But someone had to guard the sanity and prevent the whole project from falling apart.

The team met around the big table on a Friday morning to decide what the next edition should look like. I had strong opinions, but could not overrule a majority decision.

The fact remains – and most of my *Vrye Weekblad* colleagues now acknowledge it – that a freer and more democratic newsroom than ours never existed. South African journalists had never had so much freedom, both for proposing ideas for stories and for writing them in his or her own style. This freedom was sometimes, on rare occasions, abused, simply because staff members didn't appreciate that what they had did not exist in journalism outside of *Vrye Weekblad* – not even at the other alternative newspapers.

Hans Pienaar, contributor for the whole period of the paper's existence and news editor for some of it, wrote on his *Vrye Weekblad* memories: 'Sure, Max was a bit of an old tyrant. I'm a hands-on editor, he always said, the only problem was he thought he had ten hands. We sometimes had to fight and gnash our teeth, but under him one could write what you couldn't dream of [writing] anywhere else.'

It was also a bit of a game. I was the one who had to veto the worst defamatory statements, the worst swear words, the most flagrant violations of the law, the photographs that would have landed us in trouble – I was, after all, the man who had to stand in court when we got sued. I could have let it all go for the paper to become an even wackier fringe publication, but that was not why I had started *Vrye Weekblad*. I had to make sure that when we did get into trouble, it was for something worthwhile. I was the one who, every now and then, had to remember that our readers were not all bohemian freaks, Gothic punks or crazed Trotskyites.

So my colleagues pushed as hard as they could to get the risky stuff past me, which meant that there was never any self-censorship from their side. I was the chief censor. It worked well. It didn't always make me popular, though.

But while some of my colleagues might have thought that I was a bit of a prude, columnists in Afrikaans newspapers called me 'Mad Max'. A silly little man who worked for *Die Suid-Afrikaan*, Chris Louw, wrote in all seriousness that it was known among my friends and family that I had sustained brain damage in the aircraft crash. (My elder sister wrote him a letter saying: no, he was like that from birth.) Louw also said my aim with *Vrye Weekblad* was to get banned and then to get a fancy job overseas as a victim of apartheid.

And then there was our use of the *Taal*. George Claassen, head of the Department of Journalism at Stellenbosch University, who later became the deputy editor of *Die Burger*, wrote in his analysis of *Vrye Weekblad* in *South Africa's Resistance Press – Alternative Voices in the Last Generation under Apartheid* (edited by Les Switzer and Mohamed Adhikari, Ohio University Center for International Studies): 'Nowhere was *Vrye Weekblad*'s innovation more obvious than in the way it broke tradition in the use of the Afrikaans language … *Vrye Weekblad* received a lot of criticism from academics and others fighting for the survival of Afrikaans, but the newspaper used a living language that reflected the way people actually talked in South Africa and Namibia. *Vrye Weekblad* was portraying not an Afrikaans for whites only but an Afrikaans for the whole of the southern African population who could speak the language.'

I didn't make a conscious decision before the launch of *Vrye Weekblad* to promote the use of 'liberated' Afrikaans. It started happening organically; it was the natural, creative way to write.

But when we were criticised right from the early days for not sticking to 'civilised standard Afrikaans', I explained in an interview:

> There was a gap between the Afrikaans being used by the speakers of the language and the Afrikaans used in newspapers. The gap was unnaturally big and not in the interests of Afrikaans. So from the start we said: This is not our Afrikaans. We didn't say that it wasn't a good thing to have a proper knowledge of Afrikaans, on the contrary, but we said: Who are these little men who make the rules for our language? For all the years middle-aged Broederbond-types with grey shoes, appointed by some Academy, dictated to us how to spell, how to speak and how to write. And the next year they publish a new book of words and spelling rules, and we all have to follow like sheep.
>
> This did not only bring a huge schism between writers and users of the language, it also brought resistance.
>
> The only criterion is what feels good and right. Each person is an interpreter of the language on the tongue of the people. What do you do not to sound like a *dominee* or a magistrate? You close your eyes and think how you would have said it to someone on the street.
>
> It is what will save Afrikaans. Get down from the pedestal and the pulpit, move away from the academic rostrum and speak the language as it grows and as it lies warmly on the tongue.

English words and words from other indigenous South African languages could be borrowed when the Afrikaans equivalent sounded stilted or didn't convey the proper meaning of what you wanted to say. There are no proper words for 'establishment', 'constituency' or 'bandwagon', for instance, or 'sexy'. The proper Afrikaans word for 'township' is *woonbuurt*, but that gives the feel of a Waterkloof or an Oranjezicht. Afrikaners know exactly what you mean when you talk about a 'township'.

Our liberated way of using our language also stimulated a much richer, earthier and colourful use of Afrikaans, which was evident in some of our best writing. Pearlie Joubert's writing was virtually impossible to translate because of the way she played with words and filled her copy with images and symbolism.

Beverley Mitchell, who grew up in black Cape Town, said she was ashamed of Afrikaans when she grew up, and denied being able to speak it. 'One day at the University of Cape Town, I picked up *Vrye Weekblad* and thought, but I can understand this. The language was progressive, politically sensitive. It took away the stigma of ruling class and apartheid. It was poetic. And the nice Cape swear words like *moer*, *fok* and *bliksem*, part of our language, were absolutely beautiful. It made the language acceptable to me and many others. Here was a publication that accommodated us.'

Ina van der Linde, who, like me, was trained at Nasionale Pers to use only standard Afrikaans, said: 'Afrikaans was forced into a tight *borstrok* [corset] by people behind desks who thought up new words so that they don't sound a bit like English. The creativity of our language was smothered. We got to a point where we didn't know how to handle words spontaneously and creatively ... We really turned language into such a sophisticated, uptight dogma that one became too scared to sail on waters outside the known.'

In the last edition of *Vrye Weekblad*, I referred to language again: 'If there is one thing we're proud of, it is the favour we did to the Afrikaans language by de-stigmatising it, but also making it looser and more sexy.

'We were part of the movement to hijack Afrikaans back to where it belongs: the ordinary people who speak it.'

Our books pages, and later a whole books supplement printed on crisp, white paper, were, at the time, undoubtedly the best in Afrikaans. We had wide-ranging interviews with progressive writers such as Etienne le Roux, Breyten Breytenbach, John Miles, André P Brink and Antjie Krog. William Pretorius was our books editor, but we also had formidable published authors on staff: Ryk Hattingh, Hans Pienaar, Koos Prinsloo. And only the best people wrote for us: Gerrit Olivier, Fanie Olivier (he also had a column from time to time), Joan Hambidge, Ena Jansen, Marlene van Niekerk, Jeanne Goosen, Ampie Coetzee.

I was therefore astonished when, in August 2003, the prominent Afrikaans writer and playwright, Hennie Aucamp, launched a vicious attack on *Vrye Weekblad*, then dead for almost nine years. In a piece in *Die Burger*, he accused *Vrye Weekblad* of having had a 'political agenda' to 'put Afrikaans in a sphere of inadequacy' by not sticking to standardised Afrikaans. This 'sly strategy of the extreme leftist brigade' wanted to undermine 'the most valuable metaphor for the Afrikaner', his language, in order to defeat 'that arch sin, Afrikaner hegemony'.

He was right about us wanting to undermine Afrikaner hegemony. But his little conspiracy theory about the language was just stupid. He must really have become a bitter and twisted old fart, unhappy to his core that Afrikaners had lost their political power and Afrikaans all its special privileges. *Vrye Weekblad* was a giant step towards making Afrikaans vibrant and sexy again, and palatable to the many who had shunned it because of the language-of-the-oppressor stigma.

When I read what Aucamp and other old Afrikaans literary dinosaurs have to say about Afrikaans and the artificial, uptight language they use to say it in, I am reminded of an old Afrikaans saying: *Wie kan jol met 'n stok in sy hol?* [Who can have fun with a stick up his arse?]

In *Vrye Weekblad*'s second year, another important cultural movement broke the surface: the 'alternative' Afrikaans music movement. Up till then, Afrikaans music was dominated by the likes of Bles Bridges, who sang schmaltzy love songs with terrible lyrics. Then came musicians such as Laurika Rauch and Anton Goosen, who made beautiful music and used good, poetic lyrics. But no politics, no social commentary.

The alternative lot was young, angry and hugely talented – and they were rockers. Ralph Rabie was a sub-editor at *Vrye Weekblad* when he took on the new identity that made him famous: Johannes Kerkorrel, with his Gereformeerde Blues Band. André le Roux du Toit first became André Letoit and then Koos Kombuis. James Philips became Bernoldus Niemand.

They rocked and ranted and raved about PW Botha, conscription, the NG Kerk, the Broederbond and the symbols of the ruling Afrikaner middle classes.

It was powerful and changed Afrikaans music forever. They did what *Vrye Weekblad* was doing: showing a fat middle finger to the institutions of Afrikaner power.

Vrye Weekblad and the new music movement had so much synergy, so much in common in terms of the liberation of Afrikaans and Afrikaners, that we became the sponsor, with Shifty Records, of the first big alternative music tour through South Africa: the '*Voëlvry*' tour. We were also the only Afrikaans newspaper to write extensively about these musicians.

In 1992, *Vrye Weekblad* started publishing *TwoTone*, the country's only jazz magazine, as a supplement to the paper. Shado Twala was the editor. It attracted a whole new black readership, and we were pressurised – especially by black activists who had just returned from exile – to include more English in the paper. So we became a little bilingual, with an average of about 30 per cent English per edition.

I must admit that my motivation for doing this was to increase our readership – we desperately needed to average above 25 000 readers to become more attractive to advertisers. But perhaps it was a mistake. When we changed from a tabloid format to a news magazine format in 1993, we changed back to being exclusively Afrikaans. The magazine format was probably also a mistake, although it was very good-looking. But it looked a bit too respectable, I think, and lost the raw energetic feel we'd always had. By 1993, foreign funding, even for training, had all but dried up, and I was desperate to make *Vrye Weekblad* pay for itself. In that sense the magazine format was quite successful, although it also helped to get our first professional business manager, Mark Beare, and his deputy, Louwrins Potgieter, on board. After Mark's arrival I stopped worrying so much about our finances and administration, as he was just so on top of everything.

Right through the life of *Vrye Weekblad*, the leadership of other Afrikaans newspapers treated us with hostility and waged malicious gossip campaigns against us. However, socially we got on well with the working reporters. It almost became a rule with these newspapers not to report on anything that had happened to us or on stories that we had broken.

Hennie van Deventer, news editor of *Beeld* when I worked there, then editor of *Die Volksblad* and later head of Nasionale Pers's newspaper division, wrote in his book *Kroniek van 'n Koerantman* on remarks I had made to the Truth Commission on the behaviour of Afrikaans newspapers. 'Du Preez is clearly a man with a grudge,' he writes, 'seemingly because mainstream newspapers ignored his little journal's [*blaadjie*] Vlakplaas exposés and other scoops about police brutality.

'Perhaps he has a point – although such aloofness about another paper's stories is not a strange phenomenon in the newspaper business. Moreover, *Vrye Weekblad* didn't further its own stature and credibility with its student-like frivolousness [*studentikose loslittigheid*] which cannot be associated with serious journalism.'

What a damning judgement on himself: as the editor of a newspaper, he had ignored the most important story of his career because it was published in another newspaper! He knowingly allowed the government to mislead his readers just because he wanted to ignore a publication that had a looser style than his own stuffy, Broederbond mouthpiece.

It is editors like Van Deventer who should be held responsible for the shock and horror Afrikaners felt when the real face of the successive apartheid governments was revealed before the Truth Commission.

Van Deventer did criticise the government from time to time, often annoying the establishment in the process. A few other editors did too, like Johannes Grösskopf, Ton Vosloo, Willem Wepener, Willem de Klerk and Harald Pakendorf. But they all made the same grave error: they thought criticising apartheid and encouraging negotiations in their editorial commentary was enough. They forgot that only a tiny number of readers read editorials. These editors should have allowed their reporters to reflect the true situation in the country.

How do you expect your readers to accept that state-sanctioned killings of political opponents or forced removals should stop if you never told them that these things happened in the first place, or of their effects on the victims? How can you want ordinary Afrikaners to agree with the editor's statement that the government should start talking to the ANC if your news pages continue to demonise them and the people already talking to them?

But while we were shunned by most of our Afrikaans colleagues, we made dear friends among the foreign correspondents stationed in South Africa. (CBC of Canada even made a one-hour television documentary about *Vrye Weekblad*.) Scott McCloud of *Time* magazine wrote in a letter published in our last edition: 'It was with sadness that we learned from this morning's papers that *Vrye Weekblad* is coming to an end. You and your fellow editors and reporters have done such an amazing job of keeping us informed about the "real South Africa" that this leaves a large gap in our lives and our hearts.'

Recognition also came from other colleagues. The Southern African Society of Journalists (SASJ) awarded me the 1990 Pringle Award, the first and last time it was awarded to an Afrikaans newspaper.

I received several other awards. The Junior Chamber of Commerce nominated me as one of Four Outstanding Young South Africans in 1990; the Nieman Fellows at Harvard University awarded me the Louis M Lyons Award for Conscience and Integrity in Journalism in 1991; and the University of Cape Town awarded me an honorary degree in 1992. But the Pringle Award meant the most, because my peers – people who really understood South African journalism – awarded it.

In their citation, the SASJ said:

Mr Du Preez has opened up vistas and added a new dimension to journalism in the Afrikaans media by establishing *Vrye Weekblad* as a vigorous anti-apartheid newspaper in a politically repressive and economically difficult climate. The courageous venture has introduced a new direction in Afrikaans journalism and stimulated new thinking among the newspaper's pre-dominantly Afrikaans-speaking readers, exposed for the first time to a newspaper in their own language which is unequivocally committed to free expression and the ideals of a democratic and non-racial society.

Under the editorship of Mr Du Preez, *Vrye Weekblad* has consistently been a pioneer in revealing corruption and the abuse of power by those in authority. These efforts helped to reveal the existence of police death squads, unearthing a scandal the depths of which shook South Africa.

This exposé resulted in national and international headlines and public calls for a judicial commission of inquiry. As this award is being made, the Harms Commission of Inquiry is still investigating the death squads.

Not only was *Vrye Weekblad*'s exposé one of the first vital links in the chain of events which led to the establishment of the Harms Commission, but it also broke the mould of silence amongst security operatives involved in illegal activities.

The courage and enterprise of *Vrye Weekblad* under the editorship of

Max du Preez set the example for subsequent media investigations into secret security projects.

During *Vrye Weekblad*'s short existence, it has shaken public apathy, forced a re-evaluation of a nation's values and stimulated debate on vital issues. In so doing, it has exemplified the invaluable contribution a free press makes to society.

But at the end of 1993, the Appeal Court ruled against us in a defamation case that had been dragging on since 1989. It literally bankrupted us. So where to now?

I saw no other way out than to close the publication's doors. It was a few months to South Africa's first democratic elections, and foreign funding for newspapers was something of the past. Quite rightly so, I thought. But very little had changed in the advertising market – and I had no indication that we would attract more revenue that way.

I suppose if we could have found a way around bankruptcy, we might have survived. But it would have meant slashing our tiny editorial budget to such an extent that we would not have been proud of the product. I later heard that one or two of my colleagues had blamed me for making a unilateral decision to close down *Vrye Weekblad*. Apparently they'd wanted to relaunch a new publication under the *Vrye Weekblad* masthead.

Well, they didn't ask me before I announced our closure. But I suspect I would have declined their offer anyway. In my book, *Vrye Weekblad* is a proud name. That name on a soft-touch liberal magazine would have been a travesty. As I said to my staff and in an interview with the *Weekly Mail* at the time: '*Ons fade nie, ons fokof*' [We don't fade, we fuck off].

I was also blamed for walking out of talks in 1993 with *Die Suid-Afrikaan* and a monthly Nasionale Pers magazine, *Insig*, with a view of amalgamating the three titles. But they insisted that the new title be a monthly magazine and that I would not be able to keep any of my colleagues on staff. It also meant that the name would have to go – you can't call a monthly a weekly. And I knew the new publication would not have continued *Vrye Weekblad*'s brand of journalism.

There was another nagging question: How would *Vrye Weekblad* have repositioned itself after the advent of democracy in April 1994, two months after our last edition? Would there have been room for our campaigning style and irreverent journalism? Shouldn't we just say we'd achieved what we'd wanted to achieve, and quit?

I'm still not sure. But I often think that *Vrye Weekblad* would have been in the ideal position today to stimulate progressive thinking and help Afrikaners to really accept the new society, while at the same time giving the government hell on mismanagement, nepotism, corruption and bad policy decisions. Our lack of apartheid baggage would have been a major asset now.

On the other hand, a new generation of progressive young editors have taken over at *Rapport, Beeld* and *Die Burger* and dragged these publications into the New South Africa. They have become professional, modern newspapers in tune with the new society, and the difference between them and a *Vrye Weekblad* of today wouldn't have been that big.

In my farewell in the last edition, I wrote: 'There are many things I'm not sure about regarding the last five years. But one thing I do know: it was worth every moment, even the most difficult. It was exciting and rewarding and creative. *Vrye Weekblad* played a positive role and contributed to the more open society that is now emerging. I am proud that I could have had a part in the creation of a positive symbol of hope, integrity and openness.

'The other thing I do know, is that the people who were *Vrye Weekblad* the last five years, were the best South African journalism had ever known. I mean best in the sense of commitment, loyalty, idealism, work ethic, adventurousness and ability. They are special people. I shall never forget them.'

Jacques Pauw wrote: 'I will always remember *Vrye Weekblad* for exactly that which eventually caused its downfall: we never listened to anyone. Not to the advertisers. Not to the market. Not to other media bosses. Not to any politician. Not to the law or the courts or the police or the Attorney-General. I am proud of that.'

Martie Meiring said: 'If the Afrikaner needed liberation therapy, then *Vrye Weekblad* gave it. The mission was clear: you were allowed to stand up to authority; you were allowed to question and challenge vested interests, thoughts and ideologies; you were quite welcome to be a pain in the butt until your questions, all your questions, were answered.'

Vrye Weekblad was famous for its witty, irreverent and catchy posters. Martie commented: 'Readers, even those who didn't read *Vrye Weekblad*, read its posters. It was the best public reading matter ever. It made discussions around the dinner table come alive – to think up a *Vrye Weekblad* poster!'

She concluded: 'Later, when I joined *Vrye Weekblad* and experienced the inner workings of the near anarchistic environment, the creative energy struck me. Cynical, quarrelsome, fun and exciting; boredom wasn't something you felt in the office or read in the paper.

'I still think: *Vrye Weekblad* properly liberated us Afrikaners of our restrictive corset of guilt, apartheid and painful, solemn correctness.'

I had to page through all the back copies of *Vrye Weekblad* before writing this chapter. I haven't done that since our last edition appeared on 2 February 1994. It was like a reunion with a long-lost lover. I cried and laughed; I got a bit angry.

But mostly I am immensely proud.

It was a good chapter in South African journalism. Those were golden years. I consider myself richly blessed to have been a part of that experience.

24

Toying with the lion's testicles

I LOOKED INTO Dirk Coetzee's eyes. This was not what I thought evil would look like. He was quite a handsome man, with a strong, open face. I kept thinking: 'How can this man be a serial killer?' He could have been my cousin, or a deacon in the church.

Dirk had just told me his story: he had been the commander of an elite special unit in the South African security police called C1, or Vlakplaas, after the farm where they were stationed outside Pretoria. Dirk, then a rising star in the police, set up the unit in 1980 with a few white officers and seventeen former guerrillas who had switched sides, called askaris. (Their bosses murdered four of them when their loyalties became suspect.)

Vlakplaas's mission was to kill and harass opponents of the apartheid government. Like a business entrepreneur explaining his company's prospectus, Dirk told me how he had overseen the brutal slaying of Durban lawyer Griffiths Mxenge, and how he had the young activist Siphiwo Mtimkulu 'eliminated' and burned his body. The list of murders, tortures, assaults and kidnappings was long.

All my human and journalistic instincts told me that Dirk was telling the truth.

As I listened to him, I had a sudden panic attack. A part of me wished I had never had this conversation. There was no way in the world, having heard his story, that we could ignore or keep it quiet. But I also knew that the story would be one of the most dangerous to be published since the National Party came to power in 1948. It could mean the end of our newspaper, and possibly have serious personal security implications for my colleagues and myself.

I turned to my colleague Jacques Pauw and solemnly told him: '*Nou speel ons met die leeu se bal*' [Now we are toying with the lion's testicles].

But my excitement was greater than my fear. I knew, as did everyone in South African politics, and indeed everyone without blinkers in South Africa, that the apartheid government was kidnapping, killing and torturing people who opposed their policies. Who else would be responsible for the assassinations, mysterious deaths and disappearances of anti-apartheid activists? Apartheid was not a peaceful, well-meant policy of separate development, but a violent, inhuman doctrine. But nobody could ever find enough proof to expose this side of South Africa. Find the proof, and ordinary good people would be forced to look into their hearts and say, 'We cannot go along with that.'

In front of me sat a living, talking smoking gun. He was not just another wild man seeking attention with a crazy story. He had been the founder and commander of an official state-sanctioned death squad. He was a captain in the security police.

I sensed that I was experiencing an important moment that could change the history of my country. Perhaps this was why the universe had wanted me to launch an impossible newspaper project.

I had known about Dirk Coetzee for some time. Not long after we had launched *Vrye Weekblad*, Jacques told me that while he was working for *Rapport* in 1985, he and Martin Welz had met a policeman who claimed that he had information about a secret unit that killed people. *Rapport* wouldn't touch the story; nor would any other newspapers to which Dirk took his story. Dirk even confessed to two different members of parliament, but nothing was done. It was dangerous; it went to the core of what apartheid really was.

I don't know why we never went back to the story. I'd had no idea that the story would be so real and powerful, and in the drama of launching *Vrye Weekblad* and fighting for its survival, it slipped my mind completely.

But then, on 11 September 1989, my friend Anton Lubowski was assassinated. Jacques and I decided the next morning that we would make it our business to find out who had killed Anton. Jacques' first move was to look up his old mate Dirk Coetzee. Anton's assassination must have been a Vlakplaas job, Jacques said. (It turned out that it wasn't Vlakplaas, but a military death squad, the CCB. But we only found that out much later.)

Jacques had supper with Dirk in Pretoria that evening. But Dirk was no longer so desperate to tell his story. His earlier motivation to expose Vlakplaas had been fuelled by his hatred of the police generals. He had fallen out of favour after a botched kidnapping attempt in Swaziland and the killing of a diamond dealer in Lesotho, and was transferred from the security police to a desk job in the uniform branch. Now, several years later, his desire for revenge had somewhat subsided.

But Dirk was receptive to our arguments that it was in the interests of our country and a peaceful future that the truth about Vlakplaas be told. Telling his story would also restore his own standing as a professional policeman after being so maligned by his former colleagues, we told him.

Dirk agreed. But he had a precondition: his former comrades would most certainly try to kill him after he had told his story, so he wanted us to take him out of the country and find a place for him and his family to live safely.

Next major decision: how do we get Dirk out of the country and how do we find him a new home overseas? We had no money to spend, and it wasn't exactly the kind of thing for which you can seek sponsorship. Besides, Dirk would need a safe house and probably bodyguards. He also needed to be accessible for further debriefing and possible media interviews, and as a witness in any upcoming court cases or inquiries.

There was only one option. We had to hand him into the care of the African National Congress. They had the only intelligence capacity we could trust to debrief Dirk thoroughly and at the same time keep him safe. It was, after all, their members and supporters who were being murdered by Vlakplaas.

It was a crazy idea. The ANC was an outlawed organisation. Not too long before this, a man was sentenced to jail for quite some time just for scratching the three letters 'ANC' on his tin coffee mug. The ANC was at war with the apartheid government. If it became known that we had conspired with the ANC to get a security police 'defector' out of the country, we could be charged with terrorism, if not treason.

We would have to be very careful. No, paranoid. No discussions in the office, and no mention of Dirk or Vlakplaas over the telephone. If the security police or National Intelligence even had a whiff of what we were up to, the whole operation would end right there. For weeks, only three people knew about the conspiracy: Dirk, Jacques and myself.

Then a third person came into the picture: André Zaaiman. He was an officer in the SADF's citizen force until he resigned his commission and became one of the driving forces behind the End Conscription Campaign. At the time, he was working for Idasa, where I got to know him. I had an idea that he might have connections in Lusaka, and I knew he was the one guy I could trust.

André, we soon found out, had more than 'connections' in Lusaka. He was actually an intelligence operative in Umkhonto we Sizwe. As an Idasa organiser facilitating contacts across the political divide, he regularly travelled to Lusaka – and then secretly briefed the ANC on developments inside South Africa. We'd certainly picked the right guy.

André was excited, and agreed that taking Dirk to the ANC would be the correct move. A few days later, he briefed the ANC's Chief of Intelligence, Jacob Zuma. The machinery was set in motion.

Jacques spent his days with Dirk, reassuring the sometimes-volatile man that he was doing the right thing, and at the same time looking for holes in Dirk's many sensational stories. There weren't any we could find.

Friday 20 October 1989. Jacques and I arrived at the office more or less at the same time for the weekly editorial conference. We picked up that morning's edition of the *Weekly Mail*, and stared at each other in shock.

The headline read: 'Death-row policeman tells of Special Branch hit squad'. It was the story of Almond Nofemela, a Vlakplaas policeman, who was to be hanged the next day for the murder of a white farmer. His superiors had promised to save him from the gallows if he kept quiet about Vlakplaas, but obviously hadn't kept their word. So he made the dramatic statement through his lawyers and asked – and got – a stay of execution.

Nofemela also blew Dirk's cover: 'In 1981 I was appointed as a member of the Security Branch assassination squad and I served under Captain Dirk Coetzee,' Nofemela declared. All his statements supported what Dirk had told us.

It was clear that we would have to move our plans forward and publish Dirk's full story as soon as possible. Dirk was becoming very edgy, especially after being named by Nofemela.

That same evening, we organised the first meeting between André and Dirk – at Van Zyl Slabbert's thatched cottage outside Johannesburg, completely without his knowledge (he was out of town for a week). Jacques and I were already paranoid, and now a former security policeman on the run and a secret agent of the banned ANC were about to join us. The paranoia quadrupled. But we had reason to be paranoid – we established years later that the police were tapping all four of our phones at the time.

So we used elaborate coded language, and always checked whether we were being followed. André organised Van Zyl's house as a meeting point because it was secluded and he went there often anyway, but he couldn't tell us that. We met outside a filling station between Pretoria and Johannesburg, from where we proceeded to the cottage. But then someone – I think it was André, but it could have been Dirk – spotted a suspicious-looking car. A wild car chase ensued that lasted almost an hour before we were certain we weren't being followed. We were playing cowboys and crooks.

Coetzee unpacked his gruesome tales again in all their detail, fully answering André's and my questions. The next day Dirk brought his former gardener and Vlakplaas driver, David 'Spyker' Tshikalanga, to the cottage for interrogation. My stomach turned as he gave us a blow-by-blow account of how they had savaged Griffiths Mxenge, and how he had twisted the hunting knife in the lawyer's chest.

We were satisfied that Dirk's evidence was truthful and unembellished. It tallied with every other bit of information we had, and it corresponded with what he had told Jacques years earlier. It was time for action, but the ANC had still not decided that they would take responsibility for Dirk.

When André got the green light from Jacob Zuma, we booked Jacques and Dirk on a flight from Johannesburg to Durban and from Durban to Mauritius. Dirk didn't even tell his wife Karin what he was about to do. He said a tearful farewell to his sons Kalla and Dirkie (and his two poodles), and left with Jacques on a trip that would change his life forever.

On 5 November 1989, a day after *Vrye Weekblad*'s first birthday, Dirk and Jacques were on their way to Mauritius. Dirk was highly strung, and talked and drank incessantly. Jacques told me later that he'd had serious doubts about the story, sitting next to Dirk in the aircraft. Not only was he doing a recklessly dangerous thing, but he was also having second thoughts about helping an apartheid assassin escape justice in South Africa.

For a week, Jacques tape-recorded Dirk's confessions and drew up an elaborate affidavit. Then Dirk flew to London into the hands of Jacob Zuma, and Jacques came home to write the story.

It was a difficult story to keep secret. Our colleagues in the office knew something was up, but we simply couldn't risk telling anybody anything. At the last moment, we gave all our material to three hand-picked foreign correspondents whom I knew and trusted, and who would publish the story on the same Friday – just in case we were stopped from publishing at the last minute.

Vrye Weekblad's designer was told on the Wednesday that the first seven pages would be filled with one story, which would only be available on the Thursday afternoon.

Almost as an afterthought, we informed our lawyers that we were about to publish a risky story, and they came to the office. Their eyes grew wider and wider as they read the copy. They were what we called 'struggle lawyers', and they knew us well enough by then to know we didn't want their agreement to publish, merely their advice on the worst dangers we would face. They nevertheless warned us that 'all of [the story]' transgressed several different laws.

In his confessions, Dirk told how he went to the SAP's laboratories and obtained poison from the head of the police forensics unit, General Lothar Neethling, which he later administered to ANC activists.

Our lawyers wanted us to take out Neethling's name, because, they said, it was the 'worst defamation imaginable'. To their horror, I took a coin, flipped it and said: 'Heads his name stays, tails it's out.' It landed on my hand and I said: 'Heads.' Our lawyers stormed out of the office, accusing me of gross irresponsibility and recklessness.

This story was later held up as proof of my recklessness, but it had just been a game. The decision to publish Neethling's name was one I had made earlier after much thought and repeated assurances by Dirk that it was the absolute truth. This was an extremely important story and had to have maximum impact and credibility. Not naming names to play safe would undermine that. It was time to point fingers at actual living people. And I knew defamatory statements couldn't have legal consequences if they were true and in the public interest. The statements about Neethling were quite obviously both.

I was at the printers that Thursday night, 16 November, to see the newspaper get printed. I expected the police to arrive at any second to stop the presses. Nobody came. The men who worked on the press were all Portuguese-speaking and didn't understand Afrikaans, so we didn't anticipate anybody making a last call to the cops from there.

But nobody came. We followed the stacks of newspapers to the distributors and to the post office, just in case they were intercepted. They were not. I travelled some of the way with *Vrye Weekblad*'s driver, Joseph Moetaesi, while he put up our posters on lamp poles. The posters were identical to our cover: a picture of Dirk with the words '*Bloedspoor van die SAP*' [the SAP's trail of blood]. Nobody took our posters down. *Vrye Weekblad* appeared on the newsstands on Friday 17 November 1989, just as it did every Friday.

It was quite remarkable: the police, the security police, military intelligence, the National Intelligence Service, in fact the men at Vlakplaas itself, only found out that Dirk had spilled the beans on the morning we published the story. That is either an indictment of their incompetence or a compliment to our security measures.

There it was: seven pages of the inside workings and the whole bloody history of the National Party government's police death squad. Dirk's most famous quote was '*Ek was in die hart van die hoer*' [I was in the heart of the whore]. Jacques used it in the title of a book he later wrote, *In the Heart of the Whore*.

Dirk's confessions read as if they'd originated in the death squads of Chile or Argentina: murder, poisoning, arson, sabotage, kidnapping. Particularly gory was his version of how he and his cohorts had burned the bodies of murdered activists while standing around with a beer in their hand. He also spilled the beans on other police crimes. He revealed that Major Craig 'Superspy' Williamson, whose unit also blew up Jeanette and Katryn Schoon in Angola, had sent the parcel bomb that killed Ruth First in Maputo.

I wrote in my editorial: 'The testimony of cold-blooded murders and bomb explosions in other countries should stigmatise the South African government as a terrorist government in the class of Libya. It is like a cancer in the nation's bosom. We must open it up now so that it can heal. In any other civilised country the government would have resigned immediately after such a scandal. Here this is not the case. But the absolute minimum which each civilised South African now expects from the government is that a full-fledged commission of inquiry be appointed immediately and that all involved are forced to testify and be questioned in public.'

The way in which the mainstream newspapers, especially the Afrikaans ones, responded to the story, is a sad chapter in South Africa's media history. The Afrikaans newspapers only published small stories quoting the SAP's absolute denial of everything Dirk had said. Vlakplaas was merely a place where rehabilitated ANC guerrillas were housed, the police said. *Beeld* wrote that one had to be mad oneself to believe Coetzee. They all conveniently forgot that just a month earlier Almond Nofemela had stated that he was a member of Dirk's death squad.

We offered the other newspapers Dirk's affidavit, we even offered telephonic interviews with Dirk in London, but they were not interested. Dirk personally phoned the *Sunday Times* from London a week after our first story ran to offer them a full interview. They declined, and instead gave the security police all the information he had given them. Our 'alternative' sisters, *Weekly Mail*, *New Nation* and *South*, carried full reports and launched their own investigations.

The mainstream media also ignored our revelation that Eugene de Kock was the new commander at Vlakplaas, and that he had taken part in a number of murders and executions, such as the killing of eight people at Piet Retief.

I went to the Idasa conference with the ANC two weeks after Dirk's story ran, where I met Hennie van Deventer, editor of *Die Volksblad*. (Within two years, those who talked to the ANC had gone from being 'traitors' and 'useful idiots' to responsible citizens.) Dirk's revelations were the talk of the conference. Van Deventer, a senior member of the Broederbond and a prominent Afrikaner Nationalist, cornered me, and said: 'Coetzee must be lying. It simply can't be true what he's saying. I'll eat my hat if it's all true.'

In the following months, I saw a lot of that attitude, also from judges. There are two possibilities for this: either they were so far removed from the reality in the street and so ensconced in the system that they simply could not believe that such brutal behaviour existed. Or – and this is my theory – they had to go into denial because if what Dirk had said was true, they were part of something very barbaric and unchristian.

Predictably, the police launched a huge campaign to discredit Dirk. They called him a habitual liar, perjurer, traitor, gangster, psychopath and an unstable diabetes sufferer. Many newspapers played along. The Afrikaans Sunday paper *Rapport* even published a sensational story that Dirk had never left the country and was lying low on a farm somewhere, a very sick and delusional man. Dirk phoned the reporter and sent him a fax from London, but the story was never corrected. Some newspapers suggested *Vrye Weekblad* had paid Dirk large amounts of money for his story.

At *Vrye Weekblad*, the floodgates had opened. Other former Vlakplaas operatives came forward to support Dirk's revelations. Jacques traced and interviewed Peter Casselton, the man who had bombed the ANC's offices in London on behalf of the security police. Barney Horn, a counter-insurgency policeman, revealed more police murders and torture. (Horn also left the country after his confessions. He flew to Tel Aviv via Rome, but was arrested on arrival in Israel and deported back to Italy. We put pressure on the Italians to allow him to go to Holland, where Amnesty International took care of him.)

Vrye Weekblad ran confessions of dirty policemen and exposés of state terrorism week after week, month after month. In the end readers became sick of it, but we thought it was very important to at least put all the atrocities on record.

Many people found it strange that policemen and soldiers picked *Vrye Weekblad*, an Afrikaans newspaper, for their confessions. I knew why. As white Afrikaner men, Jacques and I understood where these people came from and what made them do what they did. We were fellow Afrikaners; we not only spoke the same language, *we understood the ethnic code* of Afrikaners. Also, after Dirk's story, they knew we could be trusted to publish the truth and would not sell out our informants.

Eventually the new state president, FW De Klerk, appointed Judge Louis Harms to head a commission of inquiry into state-sponsored violence. It was a circus. CCB members in wigs and false moustaches, as well as a number of policemen, appeared before the judge. It was their most useful campaign of deception yet.

Judge Harms, the poor soul, found that Coetzee was a liar, and that there was no such thing as a state-run death squad. Vlakplaas, under its new commander whom we had also exposed, Colonel Eugene de Kock, continued with their dirty work for several years after we ran Dirk's confessions.

Harms introduced his final report with the Latin phrase *felix qui potuit verum cognoscere caucus* [blessed is he who can recognise the truth]. Louis Harms wasn't so blessed. Years later some of the same characters confessed to the Truth Commission that they had all colluded to lie to Harms. We knew this at the time and said so loudly on the pages of *Vrye Weekblad*.

In the meantime, Dirk had become a proper and enthusiastic ANC member, referring to his colleagues as 'comrades'. But he could never rest: his South African colleagues tried to kill him on three occasions. He had to move house thirty-eight times, and at some point was even guarded by Scotland Yard.

While he was stationed at the ANC headquarters in Zambia, he received a parcel from South Africa. The sender, it stated on the wrapping, was a Johannesburg human rights lawyer, Bheki Mlangeni. Dirk was suspicious, refused to accept the parcel, and it was 'returned to sender'. He asked the ANC to warn Mlangeni that the parcel was suspect.

Back in Johannesburg, on 15 February 1991, Mlangeni received the parcel he had never seen before. He opened it and found a cassette player inside with the inscription 'Evidence: hit squads'. He put on the earphones, switched on the tape – and was killed instantly by the explosives hidden inside the earphones.

Vlakplaas had claimed another victim – sixteen months after we'd exposed them.

In 1996, I had a public showdown with FW de Klerk about this. He had just given evidence to the Truth Commission with his normal theme – I'm so sorry about it all, but I didn't know, and when I knew, I stopped it. After his testimony an impromptu press conference was held, and I asked him why he had misled the commission by saying that he had closed down Vlakplaas when he learned about its existence, while the truth was that they had continued killing undisturbed for two more years. De Klerk became very angry when I persisted, and his aides whisked him away.

De Klerk's dislike of me was intense. The Vice Chancellor of the University of Cape Town, Stuart Saunders, mentions this in his book *Vice-Chancellor on a Tightrope – a personal account of climactic years in South Africa*. He writes: 'Among those who received honorary degrees from UCT in 1992 was Max du Preez, editor of *Vrye Weekblad*, a newspaper published in Transvaal. He had courageously exposed the hit squads and assassinations carried out by the South African security forces. The university was honouring him for his courage in these actions and for defending democracy. Interestingly, just after the announcement was made that Du Preez was to get an honorary degree, I was at a dinner party where the then State President, De Klerk, and his wife Marike were also guests. When he came into the lounge and sat down he looked at me and said, "Why are you honouring Du Preez?" I asked him why he asked the question and he said, "Well, he's one of my enemies." I replied, "We are honouring him because he has exposed murder and hit squads and has promoted democracy. Why is he one of your enemies?" There was no reply.'

Mind you, his predecessor, PW Botha, hated me in equal measure. Of course, I knew this because of the way his government treated us when he was still in power, but he and I also had a face-to-face meeting where it was confirmed.

Botha had refused to give evidence to the TRC, for which he was then dragged to court in 1998. After his court appearance, a defiant Botha held a press conference in the courtroom, clearly basking in the national and international attention after years in obscurity. He wagged the familiar finger again (he resembled the satirist Pieter-Dirk Uys more than he did himself), and warned: 'Don't awaken the tiger in the Afrikaner, the consequences will be grave.'

I was standing a few metres away, and said to him: 'Mr Botha, has nobody ever told you that there aren't any tigers in Africa?' Those of us who thought the old coot had become senile and slow were in for a surprise. He took three steps towards me, punched me in the chest with his famous finger, and said: 'Yes, but if there were, you wouldn't have been one of them.'

It was a good retort, and everybody laughed. And then he went off about 'this man' – still punching me with his finger – who had 'spent his life making trouble for everyone' and 'stirred up feelings where he shouldn't have'. I sometimes miss the old guy.

Dirk soon became a bit of a celebrity. He was interviewed by literally hundreds of radio and television stations across the world and by every newspaper that had any interest in South African affairs. He was a happy man before he eventually came home, because the ANC top brass had promised that he would be made a general in the new dispensation.

But they dropped him. Dirk came back, despised by his former colleagues, ignored by his new comrades. He fell around doing menial jobs before getting a desk job with the National Intelligence Agency after 1994. He was also convicted of the murder of Griffiths Mxenge – the same murder the police and judges said never took place – but was granted amnesty by the Truth Commission. Dirk today is a shadow of his former self and feels deeply betrayed by the ANC. He is not the only one.

Did Dirk ever feel genuine remorse for his crimes? Only he knows. I am convinced, though, that he fully understood that his crimes were utterly senseless, and that the ideological premise for perpetrating such deeds was completely false. He did go on quite a crusade to beg the forgiveness of the families of some of his victims – and one, Griffiths Mxenge's brother, told him to go to hell.

Perhaps Dirk wasn't such a monster after all; perhaps he can with some legitimacy claim to be a victim of the prevailing ideology of the time. Because even though Dirk had moments where he boasted how evil and bloodthirsty he could be, he never actually killed anyone himself. He ordered his colleagues to kill many times, he witnessed many brutal slayings, but he never actually executed anyone himself.

Eugene de Kock confirmed this in his own way. In his book, *A Long Night's Damage*, which he wrote with Jeremy Gordin, he refers to Dirk's statement that he was 'in the heart of the whore'. De Kock says: 'That was not strictly true. For, if you want to pursue this metaphor, Coetzee was the kind of man who visits a brothel but stays in the parlour: he always had others do his dirty work for him. Furthermore, compared with me, he hadn't visited all that often. I doubt whether the whore would have recognised Coetzee in the street.'

By the time the Truth Commission started investigating South Africa's sordid past, we had exposed a large chunk of the evil of the 1980s. Every single one of the stories we published on gross human rights violations in *Vrye Weekblad* was proved true before the Truth Commission – only, in some cases we had understated the evil.

Dirk Coetzee never lied. The state president and the ministers of police and of defence lied, as did most of their generals – but not the man whom they had described as delusional and unstable.

He never received an apology from the politicians and generals who had defamed him. Not even the newspapers, which had so enthusiastically smeared his name and discredited his story, have apologised to him.

This nation owes Dirk Coetzee. Who knows if we would know so much about our bitter past if he hadn't kickstarted the process so dramatically in 1989? He certainly has nothing to show for it today. Or perhaps he should just count himself incredibly lucky not to be in jail – or on death row – for the rest of his life.

At the moment, jail is where his successor at Vlakplaas, Eugene de Kock, finds himself, serving a sentence of 212 years.

I met De Kock once in jail when I went there with Jacques to talk to him, and I met him several times when he was appearing before the Truth Commission. But the first time I met him was at Vlakplaas itself. It wasn't polite.

When the Australian rugby team played South Africa for the first time after the lifting of the sports boycott, I was a guest of the then editor of the *Pretoria News*, Deon du Plessis, in the newspaper's hospitality suite at Loftus Versfeld stadium in Pretoria. I think it was in August 1992. I was getting tired and emotional with two young Afrikaans guys who had won a *Pretoria News* competition, the prize being two test tickets in the newspaper's suite. After the game, they asked me whether I wanted to go to Vlakplaas. They explained that they were both police-men stationed there. I thought what the hell, why not – in fact, I think I wasn't thinking at all. When I said goodbye to Deon, I told him that I was on my way to Vlakplaas, just in case I disappeared. He said I was crazy to go, but my new friends were pulling me by the arm, so off we went.

I followed them through the streets and winding dirt roads in my Volkswagen Golf, and then we arrived at the farm. We walked into a noisy pub filled with policemen, and by now I knew what a crazy thing I was doing. As people recognised me, the pub grew quieter and quieter. I saw De Kock with his familiar thick-lensed glasses sitting at the end of the bar counter. He looked at me for a few seconds, and then looked away.

My hosts presented me with a potion everyone had to drink the first time they walked into the Vlakplaas pub: a potent concoction of different kinds of liquor, filled with garlic cloves. They called it *Leeutande* [lion's teeth]. I downed the drink, and, predictably, a few minutes later I had to go outside to vomit. On my way back in, my two hosts stopped me, both in a slight panic. Some of their colleagues were intensely unhappy about my presence, they said, so I had to leave very quickly while they tried to delay the hotheads who had gone to fetch their guns.

I did leave quickly – very quickly. It was about three in the morning and I drove back to Johannesburg very fast. Just after the Woodmead turn-off on the Pretoria–Johannesburg highway, a white Opel Astra pulled up right behind me and flashed its lights. I didn't know anyone who drove such a car, so I didn't stop. The Opel then moved up right next to me, and the man in the passenger seat indicated that I should pull over. By now I had a strong suspicion that these were Vlakplaas guys, so I pushed my Golf as hard as I could.

The Astra started pushing me off the road and onto the shoulder, and I had to fight hard to keep my steering wheel straight. Then the metal barricade on the Corlett Drive off-ramp came into view right in front of me. I braked hard, but the barricade flipped my car over and off the grass embankment.

I climbed out of the wreck fairly unscathed and ran, but the Opel did not stop. A police van picked me up on the side of the highway about an hour later. I told them the whole story and laid a charge, but I didn't have the Opel's registration number, and that became their excuse for not investigating the matter.

At about six in the morning, when I dragged my stiff and bruised body into bed, I lay there thinking: Could there possibly be a part of me that had a death wish?

25

The spirit of Joseph Mengele

ORDINARY CITIZENS EVERYWHERE accept that men in uniform with guns on different sides of a political or geographic divide kill each other. They might favour the one or the other side, but morally they accept that a soldier's business is to kill enemy soldiers.

But when soldiers experiment with chemicals in a laboratory that are meant to kill opponents in a clandestine fashion, people's evil-detectors sound the alarm. They start thinking of the Nazi doctor Joseph Mengele.

When Dirk Coetzee told us late in 1989 that the head of the South African Police's forensics laboratory, General Lothar Neethling, was known among policemen for experimenting with toxins, known as *Lothar se Doepa* [Lothar's Magic Potion], with which to kill opponents of the government, my evil-detector emitted a shrill wail.

Coetzee told us in detail how he had fetched some of the *doepa* from Neethling on four different occasions: three times from his office, and once from his home. Coetzee then used it on four activists: Mathew Kondile, and men known as Vusi, Peter and General.

By then I had heard rumours that the Rhodesian security forces had used poison on clothes, and injected poison into bottles of alcohol or tins of food. In 1977 alone, more than 800 black people, not all guerrillas, had died as a result of poisoned items that were distributed by the Selous Scouts. I knew the South African security forces were not above torture and murder, but I never even considered that they might have started with chemical and biological warfare.

Whatever the risk, I thought, we had a duty to expose this man, Lothar Neethling. This was pure evil. South Africans should know about this, and it should be stopped.

So we published Coetzee's testimony that Neethling had supplied him with poison. Neethling's lawyers immediately told us that they wanted R1 million in damages for defamation, as well as an apology. We went back to Coetzee and said to him: 'Dirk, old pal, now you better think long and hard and very clearly. If you're wrong on any point, you will sink us.' Dirk didn't hesitate for a second: every word of it was true, it happened exactly as he'd told us.

In the next edition, we ran a front-page headline: '*Dit wás Lothar se Doepa!*' [It *was* Lothar's potion], and repeated Dirk's statements. Neethling added another R500 000 to his libel suit.

I was decent enough not to publish the fact that Neethling was a German World War II orphan who came to South Africa when he was thirteen – it would have strengthened the Mengele angle.

The court case started in October 1990. Coetzee could still not return to South Africa, so his evidence had to be heard in London. The judge assigned to the case, Johan Kriegler, could not hear a case in Britain, so Coetzee's evidence was led before a member of the British Bar, Shaun Naidoo. *Vrye Weekblad* was represented by Bobby Levine, SC, and Frans Rautenbach, and Neethling by Willie Oshry, SC, and Manny Witz. It was very strange to be in London and to hear the darkest secrets of South Africa unfold so far from home.

The crux of the case was that Neethling denied ever having met Coetzee and ever experimenting with or producing toxins to be used by policemen to drug and kill people. But Coetzee could give a detailed description of Neethling's home and office, right down to the pictures on the walls.

Coetzee's little green police telephone book, which he'd used in 1980 and 1981, was handed in as evidence. It showed that Coetzee had written down Neethling's confidential telephone numbers during the period that Coetzee was commander at Vlakplaas. Coetzee identified the other names and numbers in the book, which all corresponded to police colleagues he'd identified the year before as people who had worked with him or had been his targets. There were two exceptions: the names of rugby players Naas Botha and Thys Burger. Coetzee said he had helped them get new telephones through his contacts in the Post Office.

Coetzee also gave wide-ranging evidence about all the kidnappings and murders in which he had been involved in South Africa, Swaziland and Lesotho. Official documents that supported his version of the detention and death of an Eastern Cape activist, Mathew Kondile, were handed in to court to prove that the official police account was false. The police had earlier told the Harms Commission that Kondile was released by them and never seen again, but the documents proved that he was still in detention two months later. Ordered to get rid of Kondile, Coetzee drugged him with drops he'd received from Neethling and took him to Komatipoort, where a policeman shot him. Coetzee burned his body to ashes on the banks of the Komati River.

Oshry cross-examined Coetzee vigorously in English, with Coetzee testifying in Afrikaans. Oshry said to Coetzee that Neethling was a respected forensic scientist and not part of the security police set-up. 'He was not a part of the happy band of warriors who went around bombing and killing people.' Coetzee replied, 'No, but he was a link in the whole security chain. As I was the killing link, so Neethling was the poisoning link in the chain.'

A month later, the case continued before Judge Kriegler – during the same week that Judge Louis Harms released his commission's findings that a police death squad had never existed. Harms called Coetzee 'mad' and 'a psychopath' who showed no remorse. Our application to the Minister of Justice, Kobie Coetsee, to give Coetzee temporary indemnity so he that could attend the court case and assist counsel with background information, was denied.

Neethling, a conceited and pompous man, took the stand. He said Coetzee was an idiot with no brains, and had thought up his stories about his visits to Neethling when he was sitting in Mauritius with a beer in his hand. He said Coetzee could have walked past his house and office while he was fabricating his evidence to see what they looked like. He had to concede, however, that Coetzee would then not have known, as he had testified, that there were wooden floors under the carpets in the house.

Coetzee's telephone book came up again when the former Commissioner of Police, General Mike Geldenhuys, testified that Coetzee could have falsified the inscriptions in between all the other numbers. But the shock came when Neethling himself told the court that he had tested the book over the weekend in his laboratory and found that it had been exposed to water or damp. An astonished Bobby Levine told Judge Kriegler that the book was evidence before the court, and had been sealed in London and sent to the registrar of the Supreme Court. Neethling had removed it illegally.

General Geldenhuys testified that Coetzee's stories were 'outrageous', because a police death squad had never existed. He said that he had been 'shocked' and 'stunned' when he saw the allegations against Neethling in *Vrye Weekblad*, because Neethling was a 'highly respected member of the police'.

Neethling also called the director of the Water Research Commission, Dr Mathys Pieterse, who testified that he knew Neethling well and always sat next to him at rugby matches at Loftus Versfeld stadium. He said Neethling was a 'world-renowned forensic expert', and would definitely not have produced a toxin that took three efforts to kill a man, as Coetzee had testified in one of the cases.

The chief secretary of the Suid-Afrikaanse Akademie van Wetenskap en Kuns [academy of science and arts], Dr Danie Geldenhuys, explained that Neethling was a highly respected member of his organisation who, in fact, had received a gold medal from the academy.

One of our star witnesses was Leslie Lesia, a paid agent of the Civil Cooperation Bureau, who had infiltrated the ANC in Mozambique and Swaziland. He testified that his handler, one Becker, had taken him to Neethling's laboratory on 23 March 1987 to fetch three cases of beer, a case of vodka and a case of brandy – all spiked with poison. A short while later, he and Becker were in the restaurant of the Airport Holiday Inn when Becker pointed out Neethling and three friends at another table. That's the man who prepared the poison, Becker told him.

He testified that he later gave some of the spiked liquor to ANC leaders in Mozambique. He saw one of them, Gibson Ncube, drinking some of it. Ncube died a week later, and Lesia helped his family with the funeral arrangements.

Jacques Pauw made a frantic trip to Harare to get hold of some of the physical evidence in Lesia's testimony. Lesia had been captured by Zimbabwe's Central Intelligence Organisation (CIO) in June 1987, and jailed until just before the start of the court case. Jacques got a series of photographs from the CIO that they had taken of Lesia's car, showing the secret compartment where he had hidden a bottle of poison. Jacques got the bottle itself, as well as a nifty ring with a removable top with which Lesia used to spike ANC members' drinks. The photographs, the bottle of poison and the ring were dramatically handed in as evidence.

Martin Welz, the investigative journalist who worked at *Rapport* with Jacques, told the court that Coetzee's story of 1984 was exactly the same as the one he had told *Vrye Weekblad*. Welz said Neethling probably didn't think supplying Coetzee with poison was wrong, but 'probably thought it was part of his job, as Coetzee thought his actions were part of his job'.

Coetzee's mother, Maria, told the court of the day in 1981 when she had accompanied her son to the police forensics laboratory in Pretoria. Dirk had told her that he had to fetch 'something' from General Neethling.

During the last week of November, the arguments for the two sides were put before Judge Kriegler. Coetzee's descriptions of Neethling's house and office were crucial bits of evidence. Advocate Oshry, for Neethling, said Coetzee could have walked past the office while he was working for the Narcotics Bureau (where Coetzee worked for a few months after Vlakplaas).

Kriegler: 'Coetzee knew there was a photograph of Easterns rugby team on the wall with General Neethling standing in the picture. He could not have made these observations by just walking past.'

Oshry: 'He could have been there when General Neethling wasn't there.'

Kriegler: 'I put it to you: he must have been there. He must have been there for a while. He also knew that there was a Concorde certificate on the eastern wall which stated that "Doctor" Neethling had been a passenger.'

Oshry: 'Someone could have given him a description of what it looked like.'

Kriegler: 'I want to put an analogy to you. A man confesses that he and a certain woman, whose husband is missing, had murdered him together. He spent time with the woman in her bedroom. He saw her naked. He says she has a birthmark on her upper body and a beauty spot on her buttock. How could he have given that description if he hadn't been intimate with her?'

Oshry: 'Why could other members of the force not have told him? There are several other pictures and mementos in General Neethling's office Coetzee didn't describe.'

Kriegler: 'The same woman in my analogy also had a birthmark on her lower body and another beauty spot on her shoulder. The fact that the man who makes the confession doesn't mention those is completely irrelevant. It is the beauty spot on the buttock that counts. These are two unique characteristics which you won't find in any other policeman's office. When someone describes them without mistakes, then we have good evidence.'

Oshry: ' But these were only two characteristics. It doesn't prove ...'

Kriegler: 'The same guy in the analogy then produces his telephone book from ten years ago. The woman's name and telephone number are in it. What do you say to that?'

Oshry: 'You have to decide whether Coetzee was there to receive poison. He could have been there on official Narcotics Bureau business.'

Kriegler: 'If he was there on official business, it would have been noted in the official records. Coetzee told you in London that the records would have shown that. Coetzee put a challenge to you in London.'

Oshry: 'We studied the documents. Those documents don't exist any more.'

Oshry said Coetzee's evidence that Brigadier Willem Schoon had phoned Neethling to ask him to give Coetzee the toxins was denied by Schoon. Kriegler said Schoon did not deny that in court; in fact, he said, he found it 'remarkable' that Schoon wasn't called as a witness, and that other policemen who had worked with Coetzee weren't called either.

Oshry said Coetzee was vague about the dates he had visited Neethling. Kriegler: 'We have a fascinating profession. If someone cannot remember something after ten years, he is vague. If he does remember, it is sinister.'

Oshry asked Kriegler to award 'a very substantial amount' in damages to Neethling, because it was 'the worst possible defamation'. The press should learn that they couldn't publish just anything. 'Max du Preez is under the impression that he can defame anybody and nobody would sue him. *Vrye Weekblad* often commits character assassination. The newspaper has been waging a campaign of mocking the general for more than a year. It had a very serious effect on him and he couldn't even look his colleagues in the eye.'

Friday morning, 17 January 1991: the day of reckoning. I had confidence in Johan Kriegler, because he had shown that he had a proper grasp of the sometimes-complicated body of evidence. I also did not get the impression that he, like the judges and magistrates before him, was filled with revulsion at what *Vrye Weekblad* was representing and trying to achieve.

It was torture. The judgment took all day. My emotions see-sawed as Kriegler went over the strengths and weaknesses of the evidence before him. And then came the words: 'The Respondent did not act unlawfully.' Kriegler went further: in extraordinary circumstances of obvious overwhelming public interest, the press has a duty to report matters that might even defame someone in a public position.

It was almost too much to bear, but I had to contain myself because we were bringing out a special edition and I had many interviews lined up.

Kriegler said he could not find a single point where Dirk Coetzee had lied in his evidence. He found that on a balance of probabilities, Coetzee had been involved in eighteen death squad actions, including four murders. He called Coetzee 'a strange man with a strange story'.

Regarding Coetzee's description of Neethling's house, Kriegler said Coetzee had fourteen out of twenty-two features correct, seven almost right and just one wrong. He said he could only have known that the house had wooden floors under the carpets if he had walked on the floors himself. 'There is only one explanation, and that is that he was there. He passes the test *cum laude*.'

The judge said that it was also clear that Coetzee had indeed been in Neethling's office and spent some time there. He correctly remembered twenty-two out of the twenty-six described features of the office. Neethling had insisted in court that Coetzee had 'cooked up' the stories about his visits to the laboratory to make his story to *Vrye Weekblad* more sexy, the judge said, but the laboratories had moved to new premises in March 1987, so that could not be true.

If Coetzee had indeed visited Neethling's office during his months working for the Narcotics Bureau, Kriegler said, Neethling would have moved heaven and earth to prove that. Instead, his suggestions in this regard were 'weak and speculative'. He said it was hard to believe that Coetzee would have loitered in the private office of a feared general. 'It was a building with restricted access and strong security, not a Wimpy,' Kriegler said. He also found Coetzee's mother's evidence that she had accompanied her son to the laboratory credible and supportive of his version. Kriegler accepted the authenticity of Coetzee's telephone book, and that he had entered Neethling's numbers in the 1981 period.

'It appears that all three central moments indicate that there was contact between Neethling and Coetzee. The blanket denial by the claimant leaves no room for doubt.'

Kriegler strongly criticised the fact that Neethling had not called key witnesses such as Brigadier Willem Schoon, Major Koos Vermeulen and Captain Paul van Dyk. The one policeman he did call, Major Archie Flemington, had lied to the court.

Kriegler said Neethling was, according to the evidence, a man of impeccable character with two PhDs and numerous awards. He described Neethling as a 'strict taskmaster' with signs of 'haughtiness'. He could understand why his subordinates feared him. 'His style is that of the machete rather than the rapier.'

But he found that Neethling had misled the court. He was unwilling to discuss certain central points because he knew he was guilty. He had not only lied to Judge Harms, he had lied to this court, too.

Kriegler himself brought up the reference to Dr Joseph Mengele: 'The spirit of Mengele arose from the first reports in *Vrye Weekblad*,' he said. What we had said about Neethling was grossly defamatory, but true and in the public interest.

No victory could ever have been sweeter. And that was reflected in the seventy-two-hour party that followed. It was about more than just winning a court case: Kriegler's judgment also cast a dark shadow over the Harms Commission findings that a police death squad had never existed, and that Coetzee was a mad psychopathic liar.

Neethling hired new counsel to launch an appeal: Fanie Celliers, SC, a man I knew socially. He boasted to colleagues in the advocates' rooms that he was 'going to win the unwinnable case'. My counsel and I were very sure that he could not get Kriegler's remarkable and thorough judgment overthrown by the highest court in the land.

We did not bargain on five stuffy old white men called Mr Justices Corbett, Hoexter, Nestadt, Nienaber and Nicholas. Exactly three years after we had published the original stories of Neethling's poisonous potions, the case was argued (no new evidence or witnesses allowed) before the Appellate Division in Bloemfontein.

Early in December 1993, the court declared that they could not determine which one of Neethling or Coetzee had lied. Chief Justice Corbett said their stories were 'mutually destructive', and that 'it was not possible to say with confidence who was telling the truth'. Hoexter said: 'In regard to what was the crucial issue in the case, Coetzee was a single witness with a grudge against the SA Police and a motive to misrepresent. He was a criminal whose misdeeds included crimes of dishonesty ... In that part of his evidence which inculpated the appellant there was grave improbability.' On Kriegler's finding that Neethling had misled the court, Hoexter said he was 'unable to agree with the adverse credibility finding which the trial judge made against the appellant. Still less I am satisfied that the testimony of Coetzee should be preferred to that of the appellant.'

The judges did not only throw out Johan Kriegler's findings of fact, they also dismissed his statements of law. Hoexter, who wrote the judgment on the five's behalf, quoted an earlier judgment by Corbett, where he'd said: 'The media have a private interest of their own in publishing what appeals to the public and may increase circulation or may increase the numbers of their viewers or listeners; and they are peculiarly vulnerable to the error of confusing the public interest with their own interest.'

Hoexter wrote that the readers of *Vrye Weekblad* 'had no possible legitimate interest in having communicated to them these untested, and largely hearsay, allegations by an informant whose credibility and motive alike were suspect'.

Corbett wrote in his report attached to the judgment: 'I, too, am satisfied that the true position in our law is that a defendant who relies on the defence of truth and public benefit bears the full onus of proving that the defamatory statements are substantially correct.'

As I explained in an editorial, 'full onus' on a newspaper, if applied, would mean the end of virtually all investigative journalism. The *Sunday Times* called it 'the most serious blow to press freedom since the states of emergency'. *Business Day* said the 'standards set by the Appeal Court, in a case involving deep public interest, could torpedo the media's watchdog role in the New South Africa'. *Sunday Nation* stated: 'The pronouncements such as those made by Mr Justice Hoexter take this country back to a past [of which] it is desperately trying to rid itself.'

The controversial judgment has fortunately since been reversed by several other judgments, the first being *Nasionale Media vs Bogoshi*, in which the new Appeal Court revived the common-law emphasis on freedom of the press. We are back to the position put down by Johan Kriegler.

In a brilliant analysis of the Appeal Court's judgment, Martin Welz wrote in *Vrye Weekblad*'s last edition:

> There are many serious errors in the Appeal Court's judgment. The Court is shockingly amateur in its reasoning and insights – apparently not only ignorant about the role of the press and how it functions, but when it comes to analysing and understanding the evidence of Captain Coetzee, ignorant of the philosophy of logic and knowledge and of the well-developed field of social science ...
>
> One of the features of Afrikaner nationalism was its need to escape from the standard and demands of the civilised world. And the Appeal Court of the Republic of South Africa, as it exists today, is that Afrikaner culture's work. Might it not be fair that the probabilities are that the Appeal Court is fatally tainted by it's own life 'beyond the law' – its forty years of loyal service to apartheid, found by the rest of the world to be a crime against humanity?
>
> Until the recent appointment of Mr Justice Mohammed, every single one of the judges currently on the bench in South Africa was appointed by, and met the approval – and racial criteria – of an undemocratic, authoritarian, racist Afrikaner Nationalist government. All of them were happy to accept that approval and appointment. Chief Justice Corbett himself became a judge in the Cape in the era of Hendrik Verwoerd, and an Appeal Judge by the grace of John Vorster ... Is it surprising, therefore, that South Africa's courts lack a broader, cultured and informed view of the world, and moral sensibility?

So, because the Appeal Court decided we had not discharged the full onus of proving Coetzee's statements as the truth, they found that we had indeed defamed

Neethling. It was determined that we had to pay all his legal costs (actually, Neethling never paid a cent, the taxpayer did) and R90 000 in damages.

Vrye Weekblad and Wending Publikasies were bankrupt. We published our last edition on 2 February 1994 – eighty-four days before South Africa became a democracy with Nelson Mandela as president.

The terrible irony was that between Kriegler's judgment and the hearing in the Appeal Court two years later, lots of new evidence came to light that proved without a shadow of a doubt that Coetzee was speaking the truth. Vlakplaas policeman Steve Bosch made a sworn statement to the Pretoria Attorney-General that he, too, had fetched bottles of poisoned beer from Neethling.

We also had an affidavit from a former state prosecutor, Johan Marnewick van den Heever, stating that he had once used Neethling as an expert witness in a large fraud case and had visited Neethling at the forensics laboratory. Neethling proudly took him on a tour of the facility and gave him several demonstrations. Then Van den Heever stated under oath: 'I was very impressed with what Neethling had achieved at the laboratory and I was very impressed with what I saw. I indicated this to him and I could see he was very proud of what he had achieved. He also in general discussed his work with me and various breakthroughs and inventions that they had achieved at the laboratory.

'It was in this context that he mentioned to me that the laboratory had developed a poison which could precipitate a heart attack. He furthermore mentioned that the poison would not be traced at a post-mortem examination.'

But we could not give this new information to the Appeal Court, because according to the rules they could only listen to arguments and review the evidence given at the trial court.

The full truth eventually came out, as it always does. During the Truth and Reconciliation Commission's hearings on the apartheid government's chemical and biological warfare programme, and the marathon court case against the military head of that programme, Dr Wouter Basson, it became abundantly clear that not only was *Vrye Weekblad*'s information correct, but it was only the tip of an immense iceberg.

After the TRC hearings in 1997, at which Neethling, Basson and several other top scientists gave testimony, I formally laid charges of murder, conspiracy to murder, perjury and fraud against Lothar Neethling at the Brixton Police Station. Nothing has come of it.

I told the Truth Commission in my submission: '*Vrye Weekblad* was closed because of Lothar Neethling's perjury. Lothar Neethling was indeed a kind of Dr Mengele, who experimented with different kinds of knock-out drops and poison for the use of security policemen to kill activists.

'We know some of the names of some of the people who were killed in this way. But we don't know how many people died after drinking Lothar Neethling's poison. He should be charged with multiple murder, perjury and fraud. Fraud for getting our money for his lies and closing down a newspaper that could have played a very constructive role in the transformation of our society today. I truly hope you can help me bring this man to justice.'

As I write this, General Lothar Neethling is living a life of luxury in his mansion in Pretoria.

PART VI

In, and out again

26

To more glamorous pastures

TWO DAYS AFTER we announced that *Vrye Weekblad* was closing down, I had a visit from an old acquaintance. His name was Christo Kritzinger, known by all as 'Mielie'. He was the head of the South African Broadcasting Corporation's television news.

I had met Kritzinger in 1977 at a press junket the SADF had organised to coincide with big military exercises they were conducting in the Northern Cape. Late that evening, bored with the macho war talk that military correspondents and soldiers like to engage in over copious amounts of liquor, I wandered off. I wasn't all that interested in military hardware, but a huge thing under canvas attracted my attention. I lifted a corner of the canvas and saw a cannon the size of which I had never seen.

The next moment two military policemen took me by the arm and marched me to the commanding officer. Kritzinger had seen me looking at the new weapon, and reported me to the commanding officer. I pretended to be a bit drunk, and said I'd been looking for a place to pee. I saw nothing, I told the commander.

The weapon was one of the earliest models of South Africa's G5 howitzer, developed secretly with the help of Israel after the SADF had struggled with the Russian-made artillery in Angola, which had a much longer range. It was developed into a formidable weapon, and South Africa is still selling it on the international arms market today.

Kritzinger clearly knew all about the secret new weapon, and when he saw a fellow journalist, one whose loyalties were suspect, peeking at it, he thought it a dangerous security breach. That's what Kritzinger and many of his colleagues at the SABC were like – right in the heart of the National Party and its security forces.

I despised the journalists at the old SABC, and wrote many defamatory things about them in *Vrye Weekblad*. They were His Master's Voice in the fullest sense of the word; they lied and cheated and made propaganda for the apartheid government.

But this was January 1994. The National Party and the ANC were governing the country jointly through the Transitional Executive Council, and all the negotiating parties had accepted the new Interim Constitution. It was three months before the elections that would, as everyone already knew, bring the ANC to power. The SABC was undergoing radical changes and preparing itself to be a true public broadcaster, rather than the state broadcaster it had been since its inception. My old colleague Jacques Pauw was already working for the SABC, and the editor at *New Nation*, Zwelakhe Sisulu, was about to take over as chief executive.

During 1993, while I was still *Vrye Weekblad* editor, I had a weekly phone-in programme on the SABC's Afrikaans radio station, which was then called Afrikaans Stereo. It was called '*Klip in die Bos*', which could loosely be translated as 'cat among the pigeons'. It was huge fun and became very popular. The vast majority of the people who called in initially only did so in order to insult me and call me ugly names. I humoured them and laughed off the insults, and slowly more and more callers accepted me. We had some really enlightening conversations.

Kritzinger had come to offer me a job as a current affairs presenter on SABC television. He was desperate to find an Afrikaans-speaker with progressive credentials, because he was coming under increasing pressure to show changes in his department. Mielie and I joked and slapped each other on the back as if we had been comrades for many years. This was the New South Africa in action.

I thought it would be exciting to help transform the public broadcaster to serve the new democracy, and I thought it would be fun to have an audience slightly bigger than the one I'd had at *Vrye Weekblad*. So I had a haircut and a beard trim, bought a suit and a tie, and joined the SABC.

It was very weird working with the same white Afrikaner journalists I had resented and criticised for so long. I felt sorry for them, because they needed to hold on to their jobs and fat perks and pension funds, and at the same time be sweet to their former enemies. But many of them soon found it as easy to serve as the lackeys of the new government as of the old.

My first appearance on television was on a programme called *Agenda*, which I co-presented with Freek Robinson in order to introduce me to viewers. Robinson had been with the SABC since the beginning of television in the 1970s. I thought it would be appropriate for me to explain to the audience what the man who had been the editor of *Vrye Weekblad* until the week before was doing at the SABC. So, when I was introduced, I looked into the camera and said that I was happy to be at 'the new SABC', because it was now a public broadcaster and would no longer only serve sectional interests. Without missing a beat, Robinson said something like, 'Of course, that's what the SABC has always been like.' Then I knew it wasn't going to be all plain sailing.

My first solo interview came a few days later. I'd had no training to be a television presenter, and had only seen the inside of a studio once before. I was unfamiliar with the autocue, the script that appears over the camera lens. My first live interview was with the state president, FW de Klerk.

I fell around a bit trying to stay with the different cameras, the floor manager's directions and reading the autocue, but then got stuck into the interview, forgetting about cameras and lights. After a few minutes I was thoroughly enjoying myself, interchanging aggressive and soft questions, trying the unexpected every now and then.

De Klerk was very good on television and a quick thinker. I thought I almost caught him towards the end. I was talking about nostalgic stuff: his family, his background, coming from the good old Western Transvaal. Then I leaned forward and asked him: 'When you push you hands into the soil of the Western Transvaal and feel the earth, what does your heart tell you? Whose soil does your heart tell you it is?' For a moment I thought he was carried away enough with all the soil-and-Boere stuff to give an honest answer. But he recovered in an instant, seeing the question for what it was, and gave a diplomatic answer about Afrikaners sharing the soil of South Africa with all their compatriots.

At the end of the interview I thought: I like this. I can do this. Outside the studio, De Klerk was annoyed and irritated with my questions, but his wife and aide both told him he had done well. And so he had. If only politicians would realise that soft, sycophantic television interviews don't do anything for them in the eyes of the public – if you can hold your own with an aggressive interviewer, you win.

My television interviews with the new president, Nelson Mandela, were in stark contrast. I simply could not be aggressive, or even mildly assertive. He was such a gigantic presence; when he talks, you shut up. Sometimes, when he paused, I would try to jump in to speed up the pace of the interview. He would just fix you with a stare and continue with what he was saying.

Of course, there wasn't really anything negative one *could* say about Mandela. He was almost single-handedly saving the country from civil war and perpetual conflict. I knew television viewers would react angrily if I did interrupt him or put him under pressure. Also, he was an old man.

I personally have a deep admiration for Mandela. Months before he was released, I wrote him an open letter in *Vrye Weekblad*. In the letter, I asked him to please take the Afrikaners with him into the New South Africa after his liberation, and explained that Afrikaners were Africans just like him, even though many of them didn't properly realise it and most didn't act like it. He should forgive them, I said, and take them by the hand into our common future.

What I didn't know then was that Mandela and several other ANC leaders in jail were subscribers to *Vrye Weekblad*. A week after his release, I received a phone call. It was Nelson Mandela himself on the line. He explained that he wanted to see me, and asked if I could possibly come to his home in Soweto. 'I wanted to come to see you in your office, but my security people refused,' he said. I was speechless.

I drove to the humble house he still owned in Soweto. He came out the door with a broad smile and an extended hand. We sat down in the small lounge. Mandela spoke Afrikaans to me, although he apologised several times for his 'Xhosa accent'.

He said he had wanted to see me as soon as he got out, because he had read my open letter to him in the newspaper, but the prison authorities hadn't allowed him to respond. 'So please don't think I have bad manners and I don't respond to letters sent to me,' he laughed.

Mandela expressed his appreciation for what I had said in my letter, and after a short lecture in Afrikaner history, told me that he saw it as one of his special tasks to help Afrikaners understand that he and the ANC were not their enemies. The new society awaiting us, he said, was as much in their interest as it was in black people's interest. 'Sometimes I think Afrikaners suffered more under apartheid than we did,' he said, 'because it corrupted their minds and souls. Black people always knew they were right to demand democracy, they always knew the suffering under apartheid was going to end. We are about to be liberated, but it will take Afrikaners longer to feel liberated too.'

For the first time in my life I looked at a politician and thought: I love this man. This is a great soul, a gift from the universe to my nation. And I haven't changed my mind about him one bit over the next thirteen years.

In 1993 he paid me a special honour. I was the guest at the annual foreign correspondents' dinner, where he was the speaker. He castigated South African and foreign journalists for the way they reported on South Africa, and then he said: 'There is a man here tonight who is an outstanding example to all of you: Max du Preez.'

I interviewed Mandela on television when he released his updated autobiography. He gave me a copy with the inscription: '*Vir my vriend Max, met beste wense, Nelson Mandela*'. But, in 1999, before the elections, when I wrote in a guest column in the *Financial Mail* that I was considering voting for the Green Party, he phoned me and sternly rebuked me: 'You mustn't confuse the people. You do not realise how many people value your opinion.' I explained that only a few white people read the magazine and that my piece was tongue-in-cheek anyway.

'No,' came the fatherly reply. 'Our democracy is too young and precious to joke about it.'

The chairperson of the board of the new SABC was a prominent ANC figure who had returned from exile, Dr Ivy Matsepe-Casaburri. She was clearly out of her depth running the SABC, but committed to transforming the corporation. Not long after she took over, she spread the word that she wanted to meet 'comrades' at the SABC to discuss transformation and the future of the SABC at an informal 'brown bag' meeting, as she called it (it meant bring your own lunch, I learnt). So it happened that I was asked to attend the small gathering. But when I walked in, she stopped and said that there must be a mistake, because she hadn't invited white people. I got the message.

My old colleague Zwelakhe Sisulu was the head of SABC news. In 1993, when

Vrye Weekblad's manager, Mark Beare, was put in charge of the European Union's shared funding for alternative newspapers, Sisulu and I came to know each other quite well. We had joint meetings in our offices several times. But the Sisulu who was head of SABC news did not know me. In the four years before he left for a top job at New African Investments Ltd, he did not speak to me once, and several times walked past without greeting me. I should have read the signs.

Jacques Pauw and I shared an office in the formidable SABC headquarters in Auckland Park, and it wasn't long before we started conspiring against some of the old SABC bosses. The first thing I started campaigning for was an end to apartheid in television current affairs. There was a programme for whites called *Agenda*, and a programme for blacks called *Newsline*. I wanted the two programmes to merge into one programme for all, but this threatened the old order, and Freek Robinson quickly mobilised the old-time black presenters who had never had any qualms about serving the apartheid government. It was an ugly fight, with Robinson's black sidekick, Leslie Mashokwe, even threatening me with physical violence and calling me a racist.

I really didn't think someone with Robinson's history and track record should still have been allowed at the SABC, however much of an institution he had become. But I decided to ignore him, even to be civil. But then a journalist of *Die Suid-Afrikaan* who later became a dear colleague, Anneliese Burgess, interviewed me on my new life at the SABC. The interview took place over lunch at my then lover's house, who had been at university with Anneliese, and we had some wine to drink. I carelessly treated the interview as a chat with a friend and spoke my mind.

Anneliese published a virtually verbatim account of our conversation, including the swear words and sharp comments, as well as an unflattering remark about Freek Robinson. Someone at *Die Suid-Afrikaan* faxed it to the head of television news, Jill Chisholm, and I was called onto the red carpet. I explained the circumstances to her, and added that only a few thousand Afrikaner intellectuals read the magazine anyway. She said someone in my position shouldn't use swear words. I said, 'Come on, Jill, you've been a journalist for decades, haven't you ever said "fuck"?' She turned her face to the window and said yes, she has said 'fuck' in her life before, but not in an interview. More seriously, she said, Robinson felt hurt, and my remarks about him were unprofessional. I promised to apologise to him, because perhaps it had been a bit unprofessional.

I went down to Robinson's office and stood in his door, looking at all the pictures of himself he had on the wall. When he looked up, I said that I had come to apologise for my remarks to *Die Suid-Afrikaan*, explaining that I hadn't meant to hurt or belittle him. Instead of accepting or rejecting my apology, he got up and said, 'It is time you realised that you are not in the alternative press any longer. You have to learn to be responsible in your new job.'

I stopped him right in his tracks, gently saying the word that Jill Chisholm confessed to have once used, but relating it also to all Robinson's ancestors. We worked in the same office for four more years, but I never spoke to him again.

This uptight, post-Broederbond atmosphere got to me, so I decided to introduce some fun. I made a thirty-minute documentary insert for *Agenda* on the Afrikaanse Taalmonument, situated on a mountain overlooking Paarl. I called it: *The Language Monument – a Monument for What?*

I interviewed the black Afrikaans-speaking writer and poet, Sandile Dikeni, at the monument. He pointed out that the small concrete balls next to the very tall main column was the artist's representation of the contribution Africa had made to Afrikaans, and said they were *drolletjies* [little turds]. Sandile said the monument did not represent the language he spoke, but Afrikaner nationalism.

The black mayor of Paarl, whose mother tongue was also Afrikaans, agreed that he did not feel the monument celebrated his language. In fact, despite the fact that he had lived in Paarl all his life and was now the mayor, he had never been to the monument before.

I also interviewed some foreign tourists who had come to see the monument. One of them, a wise old guy who said he was a Brazilian Jew from São Paolo, looked up to the top of the monument and said that the people who had built this must have been very angry with God. It looked like a man lying on his back with his penis pointing up to heaven, he said. I though this was so insightful and true, and included it in the documentary.

Achmat Davids, a language historian regarded as the foremost expert on the roots of Afrikaans, said the language did not originate among white people in Paarl, but among Malays and slaves who had to communicate with Dutch colonialists. This monument, he said, was not erected in honour of that language, but for white Afrikaner power.

I interviewed several other people, such as the famous Afrikaans author who literally lived in the shadow of the monument, Bill de Klerk.

Basically, I wanted the documentary to ask whether it wasn't time to reinterpret and recontextualise the monument in the New South Africa, because its emphasis was so strongly on white Afrikaner nationalism. I even interviewed the Minister of Arts and Culture, Dr Ben Ngubane, who agreed that the monument belonged to the old order and had to be given a 'new mission statement'.

Next, I went to see my old mate Hardy Botha, who was then in charge of the Dal Josaphat Arts Foundation outside Paarl. He could see the phallic monument, also known as the *Taal Paal* [language pole], from his studio, and didn't like it. I did not include our conversation about 'necklacing' the monument with a huge tractor tyre, or perhaps dropping a huge plastic condom over it, in the programme – I was sensitive to more conservative Afrikaners' views, after all. But I did ask him to 'redesign' the monument, and he painted a model of the monument in the most beautiful African colours with Ndebele patterns. It looked stunning, and that's how I ended the insert.

I knew I might experience a few problems with my old SABC colleagues over the documentary, so I pretended to finish it only a few minutes before I was to present it live on *Agenda*. In my intro to camera I explained that the insert would present the views of Afrikaans-speakers who had never been asked for their opinion on the monument before. The show's executive producer, Nico van Burick, was very angry about what he saw going out on air, and later publicly distanced himself from the documentary.

I thought the programme might annoy a few people, but I wasn't prepared for the hell that broke loose. The SABC switchboard was jammed with calls from people who wanted to complain, and who demanded that I be taken off the air. For weeks the letters pages of especially *Die Burger* were filled with angry letters of protest.

Dr Henno Cronjé, the chief executive of the Federasie van Afrikaanse Kultuur-vereniginge, wrote that I now stood unmasked as someone who should never have been a journalist. The programme was reason for all Afrikaners to stop paying their TV licences. According to Deon de Villiers of Paarl I clearly hated my own language and heritage. Johan Engelbrecht of Somerset-West said that his 'blood was boiling' and that I was 'awakening the tiger in the Afrikaner'. Gene Louw, MP and former Cape premier, wrote that 'the leftist liberal' Max du Preez had tried to depict the Afrikaans language and culture as *bespotlik* [ridiculous], and asked for how long the nation was going to be tortured with my presence on television. Dr Julius Jeppe of Stellenbosch called me a *vuilspuit* (I think it means a disgusting slanderer); CE Shaw of Goodwood said I was an ANC lackey; Linda van Niekerk of Jeffrey's Bay called me an ANC lapdog; and J van Deventer of Swellendam appealed to President Nelson Mandela to personally remove me from the SABC. JG du Plessis, the chief secretary of the Federation of Rapportryerskorpse, wrote 'on behalf 8 000 members' that the damage I had done to Afrikaners 'could have far-reaching consequences'.

The Afrikaner Kultuurbond and more than a hundred other petitioners then took me to the Broadcasting Complaints Commission, the ombudsman for all broadcasting media in South Africa. The commission found that the programme 'did not amount to substantial one-sidedness' and was 'not likely to affect relations' between sections of the community. 'The observations were not racialistic, but were at the most of a political nature; much freedom exists in the area of political speech. It is necessary that viewers should have the opportunity to hear a variety of views on television.'

The programme was even discussed in parliament. Democratic Party MP Dene Smuts told the House that 'the problem with alternative journalists is that the art of iconoclasm, fun though it may be, was not made for public broadcasting. Of course, I am talking about the 'Max Factor'. Max du Preez cannot resist tackling the Taalmonument and other holy cows. I enjoy Max's programmes – any progressive would – but this is not the best way to give South Africa a makeover.'

Well, all things considered, I thought the Taalmonument documentary worked quite well.

The more familiar I became with the medium of television, the more I liked it. I made documentaries on Cuba, and several African states. I interviewed most cabinet ministers, opposition politicians and visiting dignitaries. I hosted many newsworthy debates in the studio. I loved the cut and thrust of lively debates, of thinking fast on my feet. I loved constructing interviews in a manner that could disarm especially politicians and get honest answers. I even learned the dirty trick of sitting in front of a bright light or a sunny window while interviewing someone whom I needed to discomfort, because that way they could not see my face properly.

The South African politician who best understood how television worked was Afrikaner Weerstandsbeweging leader Eugene Terre'Blanche. While most Afrikaner politicians such as General Constand Viljoen were extremely uncomfortable and reluctant to be made up before a show, Terre'Blanche loved it, and directed the make-up artists on where to apply more base or darker powder. Once, when he was in the studio for a debate with several others, we lowered or raised people's chairs so that all their eye lines would be on the same level. The camera could then swing from side to side, but needn't go up or down. Terre'Blanche knew that this trick made everybody appear to be the same height. Out of the corner of my eye, I noticed that the second before we went live he adjusted his seat to sit a few centimetres higher than everybody else – he wanted people to think he was tall.

I had a strange relationship with Terre'Blanche. In 1993, he and I appeared on a live John Berks show on M-Net. I called Eugene a 'windbag' to his face, and afterwards had to run away from his incensed bodyguards. He mentioned me in a threatening manner several times during some of his rousing speeches, but whenever we met for a show at the SABC, he was always extremely courteous. In 2000, I presented a talk show on Punt, an independent Afrikaans talk radio station. I phoned Terre'blanche the day he got out of jail – that is, just before he went back – and had a long, interesting conversation with him about his experience. He even read some of his striking but rather naive poems he had written in jail over the air.

The worst interview I ever had was with Joe Nhlanhla, political head of the post-1994 government's intelligence services. He didn't give interviews to any-body, so I thought it quite a scoop when he agreed to talk to me. I made sure the programme went out live, because I had some awkward questions I wanted to ask him. No chance. He fixed his eyes on the ceiling and started relating his personal political history. After a few minutes I interrupted him with a question, but as soon as I'd finished, he just continued with his history lesson. So it went on for twenty minutes. He didn't answer any of my questions, however rude and persistent I became. In fact, he completely ignored me and said exactly what he wanted to say.

In 1995 I hosted a programme called the *Tuesday Debate*. The most successful debate was the one between Barney Pityana, then head of the Human Rights Commission, and Dennis Davis, a law professor (now judge) and prominent liberal commentator. I knew what I had to do: get them going on their old argument about liberalism and the position of whites, and then sit back. It was fireworks, and my executive producer kept on screaming for me to intervene, but I just let them rip into and insult each other. Both men later complained that I had failed to protect them. But it made for great television and got close to the heart of the matter.

But my best memory of my early days on television was when I anchored, with a few others, the twenty-four hours of live coverage of the 1994 elections. The political settlement of 1994 was the realisation of my dreams for my country, and here I was, a part of that historical process. It was such a privilege.

27

Let the truth be known

I HAVE DREADED writing this chapter since the day I started working on my book of memories. It concerns the period of my life that I spent covering the proceedings of the Truth and Reconciliation Commission. Or, rather, lived and breathed the Truth Commission day and night for more than two years.

I'm struggling to explain to myself why my mind has tried to block that time from my memory. Sometimes I think my soul had soaked up too much of the evil that was laid bare day after day.

I don't know why I took it so personally. Somehow I did not have the ability to ward off all the negative energy in the hatred, cruelty and suffering that was released – it nestled in my subconscious, replacing my positive energy and depleting my own ability to love others and myself.

On another level, it was about being an Afrikaner, being white in Africa, being the descendant of colonisers and apartheid masters. It was about my history and identity – not only who I was as a human being, but also as a citizen of South Africa. I saw the Truth Commission as my nation's opportunity to make peace with itself after so much oppression, bloodletting and suffering, and without realising, I wanted it to have the same meaning in my life. (I sometimes curse my Calvinist genes.) The TRC was supposed to be a process during which I would be able to close a chapter in my life, or, rather, a whole book. It was supposed to bring closure – the end of the first part of my life and the beginning of the next. Only it didn't.

I think I wanted the experience of the Truth Commission to be a kind of validation, the final justification of my life thus far: a life in conflict with my family, my ethnic group and my society; a life characterised by rage, secrecy, danger, isolation, hatred, resentment, bitterness – an exhilarating life with very few dull moments, but essentially a life without love, gentleness and caring.

Perhaps I was yearning for a moment that would give me permission to become who I really was. My public image of being a butt-kicking, hard-living, cynical, reckless, maverick journalist with a fuck-you attitude had permeated my whole being. I had become a caricature of my image. In the process I had nearly alienated my two children and destroyed potentially beautiful relationships. This Frankenstein could not contemplate weaknesses or insecurities; he had to suppress his vulnerability and the deeply troubling thoughts about a mother who had died when he was an infant.

All this stuff came together during the obsessive, hectic time when I led a team that produced the *Special Report on the Truth Commission*, which was aired every Sunday evening on national television. But perhaps it would have had a more positive effect on my life in the long run if the drama I was subjected to after the Truth Commission had been spared me.

We were a small team, ranging at various times from five to eight people, who were tasked to produce a fifty-minute documentary every Sunday on that week's testimony before the Truth Commission. Most of my colleagues had very limited television experience, and for some it was their first television job. The Truth Commission itself had asked experts from the BBC to advise them on how the process should be reported on television. Their advice was that it would take twenty to thirty experienced television journalists, and the equipment and a budget fifty times what we were given.

But, through sheer commitment and belief in the cause, that small team pulled it off every week. Sometimes there were two or three sittings of the TRC in different places in the country in the same week. Most of the time, it meant that we had to rush back to the office in Johannesburg on a Friday afternoon, transcribe, script and edit by Saturday night, and package the edition with me as presenter to be delivered by Sunday. On Sunday afternoons, most of us had to travel to where the next week's hearings were to be held. Occasionally there were weeks where the TRC had no hearings at all, which meant we had to make appropriate documentaries on the process to fill the Sunday's fifty-minute time slot.

South Africa's TRC wasn't the first truth commission, but it differed substantially from those held in countries such as Chile and Argentina. With those commissions, the final report was the most important, because the process itself took place behind closed doors. In South Africa, the process was open to the public and the media. The process became the most important thing; the final report was almost an after-thought. Every single day for almost three years, South Africans, whether they loved or hated the TRC, were confronted with the evidence of victims or perpetrators of human rights violations. It was on the radio, in the newspapers, on daily television bulletins, and on for an hour every Sunday night. In that process, the *Special Report* played a big role, and became so popular that some church groups later requested the SABC to change its time slot, because too many members of their congregation were staying away from church services to watch television.

The first half of the TRC process was dominated by human rights violations hearings: mothers, fathers, daughters, sons, husbands sitting in front of the cameras and microphones to tell of their suffering at the hands of policeman or soldiers – or sometimes guerrillas in the armies of the ANC or PAC. Most of it was intensely emotional: even grown, hardened and proud black men who had never cried before in their lives broke down in tears. The TRC chairperson, Archbishop Desmond Tutu, was himself overcome by emotion on more than one occasion, and his tears and sobs tore even deeper into the hearts of those present.

Many white South Africans mocked the process and questioned the authenticity of the stories and the tears. I suppose it was a defence mechanism, but it was shameful nonetheless. White politicians and opinion leaders said the testimonies of victims had little value because they weren't subjected to proper cross-examination. If they had bothered to go and sit in one of those halls to listen to ordinary people opening up their hearts, they would never have said that.

Many of those who had testified at these hearings told us that the act of sitting down at the witness table before the commissioners and members of their community – and the television cameras and radio microphones – made them feel that their society, their nation, was at last recognising their pain and honouring them for their suffering. That brought them a form of closure.

Father Michael Lapsley, whose hands were blown off in a South African bomb attack in Harare, best summed up the hearings. He said to me after testifying in Kimberley: 'Today had a unique significance. For me the significance was that there was a commission set up by the first morally legitimate government of South Africa that was honouring me and all South Africans for our pain and our suffering and our struggle. In the past when people were tortured and killed, they were denigrated; they were told these were terrorists; their pain was denied. For me, testifying before the Truth Commission is to participate in the creation of a moral order.'

Many black South Africans expressed their unhappiness with the provision of amnesty: if you could prove that the human rights violation you had committed was politically motivated and you made a full disclosure, the TRC could grant you indemnity against future criminal or civil action. I also sometimes found it hard to stomach seeing a particularly brutal security policeman go scot-free.

I remember being upset when the black youths who had killed the young American exchange student Amy Biehl like a dog in the street, just because she had a pale skin, received amnesty. But I was wrong. Amy's parents came to South Africa and engaged with those angry youngsters. Today those same killers, Ntobeko Peni and Easy Nofemela, are doing wonderful work in the community in the name of the Amy Biehl Foundation. That's what forgiveness and reconciliation are really about.

The amnesty process meant that white South Africans were forced to take the tales of horror from the past more seriously. The information now came from the mouths of white policemen and soldiers. Amnesty also brought out more truth. If it hadn't been for the full confession of some amnesty applicants, we would not have had such a complete picture of what lay in our past.

One of the most poignant stories illustrating this was that of Phila Ndwandwe.

She was a young mother and commander of an MK unit based in Swaziland. One day she told her comrades that she had received a message to go to South Africa, and she was never seen again. A lot of rumours did the rounds about her having become a police spy or an askari at Vlakplaas. Her family and that of her son's father were shamed.

Then two KwaZulu-Natal policemen applied for amnesty for her murder. They said Phila was lured to South Africa, where she was captured. They tortured her for days, trying to get her to give up her unit's military secrets, but she was brave and proud, and refused. They then shot and buried her.

Some time after this story was revealed to the TRC, President Nelson Mandela presented Phila Ndwande's young son with a medal for bravery, issued post-humously to his mother, at a huge public ceremony. If it hadn't been for the amnesty process, this boy and his father and grandparents would still have been ashamed of his mother.

One of the most gruesome stories told during the amnesty hearings had, for me, one of the most remarkable endings. Tshidiso Mutasi was a four-year-old boy when security policemen Jacques Hechter and Paul van Vuuren executed his parents in front of his eyes. Tshidiso spent the night trying to wake his dead mother and father.

Ten years later, after consulting with psychologists and TRC personnel, we brought Van Vuuren and Tshidiso, now a strapping, handsome boy of fourteen, together in the rooms of Van Vuuren's lawyers – with the cameras rolling. For a while they talked vaguely and uncomfortably about bitterness and remorse – Van Vuuren saying he wasn't even going to try telling Tshidiso how sorry he was, because it would just be words.

Then the boy said to Van Vuuren: 'I live with my grandmother and she is very old. She is my only family. You killed my parents. Who will look after me when she dies?' Van Vuuren though for a while, then replied with a wry smile: 'I suppose you will have to come and live with me then. I will have to look after you.'

I'm sure Van Vuuren wasn't actually looking forward to having this black youngster move in with his family. But his words grasped the essence of the Truth Commission: South Africans had to take responsibility for what they had done.

Sadly, the man who then represented all of white South Africa and was expected to speak on behalf of Afrikaners past and present did not do so. FW de Klerk was the perfect man to represent Afrikaners at this unique moment in history. He was more than the elected leader of the biggest white party, more than just the state president of the last white government that had negotiated itself out of power. His family history was the history of Afrikaner nationalism: his great-grandfather was a senator in the Union after 1910; his one grandfather was a founding member of the National Party in 1914, the other a member of the Free State Provincial Council. His uncle, JG Strijdom, was a prime minister, and his father, Jan, a cabinet minister and senator.

It was 1996, just two years after apartheid as a state ideology had ended and Nelson Mandela became president. The majority of South Africans appreciated De Klerk's bold decisions to make all of that possible, but they also knew that he had had little choice in the matter, and giving up power certainly didn't mean the past was forgiven and forgotten. The TRC was an opportunity, created by the new democratic government, for all of us to look each other in the eye and deal with our past, so that we could walk the path towards a new society less burdened by the injustices that had been perpetrated. Black South Africa was waiting for white South Africa to seize the moment. The person who had to do that on their behalf was De Klerk.

When De Klerk appeared before the TRC, he did apologise for the 'pain and suffering that the previous policy directions of the National Party' had caused. I sat there listening, hoping and praying that this would be a magical moment that would unlock the forgiveness and generosity of the millions who had been affected over generations by those 'policy directions'. But his speech was void of any emotion, of any sense of momentousness. They were the carefully considered words of a clever politician and a lawyer. It was a clinical apology for something others had done, even though they had 'meant well' when they started apartheid. My heart sank.

Still, Tutu called it a 'handsome apology'. But then, again in the words of Tutu, he 'spoiled it all when he qualified the apology virtually out of existence'. And that he certainly did. The dirty torturers and killers of Vlakplaas, the CCB, the Directorate Covert Collection and the security police were a 'rogue minority' who had acted outside of their orders. He hadn't known about any wrongdoing. He hadn't known about Vlakplaas or the CCB; neither had his cabinet.

The TRC evidence leader asked De Klerk: 'You're offering us an explanation that these things were committed by a few individuals, I think in your submission you talk about a few mavericks. But we are faced with insurmountable evidence that in fact torture was widespread within the security forces.' De Klerk answered: 'That's why I'm blatantly honest with you when I say that I'm as shocked as you are about these many revelations.'

What an insult to the intelligence of the truth commissioners and the rest of the nation. Did he really think we would believe him when he said he hadn't known about the deaths of Steve Biko, Onkgopotse Tiro, Rick Turner, Ruth First, Dulcie September, Sipho Hashe, Qwaqwahuli Godolozi, Champion Galela, Siphiwo Mtimkulu, Mathew Goniwe, Sparrow Mkhonto, Sicelo Mhlauli, Fort Calata, David Webster and Anton Lubowski? Or, if he had, that he'd never suspected who their killers might have been? These were the people whose deaths featured extensively in the South African media.

Referring to the first Vlakplaas revelations, the TRC asked De Klerk: 'You were given assurances about Vlakplaas by General Johan van der Merwe and you indicated that you believed him. Do you still believe General Van der Merwe? That he knew nothing about the operations at Vlakplaas?'

De Klerk replied, 'Unless I have evidence that he is lying. I found him an honourable man. I don't question his word just on the basis of rumours.'

The TRC asked, 'How reasonable is that explanation that a lowly officer, somewhere below these generals, was responsible for this entire aberration that led to all these things?'

De Klerk said, 'There is nothing reasonable in crime. It's unreasonable.'

And yet I have personal knowledge that De Klerk had received and read the letter Dirk Coetzee wrote to him in February 1991, explaining what was going on at Vlakplaas. So, even if De Klerk hadn't read a word of *Vrye Weekblad*'s extensive reports in 1988, he would have known then.

The TRC asked De Klerk, 'Is it possible in your experience as State President of the country previously that the commander of Vlakplaas would have been able to sustain, taken all the resources he needs, finances and so on, that situation on his own and keep it secret from everybody higher up?'

De Klerk answered, 'Yes, I think it is possible. It happens every day with theft.'

When questioned about the minutes of a State Security Council meeting on 12 May 1986 (which De Klerk attended), which stated that the security forces had to create a Third Force that had to be 'feared' in order to combat terrorists 'using their own methods', De Klerk said: 'We tried to adhere to Christian norms and principles. That was the ethos under which I grew up and under which I served: firstly as an ordinary member of parliament, then as a minister, and that was the ethos also in the cabinet under my presidency. I reject the implication that there was this almost immoral 'everything goes in a state of war'. That was not the philosophy within which I lived, within which I operated and within which I served.'

It was as ridiculous as General Magnus Malan, former Minister of Defence, who said that the CCB had been created to disrupt the enemy by doing things like 'pouring sugar in petrol tanks'.

As Mathews Phosa, later the premier of the province of Mpumalanga, remarked: 'De Klerk sat in Pretoria and knew everything that was going on in the ANC's Quattro camp north of Luanda, but nothing about Vlakplaas twenty kilometres away from him.'

Desmond Tutu was devastated by De Klerk's denials. 'How can he just say he didn't know? When these people were killed, I went and told him about it. It makes me sad, I am really sorry for him.'

In his book *No Future Without Forgiveness*, Tutu remarked: 'He was incapable of seeing apartheid for what it was – intrinsically evil.'

Eugene de Kock wrote that he would have wanted De Klerk to say: 'Yes, we at the top levels condoned what was done on our behalf by the security forces.

What's more, we instructed that it should be implemented. Or, if we did not actually give instructions, we turned a blind eye. We didn't move heaven and earth to stop the ghastliness. Therefore, let the foot soldiers be excused. We who were at the top should take the pain.'

Leon Wessels, a former Deputy Minister of Law and Order, and after 1994 the Deputy Chairman of the Constituent Assembly, came closest when he confessed to the TRC: 'I do not believe that the political defence of "I did not know" is available to me, because in many respects I believe I did not want to know. In my own way I had my suspicions of things that had caused discomfort in official circles, but because I did not have the facts to substantiate my suspicions or I had lacked the courage to shout from the rooftops, I have to confess that I only whispered in the corridors.'

I thought so then and I still think so now: FW de Klerk had wasted the most important moment a white South African leader will ever have to speak honestly to the black majority and ask them for forgiveness and full acceptance. It could have made such a huge difference. That moment will never come again.

Eugene de Kock became the star of the Truth Commission process. He astounded everyone with his brutally honest evidence and confession, as well as his explanations of what motivated the death squad and his assessment of the political culture of the time. I support the efforts to grant him a presidential pardon for those crimes for which he was not given amnesty. He sits in jail while his political masters, men such as Magnus Malan, Adriaan Vlok and the generals, are living in luxury on fat state pensions.

I was also asked to make a submission to the TRC's hearings on the media. I talked about the revelations made by *Vrye Weekblad*, and said: 'If the mainstream newspapers and the SABC had reflected and followed up on all these confessions and revelations, every single one of which had subsequently been proved to be true, the government would have been forced then to put a stop to the torture, assassinations and dirty tricks. It would have saved many, many lives. And South African citizens and politicians would not have been shocked or pretended that they were shocked at the revelations before the Truth Commission the last year …

'If the mainstream South African newspapers had done what good newspapers all over the world are supposed to do, nobody today would have been able to say: "I did not know." Only the so-called alternative press lived up to this duty, and they did it with a fraction of the staff and infrastructure of the big newspapers.'

People often look at our still divided society and say: 'The Truth Commission was a failure; there has been no reconciliation.'

I believe that it would have been completely impossible for our society to be where it is today if we'd never had that process.

28

The poor man's Stalin

I'VE ALWAYS VIEWED South Africa's public broadcaster, the SABC, as one of the country's prize assets. It has a massive news infrastructure, which can reflect the society as no other media can. It serves all the country's languages and cultures, and can afford to offer educational and informative programming instead of just running junk to attract viewers and listeners. In 1994, it had the potential to be the prime agent for positive change in the new democracy.

During the first three years after liberation, it was exactly that. A number of top-class, progressive journalists joined the corporation, and despite the obvious inadequacies of the chairperson of the board, Dr Ivy Matsepe-Casaburri, and the chief executive, Zwelakhe Sisulu, the SABC was rapidly transforming itself from a servant of the government into a servant of the people.

I was happy to be working for the public broadcaster, and stayed out of all the office politics by getting stuck into my work: first *Agenda*, then *The Tuesday Debate*, *Q and A*, and finally the *Special Report on the Truth Commission*. The *Special Report* received the sought-after Foreign Correspondents' Association of South Africa's Award for Outstanding Journalism, which President Nelson Mandela awarded me.

But things had started deteriorating by 1997. Professor Paulus Zulu, a Natal academic with no media experience whatsoever, replaced Matsepe-Casaburri. Things got too hot for Sisulu, and in 1997 he left to head the media branch of Nail, a prominent black empowerment company. His deputy, Govin Reddy, a man I knew and respected, was definitely the man to succeed him. I first realised that the rot was setting in when Reddy was blatantly disqualified because he was an Indian South African. A grossly incompetent minister of religion, who had run Radio Zulu during the apartheid years, Hawu Mbatha, was asked to take Sisulu's place.

But Sisulu planted two evil seeds before he left, which would bring forth much poisonous fruit. He appointed a former ANC military commissar, Snuki Zikalala, in the powerful job of integrating television and radio news, and Sisulu's blue-eyed boy at *New Nation*, Enoch Sithole, as head of licensing – a 'sleeper job' to prepare him for greater things. Soon Govin Reddy departed because of the injustice done to him, followed by Barney Mtomboti, a senior and respected journalist who was editor of radio news, who left because of Zikalala's interference.

Sisulu also replaced my old friend Joe Thloloe, one of South Africa's most respected journalists and head of television news, with Allister Sparks, former editor of the *Rand Daily Mail* and award-winning foreign correspondent. I still don't know why this was done, but I worked very well with both of them. Eventually Sparks was also axed.

As *Special Report* was nearing its end in mid-1998, I conceptualised a new weekly programme of investigative journalism and documentaries with my two old comrades, Jacques Pauw and Anneliese Burgess. Sparks liked the idea, appointed me executive producer, and *Special Assignment* was first broadcast in August 1998. It was a successful recipe and quickly became popular and influential, sweeping the awards for television journalism.

Special Report and *Special Assignment* worked so well and the staff were happy because they operated with little interference from bureaucrats. Under Thloloe and Sparks, both programmes were given substantial independence inside television news; even by Phil Molefe, known to his friends as Chippa, when he took over from Sparks. I was an executive producer in the proper, international television tradition: I recruited staffers and controlled the programme's budgets and its editorial content. I was the editor of the programme.

The year 1999 heralded the inauguration of a new president, Thabo Mbeki, but also the rapid decline of the SABC. Was that a coincidence? In hindsight I must say I believe a lot of the ANC apparatchiks were impatient with Nelson Mandela's gentle and reconciliatory style, and could not wait for Mbeki to take over so that they could establish an ANC hegemony. That certainly happened at the SABC, but also elsewhere in the national public administration.

This is one such story.

In 1999, an old loyal servant of the apartheid SABC, Themba Mthembu, was appointed Phil Molefe's deputy of television news and current affairs. (Molefe, too, had worked at the SABC during the apartheid years.) Mthembu saw it as a challenge to undermine the independence of executive producers and journalists, and started to insist on control over budgets and editorial content. He wanted to be present at our weekly 'post-mortem' and planning sessions, but never pitched up for one. He insisted on giving final approval before a programme went out, but most of the time they were completed an hour or two before broadcast, long after he had gone home.

In February we had a crisis when we were threatened with a court interdict on a story we were to broadcast that night. At the last minute we decided to broadcast another programme instead, in order to give the lawyers time to sort things out. The next day, Mthembu cornered me quite aggressively in the newsroom, and insisted on an explanation of why we didn't broadcast our original programme. I explained the legal drama to him, but he decided that he had enough of an audience in the room to assert his power. I wasn't telling the truth, he said, like a rural schoolmaster. The staff of SABC3 (the channel on which our programme went out) had given him a different version.

I looked at this stupid, self-important pen-pusher, and told him: 'Well, fuck SABC3 if they don't know what's going on.' Mthembu replied: 'I take umbrage at your language.' I turned around, and, as I walked away, I said, 'I don't give a fuck what you think of my language. Get a life.'

The poor sensitive soul ran as fast as he could to complain to Molefe. The following day I explained the circumstances and apologised for using 'the f-word'. Molefe and Mthembu formally accepted my apology. (I wondered how Mthembu would have coped in *Vrye Weekblad*'s – or *Special Assignment*'s – rowdy newsroom. He desperately needed a Pearlie Joubert in his life, I thought.)

A few weeks later I was in Harare making a documentary on Robert Mugabe. I received an urgent call to return to deal with a crisis. Mthembu had marched into the *Special Assignment* office and ordered my colleagues to rebroadcast the previous week's programme, because he wasn't happy with the programme that was supposed to go out that night. Two respected black freelance producers had made the documentary, which investigated witchcraft. Mthembu raged that visuals of the ritual slaughtering of a goat were 'offensive', and that the producers had 'confused witches with sangomas'.

Phil Molefe later publicly defended Mthembu's decision by saying that the visuals of the slaughtered goat 'would have offended four million South African Muslims'. I'm sure the few hundred thousand Muslims in South Africa would have enjoyed hearing that they all hated meat, and that their number had grown so radically.

I wrote a memo to the head of SABC television, Molefe Mokgatle, with copies to Molefe and Mthembu. I said that Mthembu's decision was 'a grave error of judgement' and an embarrassment to the SABC, and asked him to lay down a procedure to be followed before a programme could be ripped off the air.

The two producers, Bibi Lethola and Muzi Sithebe, took their gripes to the newspaper *Sunday World*. Editor Fred Khumalo watched their documentary, and wrote in his column that Sunday that he found it 'gripping television'. It did not confuse sangomas with witches, he said, and he further declared that 'the canning of the programme is an autocratic abuse of power, a reversal of the gains we, as a society, have made with regard to extending freedom of the press and freedom of information'.

Khumalo's words would spell the end of my career at the SABC. That same Sunday afternoon, Snuki Zikalala and Phil Molefe, after several beers, boasted at a party of comrades that they were going to 'crush this Boer'. Another comrade gave me a full report of their conversation the next day.

Ironically, the previous night *Special Assignment* was the only current affairs programme out of seven on five different television channels to get a mention at the annual Avanti Awards. We won six awards and a Special Mention for Consistent High Quality Journalism.

Alerted by Zikalala's remarks and the mounting rumours, my colleagues and I tried to see Molefe or anybody else in power, but everyone avoided us. Jacques and I eventually cornered Zikalala, who said he knew nothing about a problem with *Special Assignment*.

I got to know Zikalala during my time with the Truth Commission. A former MK soldier, Olefile Samuel Mnqibisa, had testified before the human rights violations hearings in Soweto on 25 July 1996 that he was stationed at an ANC camp in Zambia in 1978. Zikalala was one of his commanders. Mnqibisa said that when he and other soldiers criticised Zikalala and others for the poor conditions in the camp, they were thrown in jail, where Mnqibisa was subjected to solitary confinement and ill treatment. He listed the following people 'who abused me': Joe Modise, Keith Mikwepe, Snuki Zikalala and Solise Melani.

Zikalala was a senior colleague of mine, so I talked to him before our next broadcast. He said Mnqibisa was lying, and he would personally clear his name before the TRC. We decided not to broadcast Mnqibisi's statements on *Special Report* until Zikalala had had a chance to appear before the TRC. He never did. He was one of thirty-six ANC members who applied for a blanket amnesty by the TRC, but it was declined because they did not stipulate their crimes, as was required.

On 15 April I sent an urgent fax to the SABC's group executive, Hawu Mbatha, and a few hours later my colleagues Shenid Bhayroo and Jacques Pauw and I met with Mbatha, Zikalala, and the new head of news, Enoch Sithole. They faked complete surprise at our concerns – they knew nothing about the matter. But when I asked them about the threats uttered at the Sunday party, Sithole stated that Molefe had advised him that our contracts with the SABC should be 'renegotiated to re-establish editorial control'.

Mbatha, who contantly wore a silly grin and clearly had no idea what was going on, said to me: 'The SABC is a decent and disciplined organisation. Nobody gets to the end of his contract to find he has no job.' I asked him: 'So we are just being paranoid, Reverend?' The three men smiled and nodded their heads.

Relieved, we made our way back to our offices. A few minutes later, I was summoned to Molefe's office. Vasu Moodley, the general manager of television news, and the human resources manager, Theo Erasmus, flanked Molefe, who had just returned from an extended lunch. Molefe appeared agitated, constantly sipping water, pacing the office or holding on to a chair. He never once looked me in the eye. He thrust a piece of paper in my hands. It stated simply: 'This letter serves to notify that the SABC has decided not to renew your existing contract or to conclude a new one.'

Just two months before that, Jacques and I had had a long lunch with Molefe. He could not stop talking about how proud he was of *Special Assignment*, and how good it was to work with old comrades like Jacques and myself. He always called me 'Maxie'.

But not today. I asked him: 'Why do you do this?' He said that I was arrogant and difficult to work with. I asked him, 'How would you know, Phil, I haven't seen or talked to you in two months. You're never around.' Then it came out: I had 'used the press' against him (referring to Fred Khumalo's remarks), and wrote a memo to his superior, not to him. I looked at Moodley, an old friend, but he just looked down at the carpet. I looked at Theo Erasmus and said: 'Theo, you know this is highly irregular.' He just shrugged. Erasmus was later rewarded with the job of channel head, and is now the head of the private Afrikaans channel, kykNET.

By the time I got back to my office, the news was all over the SABC. An hour later, the newspapers started phoning me at Jacques' house, where my shocked colleagues and I had gathered. I confirmed that I had been fired. I thought that if I didn't tell them why, they might suspect that it was because of a scandal, so I told them what Molefe had told me.

A huge public storm broke out over the affair. It was on the front pages of all the newspapers, and the posters proclaimed it on the lamp posts: 'Max axed', 'Max fired from SABC'. The week afterwards, Molefe told me that he would have reinstated me if I 'hadn't run to the newspapers'.

I sent Mbatha a fax, asking him why he had lied to me. He convened a meeting with me, Zikalala, Sithole and the SABC's lawyer, Ronnie Bracks, and told me to come alone. When I reminded Mbatha of his statement that nobody got to the end of a contract finding he has no job, the smiling reverend said: 'But you did not get to the end of your contract to find you have no job. You still have ten days to go.'

At the meeting, Zikalala said that it hadn't been Molefe's decision to fire me, but that 'television news management' had made the decision. I asked him who that was, but lawyer Bracks instructed him not to answer.

It later turned out that Zikalala himself had pushed for my dismissal. He explained to senior black colleagues, who in turn told me, that it was 'symbolically important' for the 'Africanisation of the SABC' to 'crush' the most senior white journalist at the corporation 'as an example' to other whites. (In October 1997, he told an interviewer from the *Mail & Guardian* that he 'used to hate everything to do with white people' and that 'it's not easy to shake that passion'.

That night I was sitting in my office one floor below the newsroom and the studios from where the news bulletins were broadcast. A TV news reporter brought me the script for the evening bulletin, edited by Themba Mthembu. It was about my dismissal, and read: 'Molefe has again refused to discuss the matter with the media. It's however believed that Du Preez's contract was not renewed because of several incidents of gross insubordination towards management. This included the incident in which he swore at the head of news and current affairs, Themba Mthembu, in the newsroom.'

I was outraged. I told the reporter to tell Mthembu that the story was complete nonsense, and that I was fifty metres away and willing to respond. Mthembu's spiteful response was to add another tail to the story: 'Shocked members of staff saw an irate Du Preez in the middle of the newsroom pointing a middle finger at Mthembu and using an f-word.'

So the SABC's news bulletins were now available to bureaucrats for distributing lies about their own staff, with whom they were in a labour dispute – without giving the staff member a chance to respond. I had never experienced more blatant abuse. I later took the matter to the Broadcasting Complaints Commission. In a subservient decision, they found that there was 'no lack of editorial independence' because 'there was no evidence that an external source was active in influencing the news editor'. They refused to deal with my complaint that their facts were wrong, but decided that the SABC should have obtained a comment from me, thus '[contravening] the requirement of balance'.

Mthembu, egged on by Zikalala, ordered the staff at television news' finance department to look through my five-year employment record at the SABC to find 'any sort of financial irregularity' that they could use against me. Of course they found nothing, but the head of finance at TV news fully informed me of these efforts to discredit me.

The support I received from colleagues in journalism – both black and white – and from the public was overwhelming. *City Press* called Zikalala 'Adolph Zikalala' in a satirical column, and wrote in an editorial: 'The Max du Preez case is something of a reality check for those who believed that a wholly enlightened, progressive leadership is now in place at the SABC. Many nasty habits of the old SABC are clearly well entrenched in the corridors of power in Auckland Park. And the new mandarins have slipped into them with remarkable ease.'

The Star, under the headline 'Max-imum folly?' wrote in an editorial: 'The SABC's decision to axe Max du Preez is a sad event for South African broadcasting. His presence as an outspoken champion of investigative journalism will be missed on air.'

I was invited to write a piece for the *Mail & Guardian*, and ended it by saying: 'I was in Harare just before this drama began. I got a sense of what Mugabe and his cronies in the inner circle of ZANU-PF have done to Zimbabwe. I smelled Robert Mugabe in the corridors of the SABC this past week. South Africa cannot afford it.'

The *Sunday Independent* wrote in its editorial:

Vigorous democracies can be identified by the way they treat their most troublesome advocates of justice and fair play. Award-winning journalist Max du Preez is such a person. His career has been marked by controversy and drama. He is not known as 'Mad Max' for nothing.

But the qualities that have been constant throughout his tempestuous career are journalistic courage and integrity of a rare kind in South Africa. His particular brand of 'madness' is a beacon of sanity and a mirror in which we can all see ourselves and be reminded of some of the ugly similarities with the apartheid era that are creeping into our emerging nation – such as the naked greed displayed by the directors of Nail in scrambling for a R130 million share option issue.

Du Preez is individualistic, passionate and totally committed to a non-racial and democratic South Africa. His award-winning series on the Truth and Reconciliation Commission was one of the most powerful current affairs programmes. And *Special Assignment* was developing into a first-class investigative programme.

As the editor of *Vrye Weekblad,* Du Preez often fought a lone crusade in taking on some of the ugliest monsters of the apartheid era when it was not popular – and very expensive in libel actions and legal costs – to do so. He has proved time and again throughout his career that he is incorruptible in the face of persuasions or coercion, whether it comes from management or the government.

That is why he has such wide support among the public. And that is why he is respected by journalists who care about the principles on which the profession is based. The fact that he lost his temper with some of his SABC managers, is no surprise. Du Preez is fiercely independent and has never erred on the side of diplomacy in dealing with those below or above him.

The issue is whether the public broadcaster is serving all sections of the society without fear or favour or whether it has fallen into the hands of a clique of the ruling party and a board so emasculated that it will opt for political correctness rather than confrontation. In the case of Du Preez, the damage has been done and the chief victim will be the public broadcaster itself. The SABC will be poorer for axing Max.

My old boss, former television news head Joe Thloloe (now head of news at e.tv), wrote in his column in *Sunday World*:

When Max du Preez talks about his farm and the pleasures of getting food and animals to grow, he is transformed into a true African. I've spent hours listening to him become mystical as he describes the texture of the soil trickling through his fingers and the sun rise on his farm in the Eastern Free

State. I've also spent hours wrestling with him, arguing about journalism and its future in this country.

Few people can match his passion when he talks about stories and their telling through the printed word or the camera. He is truly caught between two loves.

Max has been dogged by controversy, from his days as a reporter on *Beeld*, through his days as founder and editor of *Vrye Weekblad*, right up to now at the SABC's television news. Many say he is difficult to work with and has no respect for authority. For him there are no holy cows. But even his worst enemies will concede that he is an outstanding journalist. And South Africa has been richer because of his contributions to the craft of journalism.

He enriched South Africa with his newspaper *Vrye Weekblad*, that shunned *suiwer* Afrikaans as it charged at the Afrikaans establishment and told the Afrikaners the true story of apartheid. Max and his small band of journalists were the outcasts who had turned against their own and had to be crushed. Particularly when they unmasked apartheid's death squads. Max lost that battle when *Vrye Weekblad* was closed down after it had lost a suit against it by General Lothar Neethling. *Vrye Weekblad* had alleged – and has since been vindicated – that Neethling supplied poisons used by the notorious assassins of Vlakplaas.

Perhaps the closure of *Vrye Weekblad* was a blessing for South Africa because with its demise Max joined SABC Television News and was thrust into the living rooms of the majority of this country. He took to television like a duck to water and made effective use of the wider canvas at his disposal.

He's now been axed from television news or, to be formal, 'his contract has expired and will not be renewed'. Sad indeed. It is certainly not because of the quality of his work, the programmes that we see on our screens. It is because of a bizarre power game being played at Auckland Park ...

Are the new bosses of television news not used to the robust cut and thrust of the newsroom? Old hands will tell them that great stories and great programmes are born only in this heat.

Sensitive managerial egos and meek and docile journalists can only produce propaganda, not good journalism.

John Carlin, former South African correspondent for the British *Independent*, wrote in his column in the South African *Sunday Independent*:

My friend Max (yes, I blush to own it, he is my friend) has been getting into a spot of trouble, I read. Apparently, he said a rude word – or rather, two – to one of his bosses, and was promptly fired. Quite right too. Can't have that sort of thing going on at the upstanding, venerable SABC, can we?

Or so, quite properly, I thought. Until I acquired some intelligence on the fellow he had abused. It turns out, from what I reliably hear, that he is one of those hamsters who used to sing the songs of the system that Voltaire might have described as the *ancien regime*. You know, one of those hamsters who freedom fighters like Winnie Mandela used to consider fair game for a clubbing.

So here, seen through the filter of this new intelligence, is how I see the strange story of the calamity that befell Max du Preez. On the one side you have an Afrikaner who during the era of PW Botha started an Afrikaans newspaper that supported the ANC; on the other side is a black man who during the PW Botha era worked at a Zulu radio station that helped to prop up apartheid.

The Afrikaner bloke moves from his plucky little paper, basking in the warm praise of none other than Nelson Mandela, to the SABC, where he ends up running the best news programme on the South African airwaves. The black bloke also moves to SABC television. He is appointed Max's boss. This, in and of itself, seems splendid. Max needs a boss. He needs a good thrashing – as anyone who has worked under him will attest.

Yet everyone who has worked under Max will also attest that he is generously endowed with, among other things, courage, talent, energy and integrity. So what happens if you put a man of Max's qualities in the same room as one of apartheid's hamsters? What happens if the hamster then has the presumption to order Max around?

It's obvious what happens. We're talking chemical reactions here. We're talking unstoppable forces of nature. He utters the two words which capture most precisely feelings of utter scorn that someone like Max is entitled to feel towards SABC's resident hamsters …

Here is the moral of the story. Max belongs to South Africa's heroic period; he is a character worthy of having walked on the Mandela stage. The tawdriness that is the master spirit of this age is beneath a man of his outstanding qualities.

So here is the answer. Max, as those of us who know him are only too tediously aware, has always been banging on about doing the Boere 'thang' and retiring to his farm.

Now is the time. The hamsters have done you a favour, Max. Get out of town. Ride off into the Free State sunset, praising the Lord.

In an interview with *Rapport* and *City Press* on 5 May, the new CEO of SABC news, Enoch Sithole, said that the criticism of my dismissal only came from the 'white liberal establishment'. He said that not one of his critics had the credentials to criticise him (he had been a cub reporter for two years at *New Nation*, and served for two more in administrative positions at the SABC).

Sithole said that the SABC did not need me. 'The people at *Special Assignment* are as jubilant as before without Max. Jacques Pauw does the job equally well.' (In fact, *Special Assignment* has three joint executive producers.)

My former colleagues contested Sithole's assertion, though not in the media where his statement was published. They sent a confidential memo to the SABC board and management stating that they stood by their earlier request to management that I be reinstated as executive producer. 'We are distressed that positions have been advanced on our behalf by television news management in interviews or articles published in *Sunday World*, *Rapport* and *City Press*. None of the authors of these stories have ever visited our offices to assess the mood and state of affairs within. Numerous statements are made in our name, and they do not reflect our opinion. We feel the programme's name and the team's integrity have been used in something of a propaganda war between yourselves and your critics.'

I suddenly found that I had interesting friends, all of whom rallied round the demand for my reinstatement. The Azanian People's Organisation (AZAPO), a Black Consciousness party, accused Sithole and his colleagues of both racism and tribalism. 'If Max du Preez was a 'comrade' during 'trailblazing to Lusaka' and as editor of *Vrye Weekblad*, then why is he not acceptable today in a non-racial society?' The Freedom of Expression Institute, the South African Union of Journalists, the Workers' Library and the Friends of the Public Broadcaster were among those who crusaded for my reinstatement. They even formed the Reinstate Max du Preez Committee, and held protest meetings.

I took my case to the Commission for Conciliation, Mediation and Arbitration (CCMA), a statutory body for resolving labour disputes. That was an even bigger circus than the Sithole and Zikalala show. My case was simple: I wasn't, as the SABC had suddenly suggested, an independent freelancer who did contract work for the SABC. I had signing powers on a huge SABC budget and the responsibility of hiring and firing people on my programmes. My contract – as was the case with most of my colleagues in current affairs – had automatically been renewed four times, and the understanding was that if management were unhappy with someone, standard labour practices would be followed before the contract is not renewed – and then with proper notice. My colleague Jacques' contract, for instance, had expired a month before this debacle, but was viewed as 'paperwork' that could be done later, and he simply carried on working and getting paid.

The CCMA denied me the right to a lawyer, as is its practice, but allowed the SABC to have one. Their lawyer objected when I referred to my notes as I was putting forward my case, and the commissioner agreed, forcing me to hand in

THE POOR MAN'S STALIN

my notes as an affidavit. I was not allowed to speak at all. But the SABC lawyer proceeded to read from his notes, and my objection was overruled.

I wasn't allowed to call witnesses, but the SABC called Themba Mthembu, who stood there and told the commission under oath that he hardly knew me; that he had no say over or input in *Special Assignment*; had never attended a meeting with me; and had never monitored my attendance at work, as he did all other employees, on a 'duty roster'. I was just an independent contractor, he said, who happened to work from the SABC offices.

I knew from the behaviour of the commissioner that this was a kangaroo court and that I was going to lose. So, when Mthembu spoke, I told him to his face that he was lying, despite the lawyer's pompous objections. I was not allowed to cross-examine him.

Of course I lost. The CCMA commissioner found that I was an independent freelancer who was simply paid for contractual work, which I delivered to the SABC. I was not obliged to perform the work myself, but could avail myself of the labour of others to do it.

It was shocking.

The SABC board came under such pressure that they appointed a Special Task Team to investigate my case and journalistic independence at the SABC. In its submission to the task team, SABC management said that I was lazy, got paid too much and disrespected my superiors. In November 1999, the task team announced that it had 'found no evidence to support allegations of unfair labour practices and infringement of editorial independence by its management'. Of course not.

Snuki Zikalala, Enoch Sithole and Phil Molefe had a huge 'victory party' to celebrate the findings of the task team. Zikalala – or 'Doctor Zikalala' as he called himself (he claims he has a PhD from a Bulgarian university), continued to single-handedly drive the SABC to virtual destruction. He referred to his subordinates as 'cadres' in an opinion piece he wrote for *Business Day*, in which he pleaded for a 'press corps that can work with government'. Snuki was a commissar again.

But when the rot became too obvious even for the Mbeki government and the SABC board to ignore, they got rid of Zikalala – he was appointed media spokesman for the Department of Labour.

My other enemies did not last much longer either: Sithole left after it became known that he had been less than honest about his academic qualifications and South African citizenship; Mbatha was unceremoniously dumped; lawyer Ronnie Bracks left under a dark cloud; and Phil Molefe was demoted. The law of karma at work.

I should have followed my friend John Carlin's advice and shrugged off the whole drama as beneath my dignity. But I didn't. It traumatised me. I felt betrayed. In my heart, it felt as if my contribution to this new society of ours was denied by the stroke of a pen. I was now classified as a 'counter-revolutionary'. The comrades had forced me into a white Afrikaner box again.

But perhaps what disturbed me the most was the realisation that my dreams of a new, open, progressive society after apartheid were false: the nasty white men in power had merely been replaced with nasty black men.

29

Enemy of the people

NOVEMBER 1989 SAW the last big 'bridge-building' meeting between the exiled ANC leadership and a delegation from inside the country. It was organised by Idasa, financed by Madame Danielle Mitterand, and held outside Paris. It was a riot.

The discussions were interesting and informative, but the main event occurred after hours. Foremost among the party crowd was Trevor Manuel (wearing a yellow T-shirt proclaiming 'Viva no compromise!'), Jay Naidoo, Fink Haysom, Azhar Cachalia and Alec Erwin. Trevor, Jay and Alec became ANC cabinet ministers (and brilliant ones), Fink the president's legal adviser, Azhar a judge.

We were not exactly good ambassadors for our country. One evening after a formal state function in a 400-year-old building, a group of South African activists was asked to stop toyi-toying because the precious chandeliers in the historic building may just fall on them. I stood next to a Cape activist at a table where the garçon was serving precious cognac older than most of us. My Cape friend was upset that they didn't supply Coke as a mixer with the brandy.

When the French prime minister invited us to a banquet, we almost caused a diplomatic incident. Our bus stopped outside the building, and we walked up the steps to where a man was awaiting us. Two of our colleagues thought he was the concierge, and handed him their overcoats – which he took. It was the French prime minister himself.

Fink, Azhar, Jay and I, all liberated New Age men, were so ashamed of our behaviour one night late in a Paris nightclub that we formed a club to redeem ourselves – Jocks Against Sexism. We've even had a few reunions in Johannesburg.

The main event of the week was a meeting in the French parliament to commemorate the anniversary of the French Revolution. The leader of the ANC delegation, Thabo Mbeki, was to deliver the keynote speech. But it had been a long night, and when the bus was about to leave our speaker still hadn't arrived. Some of us went to look for him – and found him, with a companion, not willing to rise and shine. Pallo Jordan had to stand in for him, and made a brilliant off-the-cuff speech.

It was an amusing incident, but nothing more. There were few angels in politics, and even fewer of them attended the Paris conference. The man was a leader of a major liberation movement, after all – cut him some slack.

By 2001, the African National Congress, by then in power for seven years, was showing signs that it was slowly evolving into an ordinary political party instead of remaining a liberation movement. That meant that internal power struggles and party gossip would become public, as is the case with any political party in a democracy. The Minister of Safety and Security, Steve Tshwete, for instance, announced that he was investigating a plot by three ANC stalwarts, Cyril Ramaphosa, Tokyo Sexwale and Mathews Phosa, to oust Thabo Mbeki as president. It was bizarre.

Early in 2001, the inimitable president of the ANC Women's League and former wife of the former president, Winnie Madikizela-Mandela, wrote a letter to Deputy President Jacob Zuma, vehemently denying that she was spreading gossip about President Thabo Mbeki. Unfortunately, the letter was leaked to the media. Among the top ANC leaders who tried to stop publication of the letter was Police Commissioner Jackie Selebi, who approached the newspapers 'in his personal capacity to express concern about the possible damage publication of the rumours might cause the president'.

But some newspapers did quote from the Winnie letter. She wrote that Thabo Mbeki had accused her at a national working committee meeting 'of telling Linda Zama at Comrade Ismail Meer's funeral that he [Mbeki] had taken Comrade Shilowa's wife one evening and brought her back at 5 am'.

Madikizela-Mandela claimed that the rumours about the president had been circulating for some time at ANC headquarters, Luthuli House, and had even reached the media. 'The City Press reporter, Richard Nkadana, was about to publish them but was pursuaded not to do so,' she wrote. 'Worse, Mr Nkadana had been given not only the name of Mrs Shilowa, but of four other women, one of whom was Linda Zama, the others, ministers and deputy ministers!'

But it was not the first time the president's private life appeared in print. Noseweek magazine's February edition also referred to Mbeki's close relationships with several women, some of whom, the magazine said, were either in his cabinet or married to top officials.

I was also aware that members of the VIP protection unit had complained to journalists that they were asked by the presidency to act as bodyguards for a female journalist at the SABC and make sure that her privacy was respected.

Then, in April, Deputy President Zuma issued a surprise statement that he was not seeking to oust President Mbeki as president. For most people it seemed to come out of nowhere, but I knew it was related to Winnie's letter to Zuma – there had been speculation that Zuma's office had leaked the letter to damage Mbeki.

On Sunday 10 April, I was invited to be part of a radio discussion on a programme called The Editors, with Nigel Murphy as host. The journalist Caroline Dempster was the other guest.

Murphy referred to Zuma's statement, saying, 'This extraordinary story of the Deputy President saying that he wasn't challenging Mr Mbeki for his position … What do you make of that?'

I said: 'It's one of the most important stories of the year; it really is an important story.'

Caroline Dempster: 'Well, I'm going to hand it over to Max, because I read it with some incredulity.'

Murphy: 'We all did.'

Dempster: 'It was a reaction before it even happened, and as much as we're used to reading statements coming out of the president's office these days that seem to be quite startling … I mean, Max, take over, you know more about this, enlighten us.'

Du Preez: 'Well, you know, nobody really knows. But the indications are, and I've had it for some time, that there is some tension inside the ANC, and I think Jacob Zuma slightly overreacted to this. He was talking about intelligence reports suggesting this and lobbies trying to forward this opinion that he was challenging the president. So there's a lot going on inside the ANC.

'I think there is a perspective among white South Africans, almost the media as a whole, that Thabo Mbeki is untouchable, that, in the African mode, he will be president until he decided not to be. Clearly that's not the case. There is a lively debate inside the ANC …'

Murphy: 'Brought about as a result of his stance on AIDS and …?'

Du Preez: 'Yes, but also because he is seen as a womaniser. It is publicly known – and I think we should start talking about this – that the president has this kind of personal life. I'm not saying it's scandalous. He's a womaniser. Winnie Madikizela-Mandela sort of suggested that in her letter that was released – which is part of this whole struggle.

'Now the question is, can Jacob Zuma threaten Mbeki? We're talking about 2002 here, when the leadership issue comes up. And this is about the time when people would start jockeying for position. Can Jacob Zuma do it? Who are the other guys? What about Cyril Ramaphosa? Mathews Phosa was a strong contender. And the Mbeki camp just cut him down. There's a lot of that stuff going on.

'I think it is one of the important developments in our country. On the one hand, it's nice to see [that] an organisation like our former liberation movement is open enough and they can have this kind of thing – that it's not like ZANU-PF or SWAPO, a monolith. On the other hand, I think it could make our very insecure president even more insecure and more thin-skinned when he knows he's being challenged inside his own party.'

After the programme, Murphy said it had been a good show, and he and I had lunch in Sea Point. On the Tuesday morning I flew back to Johannesburg. I collected my baggage and walked to the car park. Just as I was leaving the arrivals building, a black man in a suit carrying an attaché case walked right towards me. I stepped aside for him to pass, but he bumped me with his shoulder and I tripped over my feet. He looked at me and hissed, 'Bloody racist.' I was stunned. I had no idea who he was or what had motivated him.

But as I drove into Johannesburg, I saw a poster advertising *The Citizen*: 'Mbeki a womaniser, says Max du Preez'. My heart sank into my shoes. That was the last thing I needed.

The Citizen had obtained the transcript of *The Editors*, and lifted out the part where I talked about Madikizela-Mandela's letter and the president's womanising. There was nothing wrong with quoting me discussing issues on public radio, but it was devious to pluck something like that out of nowhere and sensationalise it in a front-page lead – after all, that story had already been in the newspapers. For once I understood what politicians meant when they complained that they were 'quoted out of context'.

Within hours, an extraordinary barrage of abuse was hurled at me. The first to jump in was the ANC's official spokesman, Smuts Ngonyama. I was 'a disciple of apartheid', he said. 'An attack on President Mbeki is an attack on the ANC and will not be tolerated. Max du Preez and his old friends have clearly embarked on a war path and such statements on the ANC are a declaration of war.'

Ngonyama accused me of 'irresponsible and undermining behaviour which bordered on hate speech and malicious character assassination', and said that I 'meant to cause harm to the image of the president, the ANC and the country as a whole'. He also accused me of 'hatred for the president, this country and all the millions of people who by popular choice made President Mbeki our president. From Du Preez's allegations, the ANC has learnt that among some sections in our society respect and dignity are accorded only those with a certain type of pigmentation and being black and powerful qualifies one to be the recipient of a barrage of insults and abuse.'

He was the ANC's Clown Number One. Next came Clown Number Two, KwaZulu-Natal leader Dumisani Makhaye. I was 'a political commissar of apartheid', he declared. 'The ANC in KwaZulu-Natal accepts the declaration of war by Max du Preez and his political masters who have unleashed an unprecedented vitriol against the ANC, its leadership, the president and its supporters.

'The ANC, for a long time, has been a cushion between the anger of our people and the political commissars of apartheid masquerading as journalists. For too long the ANC has been a shock absorber of anger of our people against such journalism. Unfortunately, the ANC may be losing this role. Let the people decide the fate of such gutter journalism without let or hindrance.'

Makhaye called on the leadership and all structures of the ANC 'to explore all avenues, including legal action' against me. 'The fact that President Thabo Mbeki is hated by all racists and their lackeys with a special venom is an indication of how valuable he is to our struggling masses.'

The ANC Youth League insisted that I be charged with high treason. The Western Cape ANC's provincial secretary declared: 'For anyone to be able to state as fact that the president is a womaniser and get away with it, is unacceptable. Some of our laws need further scrutiny.' In a radio interview he said that there should be an Act of Parliament to protect the president's dignity.

(Ironically, two years later, the same Western Cape ANC leaders who had issued these statements approached me to help them with a municipal by-election in the Little Karoo. This is a crazy country.)

An interesting reaction came via a statement issued by the women cabinet ministers and deputy ministers. I had not said anything about them at all, yet they felt they had to fight back – they were reacting to Madikizela-Mandela, but I was the convenient whipping boy: 'Our concern is heightened by the fact that the unwarranted attacks, innuendo and insults are at the same time directed at women who occupy positions of responsibility in both the public and private sectors. Among the assumptions feeding the rumour mill is the chauvinistic attitude that female citizens who occupy these posts do so as a result of favours extended to men in senior positions.' Referring to me, they said: 'It is of serious concern to us that some of these individuals exploit the freedoms that were achieved at great cost – to the men and women who are today the objects of their ridicule – for purposes of subverting confidence in the institutions of our democracy.'

Winnie Madikizela-Mandela also reacted to something I didn't say. She denied that she had leaked the letter to Zuma to the media, and she denied that she was involved 'in a plot to overthrow the president'. The stories that Mbeki was a womaniser 'are the work of right-wing elements trying to destabilise the ANC by dividing it against itself'.

The brouhaha reminded me of two old Shona proverbs: 'He who is scared of the hyena's howling is he who has smeared himself with fat.' And, 'The cheetah enjoys pulling others around, but when it is being pulled around, it complains that its spots get soiled.'

On 12 April 2001, I responded in my column, *Maximum Headroom*, which appeared in *The Star*, the *Cape Argus* and the *Daily News*. I wrote:

I have forgotten what a strange society this is. During a radio programme on Sunday I made a remark about something that most informed people in the country already knew. Two days later I see a silly newspaper putting the remark – and my face – on the front page.

Ridiculous, I thought. And not the kind of journalism I admire – *The Citizen* clearly wanted to take a swipe at the president, but did not have the courage to do it without riding on someone else's back.

And then on Tuesday night I started receiving the ANC and Winnie Mandela's statements. I'm a racist, I'm part of a right-wing plot, I'm guilty of hate speech, I hate my country and all its citizens, I'm declaring war. I had to pinch myself.

Let me explain. I was part of a panel discussion on a programme called *The Editors*. We talked about the US–China tensions, about the racial tensions in Pietersburg and elsewhere, about the Pagad killings and other current stories. Then the programme leader touched on the rather bizarre statement made earlier last week by Deputy President Jacob Zuma announcing that he wasn't actually challenging Thabo Mbeki's leadership of the ANC. I was then asked for my opinion on what was happening inside the ANC – surely the Zuma statement was proof that there was tension inside the party? Could it be because of his bad handling of the HIV/AIDS issue, I was asked. Perhaps that too, I answered, but there is a lot of infighting in the party and unhappiness because of Mbeki's womanising. I reminded listeners of Winnie Madikizela-Mandela's equally weird letter to Zuma that was leaked to the newspapers in which, among other things, she wrote that Mbeki 'accused me of telling Linda Zama ... that he had taken Comrade Shilowa's wife one evening and brought her back at 5 am'.

I read parts of that letter in South African newspapers. I also read in *Noseweek* magazine's February edition that Mbeki 'has, or has had, close relationships with several women who are either in his cabinet circle or who are married to top officials'. The magazine added: 'We have been told that Mrs Mbeki recently consulted a spiritual adviser about an all-night visit her husband made to the home of one of his female colleagues.'

My point is that I was hardly saying something that had not been said in public before – and frequently discussed in Johannesburg black high society circles and the ANC itself in recent months. I wasn't making any moral judgement – I wasn't even suggesting scandal. Winnie Mandela's letter suggested scandal, not my remarks.

The political elite of South Africa, the intelligence community – yes, Thabo Mbeki's intelligence community – and senior journalists have known about this side of our president for a long time. But the citizens, the voters, are kept in the dark. This happened during the previous regime too – journalists, politicos and spooks knew of cabinet members' indiscretions and knew exactly which minister slept with whom and when and how it was covered up. I was one of very few who wrote about their scandals – can anyone remember that I was sued for defamation a dozen times by the former regime's top brass, including the president?

Why should the citizens of South Africa not know about something as important as a potential weakness of their head of state while most of the political and security operators know about it? What if, for example, a top politician has an affair with a key political correspondent at a national news institution – isn't there a potential danger there we should know about? Do we really want to be like the former Zaire where everybody knew about Mobutu Sese Seko's shenanigans, but it never appeared in a newspaper?

I can understand that the president is upset. But for the ANC apparatchiks to issue a statement that I'm a racist who hates my country and its people and that my remarks bordered on hate speech is just stupid and ridiculous. It's not only an insult to everybody who can read, it's an insult to the man they're trying to protect. Why didn't they just do the president a favour and shut up completely? Like the people around former French president Francois Mitterand did when their newspapers wrote about his affairs?

Thabo Mbeki should realise that we have a different political culture as a nation now, and that we value our right to know what goes on in the corridors of power more than before. And it was his doing, his and all the other leaders of the ANC past and present who brought us freedom and democracy and transparency and a magnificent constitution. We honour them for it, but then they have to honour our new political culture too.

Such as respecting the principle that the party is not the same thing as the state. And that public threats directed at a journalist is behaviour we expect of ZANU-PF thugs, not of a spokesman of our ruling party.

The radio talk shows, the newspapers' letters pages and the Internet chat rooms buzzed for weeks about the story. Some black people cursed me as a racist, but mostly people, both black and white, condemned the ANC's accusations that I was a racist. Two of my black journalist colleagues, Abby Makoe and Kaizer Nyatsumba, wrote opinion pieces in my defence. The deputy editor of *The Star*, now editor of the *Sunday Times*, Mathatha Tsedu, sided with the accusers and called my column the 'worst gutter journalism' he had ever seen. He was also the only journalist who thought that there was merit in the SABC firing me. I guess he's not a fan of mine.

At the time, I was a presenter of a talk show on kykNET television, called *Dwarsklap*. I invited my old friend Terror Lekota, now Minister of Defence, to take part in a debate. His office said he couldn't make it, but a top ANC source told me that the word was out that no cabinet minister of senior ANC person should have anything to do with me. A week later, I bumped into a cabinet minister whom I had known for many years. He hugged me and thought the whole thing was a huge joke. When he saw I wasn't very pleased with what his party had said about me, he said: 'Oh, its just ANC infighting. Don't take it seriously.'

Van Zyl Slabbert, who was chairman of *The Citizen*'s publishers, Caxton, wrote a letter to the paper to distance himself from their report, and apologised for the hurt it had caused. The editor later apologised to Mbeki.

I didn't apologise. I didn't think I had anything to apologise for. But was it a mistake to make those remarks? I don't think it was wrong if one considers that it was said in the context of a radio programme broadcast at half past twelve on a Sunday, with a small and intelligent listenership. It was also perfectly legitimate in terms of the context of the discussion and the wording I used.

The problem came when *The Citizen* sensationalised my words out of context. If I knew something like that would happen, I wouldn't have said it. But I should have foreseen that it might happen. So, yes, it was a mistake. And I've paid for it.

But it has also helped a lot of people, including me, to understand the dynamics inside the ruling party under the leadership of Thabo Mbeki. During their days in exile, when spokespersons or regional leaderships issued wild and weird statements, the ANC did not take responsibility for them. That habit has not died. They do not hesitate to play the race card when under pressure – in fact, race is their first line of defence. The same Dumisani Makhaye savaged his own comrade, Communist Party veteran Jeremy Cronin, as a typical middle-class white when Cronin said in an equally obscure interview with an Irish academic that he was concerned about the 'ZANU-faction' in the ANC.

Another lesson I learnt was that one shouldn't underestimate the fierce divisions within the party. It is utterly ruthless, and it can only get worse. I understand now that I was a lightning conductor for some of the fury – and being a white Afrikaner made me a very convenient target.

3 0

Into the sunset

AT NOON ON 24 AUGUST 1978, as I sat with a broken body in an aircraft wreck, the only thing that went through my mind was: I haven't lived enough.

Twenty-five years later, I still think that. A lover once said to me that I was born with a midlife crisis, so at least I don't have to worry about that hitting me any time soon. There's a lot of living to be done in Africa in the next few decades.

I've had a couple of raw deals so far. But it was a small price to pay for the way I chose to live my life. It is not commonly believed to be so, but I have no doubt that it is easier and simpler not to serve a master; not to do anyone else's bidding, choosing instead to express the truth as and when one sees it.

Few journalists really appreciate how special their job is. You get to be a politician without having to lie; a psychoanalyst with no concerns about your own sanity; a pastor whose private life no one will ever question; a storyteller who never has to look for a story. But if you're a journalist in it for the money or status, you will be very unhappy.

I had the good fortune of being a part of two great chapters in South Africa's media history: *Vrye Weekblad* and the *Special Report on the Truth Commission*. Journalists around the world always dream of being a part of something that really makes a difference, of history in the making. I had that opportunity twice.

I am sad that many Afrikaners and white South Africans have been so slow in embracing the new society with enthusiasm and a sense of ownership. It started so well after 1994, under the presidency of Nelson Mandela. But the process was stunted when the white political leadership and the Afrikaans newspapers shunned and attacked the Truth Commission. They squandered the opportunity to cleanse themselves and wash off the smell left by the actions of their ancestors. If they had unburdened themselves and opened their eyes to the eagerness of black South Africa to forgive and accept them, they would have been so much more positive today. Instead, so many of them are fearful, insecure and defensive.

Still, if the veneer has been rubbed off the miracle of post-apartheid South Africa, and a few cracks are showing, South Africa today is still living a miracle. A hundred, two hundred years from now, history students will be amazed at how a society had managed to overcome an ideology as vicious as apartheid without fighting a civil war, and building a stable society on its ashes.

I never cease to think in great wonderment how spectacular it is that I was born where humanity originated – that one part of me stayed here always, while the other wandered the globe, just to come home again 350 years ago.

I feel blessed to have experienced how my nation successfully overthrew a race-based autocracy, replacing it with a proper democracy with a magnificent constitution. I feel privileged to have been an actor – even though I had just one line to speak – in the grand play that was the creation of the New South Africa, and which starred great people such as Nelson Mandela and Desmond Tutu.

I am immensely proud of the people who live on the southern tip of Africa. God painted with grand and generous strokes, with lots of flair and a sense of drama, when He created us.

I sometimes worry about the terrible poverty so many of our people still suffer, and about the naked greed and self-indulgence of our new rulers and our new elite. I worry about violent crime and corruption, and old and new racism.

But every day I sense that the people of South Africa are steadily moving along on a path of tolerance and loyalty to a shared nationhood and a constitution cast in stone. As our confidence grows and our insecurities diminish, we will be able to share more.

Four years ago, I admonished our politicians in a newspaper column to stop excluding non-black South Africans when they refer to 'Africans'. I was cursed and called names. Today, if someone stands up and says only black South Africans can call themselves by that honourable title, he or she is called names.

I've been called many names in my life. I call myself a native of Africa: pale, but no less native.

Abbreviations

Aktur:	Action Front for the Preservation of the Turnhalle Principles
ANC:	African National Congress
ARAC:	Africa Risk Analysis Consultants
AWB:	Afrikaner Weerstandsbeweging
AZAPO:	Azanian People's Organisation
BOSS:	Bureau of State Security
CCB:	Civil Cooperation Bureau
CCMA:	Commission for Conciliation, Mediation and Arbitration
CIA:	Central Intelligence Agency
COSATU:	Congress of South African Trade Unions
CP:	Conservative Party
DCC:	Directorate Covert Collection
DTA:	Democratic Turnhalle Alliance
FAK:	Federasie van Afrikaanse Kultuurvereniginge (Federation of Afrikaans Cultural Associations)
FAPLA:	Forças Armadas Populares de Libertação de Angola (People's Armed Forces for the Liberation of Angola)
FM:	*Financial Mail*
FNLA:	Frente Nacional de Libertação de Angola (National Front for the Liberation of Angola)
Frelimo:	Frente de Libertação de Moçambique (Liberation Front for Mozambique)
HNP:	Herstigte Nasionale Party
Idasa:	Institute for a Democratic Alternative for South Africa
IFP:	Inkatha Freedom Party
KZA:	Komitee Zuidelijk Afrika
MFA:	Movimento das Forcas Armadas (Movement of the Armed Forces)
MK:	Umkhonto we Sizwe (Spear of the Nation – ANC's armed wing)
MPLA:	Movimento Popular de Libertação de Angola (Popular Movement for the Liberation of Angola)
NEC:	National Executive Committee

NG Kerk: Nederduitse Gereformeerde Kerk (Dutch Reformed Church)
NGO: non-governmental organisation
NI: National Intelligence
NIS: National Intelligence Service
NP: National Party
NUSAS: National Union of South African Students
PAC: Pan Africanist Congress
PAIGC: Partido Africano da Independencia da Guiné e Cabo Verde
(African Party of Independence of Guinea and Cape Verde)
PFP: Progressive Federal Party
PLAN: People's Liberation Army of Namibia
SABC: South African Broadcasting Corporation
SACP: South African Communist Party
SADF: South African Defence Force
SAP: South African Police
SASJ: Southern African Society of Journalists
SWA: South West Africa
SWANU: South West Africa National Union
SWAPO: South West African People's Organisation
TRC: Truth and Reconciliation Commission
UCT: University of Cape Town
UDF: United Democratic Front
UNITA: União Nacional para a Independência Total de Angola
(National Union for the Total Independence of Angola)
VOC: Vereenigde Oost-Indische Compagnie (Dutch East India Company)
Wits: University of the Witwatersrand
ZANU-PF: Zimbabwe African National Union-Patriotic Front

Glossary

baas: boss

baasskap: domination

boerseun: Afrikaner boy

burgher: citizen

bywoner: tenant farmer

doepa: potion

dominee: reverend

dompas: passbook

eina: ouch

Hollandse meide: Dutch girls

kaffir: derogatory term for black people

landdrost: magistrate

Lifacane: the great upheaval

mampoer: moonshine

Mfecane: the great upheaval

moruti: reverend

oom: uncle

pandoer: Khoikhoi soldier

poephol: arsehole

rooinek: derogatory term for English-speaker

sitkamer: lounge

soutie: derogatory term for English-speaker

stoep: verandah

suiwer: pure

taal: language

tsotsi: young criminal

vaatjie: small barrel
veldkornet: field cornet
verligte: progressive
volk: nation
volksraad: House of Assembly

Index